Myth and Reality in the Contemporary Islamist Movement

MYTH AND REALITY IN THE CONTEMPORARY ISLAMIST MOVEMENT

Fouad Zakariyya

Translated and with an Introduction and Bibliography by
Ibrahim M. Abu-Rabi‘

Pluto Press
LONDON • ANN ARBOR, MI

First published 2005 by Pluto Press
345 Archway Road, London N6 5AA
and 839 Greene Street, Ann Arbor, MI 48106

www.plutobooks.com

Translated with a grant from The Gateway Trust

British Library Cataloguing in Publication Data
A catalogue record for this book is available from the British Library

ISBN 0 7453 2247 6 hardback
ISBN 0 7453 2246 8 paperback

Library of Congress Cataloging in Publication Data applied for

10 9 8 7 6 5 4 3 2 1

Designed and produced for Pluto Press by
Chase Publishing Services, Fortescue, Sidmouth, EX10 9QG, England
Typeset from disk by Stanford DTP Services, Northampton, England
Printed in the European Union by Gutenberg Press, Malta

Contents

Translator's Introduction

"A rising mass movement attracts and holds a following not by its doctrine and promises but by the refuge it offers from the anxieties, barrenness and meaninglessness of an individual existence. It cures the poignantly frustrated not by conferring on them an absolute or by remedying the difficulties and abuses which made their lives miserable, but by freeing them from their ineffectual selves—and it does this by enfolding and absorbing them into a closely knit and exultant corporate whole." Eric Hoffer, *The True Believer: Thought on the Nature of Mass Movements* (New York: Harper and Row, 1966), 44.

"The common strain that binds together the attitudes and ideas which I call anti-intellectual is a resentment and suspicion of the life of the mind and of those who are considered to represent it; and a disposition constantly to minimize the value of that life." Richard Hofstadter, *Anti-Intellectualism in American Life* (New York: Alfred A. Knopf, 1963), 7.

Fouad Zakariyya's *Myth and Reality in the Contemporary Islamist Movement* offers a sustained critique of the intellectual, political, and social foundations and contemporary manifestations of Islamism in the Arab and Muslim worlds. This work is a genuine contribution to our social and political thought: it sensitizes us to the complex relationship between religion and society in the post-colonial Arab world and the rise of new social movements that vie for power in the name of religion. Written in the aftermath of the assassination of former Egyptian president Anwar Sadat in 1981 and at the height of the global debates about the relevance of Islamic revivalism in contemporary Muslim societies, especially after the triumph of the Islamic revolution in Iran in 1979, this book sheds important light on the multiple voices of current Islamism, their theological worldviews, ideological currents, and attempts to construct an Islamic social and political order in the contemporary period.

In addition to treating the mainstream Muslim Brotherhood Movement, founded by Shaykh Ḥassan al-Banna in Egypt in 1928,[1] Zakariyya's book delves into the religious and political formations of such militant

Islamist movements as the Jamā'ah al-Islāmiyyah and the Egyptian Jihād, which have been mushrooming in Egypt and the rest of the Arab world since the 1970s and whose impact on the world was seen in the September 11, 2001 tragedy.[2]

While academic studies of Islamism abound, none compares to Zakariyya's thorough inquiry into the nature of contemporary Islamism, its theological foundations and contemporary political and social practices. A well-known Egyptian philosopher and a leading Arab intellectual, Zakariyya is in a unique position to shoulder the task of critically analyzing contemporary Islamist movements.[3] Although Zakariyya himself does not belong to the Islamist camp, it makes sense to place this book in the genre of self-criticism in contemporary Arab writing since it wrestles with many intellectual, theological, and ideological issues that are at the heart of contemporary Arab and Muslim intellectual history.

It is difficult to pinpoint the genesis of the genre of self-criticism in modern Arab intellectual history. However, many consider the 1967 defeat with Israel as its starting point. The 1967 defeat forced a number of contemporary Arab thinkers to reconsider those issues and questions that had long been taken for granted, and some thinkers have gone as far as to question the relevance of the Sacred to contemporary social and political life. The Arab left, the Islamic trend, and the nationalist trend were all negatively affected by the reasons behind defeat and sought in their different ways to diagnose and remedy the situation. The Arab intelligentsia was anxious to produce a new intellectual project of self-criticism and rejuvenation. The Arab left shouldered the responsibility of self-criticism and analysis, and defeat gave the Islamic tendency its best historical moment in decades. In short, a mixture of critical traditions stalked like specters across the wounded paths of Arab consciousness. From the leftist side, Yāssīn al-Ḥāfiz wrote *Ideology and Defeated-Ideology*;[4] Sādiq Jalāl al-'Azm wrote *Self-Criticism After Defeat*[5] and *Criticism of Religious Thought*,[6] and Abdallah Laroui wrote *L'idéologie arabe contemporaine*.[7] Islamist thinker Yūsuf al-Qaraḍāwī wrote *The Islamic Solution*,[8] and nationalist thinker Costantine Zurayk wrote *Revisiting the Meaning of Disaster*.[9]

In his various writings on Islamism and the need to revive rationalism in contemporary Arab thought and culture, Zakariyya often refers to passages from most of the above listed writings. His own *Myth and Reality in the Contemporary Islamist Movement* falls squarely within the tradition of critical writing on the status of religious movements in the Arab world. Here, he is not just critical of Islamism *per se*, but of the political and economic conditions that led to the rise of religious extremism in the contemporary Arab world. In Egypt, his home country, Zakariyya was critical of Nasserism because of its lack of respect for public freedoms and the way it diminished the role of democracy during its almost two decades of power.[10] Likewise, he was critical of the Sadat regime, particularly of the way it handled the religious question in Egypt in the 1970s and its wholesome and uncritical embrace of the United States, which led to the signing of the Camp David Accords between Israel and Egypt in 1979. Zakariyya argues that Sadat was partially to blame for the religious crisis in Egypt in the 1970s because he led the Islamist movements to believe that he was for the implementation of Sharī'ah in Egypt, which the different Islamist movements saw as the beginning of the formation of the Islamic state in that country.[11]

In this book, Zakariyya focuses on the post-1967 socio-political and religious scenes in the Arab world. He devotes a great deal of time to treating the intellectual and religious underpinnings of Islamism in Egypt in particular and in the Arab and Muslim worlds in general in the 1970s and 1980s. Here he offers a well-constructed thesis on the status of Islam and, in particular, of Islamism in the modern Arab and Muslim worlds.

Zakariyya's main arguments in this book can be summarized as follows. First, religion in the contemporary Arab and Muslim worlds forms a great part of the public sphere; for various reasons, both state and society permit the public expression of religion. Second, although religion contains positive social and ethical values, both the state and Islamism have exploited religion to advance and/or protect certain political and economic interests. Third, since the beginning of the decolonization process almost half a century ago, the political Arab and Muslim elite have failed to offer a coherent nationalist program or ideology to rid their societies of economic dependence and political stagnation. Fourth, authoritarianism has been the hallmark of the power elite in Arab and Muslim societies. Democracy has not been anchored in contemporary Arab and Muslim societies, and to take hold in the Arab and Muslim worlds, democracy must be homegrown. Fifth, because of widespread social, economic, and demographic changes that have taken place in the past five decades, religion has gained more public prominence than ever before. In the ensuing social and economic dislocation experienced by a significant number of people, religion has offered hope and solace Sixth, the relationship between state and Islamist movements in the Arab world has been awkward at best. The state is primarily responsible for the consolidation of authoritarianism and political repression, which made the rise of Islamism possible if not welcome by a large number of people. Seventh, although the Islamist movements are diverse by nature, they exhibit common characteristics relating to their interpretation of the Sacred Text and the role of Sharīʻah in contemporary life. All agree on the idea of constructing an Islamic political system and argue that Islam is both "religion and state." Eighth, Sharīʻah contains general rules that cannot be simply implemented without a thorough rational critique and appreciation. Ninth, as opposed to the religious formulations of the nineteenth-century Islamic reform movement spearheaded by such thinkers and activists as Jamāl al-Dīn al-Afghānī, Sayyid Ahmad Khan, and Muḥammad ʻAbduh, contemporary Islamism advocates the implementation of Sharīʻah as a prelude to the foundation of the Islamic state. Finally, Zakariyya advocates the depoliticization of religion in contemporary Muslim societies in order to avoid political exploitation and to keep religious ethical and normative values alive.

While not against the ethical and ritual practices of Islam in the contemporary world, Zakariyya does object to the politicization of religion and the implementation of Sharīʻah. After a discussion of recent attempts to implement Sharīʻah in such countries as Sudan, Saudi Arabia, and Iran, Zakariyya advocates secularism as the only solution to the current impasse in Arab and Muslim societies. Zakariyya calls for a strict separation between politics and religion and proposes secularism as a state of mind that must proliferate in the Arab world in order to catch up with the achievements of modernity.

In this context, Zakariyya argues that secularism is an historical and civilizational requirement at the present stage of Arab and Muslim societies. His formulation represents the most subtle and serious attempt to salvage the contemporary Arab secularist movement from its current historical impasse. He considers the resurgence of Islamism and not the failure of "Arab modernism" to be the most serious threat to the integrity and viability of secularism in contemporary Arab society, and hopes the Islamic past will jump-start the contemporary Arab secularist movement. He argues that from Islam's inception, secularism has been pivotal. Contemporary Arab secularist thinkers need not be carbon copies of Western secularists, but must revive the secularist tradition of the Muʻtazilites, Ibn Rushd, al-Fārābī, and others.[12] This is a tempting thesis, although a very difficult one to defend now in view of the indebtedness of the modern Arab secularist movement to Western thought and political hegemony.

In principle, Zakariyya does not object to borrowing from Western civilization as long as this borrowing meets the criteria of rationalism and progress. Rationalism is universal and it is high time for the Arab intelligentsia to historicize the Islamic past without paying it blind deference.[13] In *Myth and Reality in the Contemporary Islamist Movement,* Zakariyya treats the following main themes: recent attempts at applying the Sharī'ah, the mass orientation of resurgence, "Petro-Islam," and science, reason, and revelation.[14]

In addition to offering a critical evaluation of the relationship between religion and society in the post-colonial Arab world, the current work is also an inquiry into the roots of anti-intellectualism in contemporary Islamist discourse, which Zakariyya considers to be a lack of respect for the mind. Zakariyya preaches a form of critical and creative intelligence to be used as a yardstick against which the achievements of contemporary Islamist movements must be measured. What is critical intelligence? According to one American historian, "Intellect ... is the critical, creative, and contemplative side of mind. Whereas intelligence seeks to grasp, manipulate, re-order, adjust, intellect examines, ponders, wonders, theorizes, criticizes, imagines."[15] Throughout *Myth and Reality in the Contemporary Islamist Movement*, Zakariyya argues that religious movements as mass movements do not cultivate critical consciousness in their followers; on the contrary, they encourage obedience to a leader or doctrine without paying sufficient attention to the underlying socio-economic and political causes of the problems. To him, these movements offer refuge "from the anxieties, barrenness and meaninglessness of an individual existence" while emphasizing blind obedience to a leader or to an incomprehensible doctrine, though Zakariyya does not think that Islam *per se* encourages this type of attitude, which can best be described as "the suspension of human reason."

Zakariyya perceives Islamism as a broad religious and social movement with distinct political objectives that have been boosted by the rise of the oil states to prominence in the 1970s and 1980s. In this sense, Islamism is a broad social movement, not clearly delineated from politics. Here, he does not draw a distinction between establishmentarian Islamist movements and anti-establishmentarian movements. These movements are far from interested in preparing a generation of leaders who can navigate the ship of the movement through rough seas.

It is difficult to describe accurately the reasons behind the rise of Islamism in the 1970s. However, one must take note of the failure of the Arab project of modernity begun after independence and of the fact that the Gulf States offered money and not religious leadership. The rise of these movements was not a revolt against modernity *per se* but against a failed modernization project, the increase in the gap between poor and rich, the increase of the power of the elite in Arab societies, and the increase in the role of military violence against the civilian population. The situation in the Arab and Muslim worlds has not improved with globalization; I expect a re-resurgence of mass social movements in the name of religion as an expression of a widespread social anger and frustration with the status quo.

Throughout the book, Zakariyya is quite critical of certain political regimes in the Arab world, especially those in the Gulf States, though he is too subtle to dismiss the "modernization achievements" of Gulf regimes. As a professor of philosophy at Kuwait University in the 1970s and 1980s, he enjoyed some of these benefits. His quarrel is not with the idea of modernizing the Gulf States as much as it is with the actors behind modernization, that is, the political elite and their spurious methods. He is right to contend that these elite and their supporters in larger society, the conservative ulama, are too misguided to appropriate the Enlightenment's intellectual premises *en masse*.

In critiquing the Gulf ruling elite, Zakariyya's point of departure is quite similar to other Islamist thinkers who are critical of the political status quo. He argues that social justice must be the hallmark of social and political action in the Arab world. However, contrary to many Islamists, he thinks that the Arab political elite (especially in the Gulf), have lent a hand to both "official Islam" and Islamic resurgence in order to achieve political stability. He says that many current rulers appeal to Sharī'ah as a last attempt to preserve power. By doing so, they intend to exploit the Islamist movement for its mass appeal. In this regard, he forcefully argues that,

> There is an ocean of difference between the current systems of government in the Arab world and the values of freedom, justice, and equality as preached by all religions, philosophers, and reformers throughout history. Nevertheless, the proponents of the implementation of Sharī'ah in our land do not heed the astonishing failure of previous experiments. On the contrary, their voices became extremely loud when the implementation of Sharī'ah in the Sudan under Numairi turned into an international scandal.[16]

Zakariyya further argues that proponents of Sharī'ah use the sacred text, the Qur'ān, as a springboard for their thinking while remaining totally oblivious to the social and cultural manifestations of Islam throughout Islamic history. The Qur'ān and, for that matter, Islamic tradition, cannot provide adequate solutions to the many dilemmas besetting the modern

Arab world. To adopt this view is to become ahistorical, at best.[17] He takes a critical position *vis-à-vis* the applicability of the Qur'ān and the viability of Islamic tradition in the modern era. A critical thinker must subject both the Qur'ān and tradition to strict historical criticism if he or she is to learn from them. Zakariyya basically encourages the same critical methodology adopted by both Mohammed Arkoun and Naṣr Ḥāmid Abū Zayd in the analysis of Islamic religious tradition.[18]

Many a ruler has practiced absolutist rule and made a mockery of the lives, property, and freedom of Muslims. Zakariyya reminds the "Islamist camp" of the distinction they must draw between "textual Islam" and "historical Islam." He argues that implementing Sharī'ah falls in the domain of "historical Islam," and that as a practical issue, "invoking the power of the texts [that is, the Qur'ān and the *Sunnah*] is insufficient."[19] In Zakariyya's opinion, what is dangerous is the mass emotional appeal exerted by Islamic movements. As a result of this mass appeal, the discussion around the Sharī'ah issue "remains generalized and elastic, although, if it is subjected to rational analysis, it remains ambiguous and messy."[20] Zakariyya, representing the secular academic community in contemporary Arab society, contends that the mass appeal of an idea or ideology does not necessarily make it valid. He argues, along Marxist lines, that as a result of deplorable economic and political conditions in the Arab world since 1967, the Arab masses have suffered "absence of consciousness" (*in'idām wa'y*), and that the recent resurgence of Islam is "a clear reflection of the lack of consciousness among the masses. The spread of these movements becomes inevitable after more than thirty years of oppression, the suspension of reason, and the domination of a dictatorial political system."[21]

Zakariyya further criticizes Islamism by accusing its principal leaders of mental poverty and of lacking rational values, "In my view, their major problem is that they do not take full advantage of their mental faculty, which they often suspend to the point of complete paralysis."[22] The "monolithic mind" of Islamic resurgence is accustomed to unquestioned premises and to the belief that "doubt is a mistake, criticism is a crime, and questioning is a crime."[23] In other words, these movements are far from embracing the central tenets of modernity as defined above. He relishes the principle that Arab society has only one option for modernization: the uncritical wholesale acceptance of the central premises of secularization and modernity. What this entails is in effect a total disregard of the application of religious values to the governing and daily functioning of Arab society. In addition, he accuses Islamism of being complicit with the ruling political elite in the Arab world. This assumption is problematic.

In the same vein, Zakariyya argues that Islamism has been on the rise in many Gulf States, and that it has principally turned a deaf ear to the misuses of Islam in the public sphere. However, he does not draw clear distinctions between Islamism, as a movement of religious revivalism, and official Islam, as a body of official clergy, which supports the status quo. Zakariyya points out the importance of the Gulf States in the international arena, thanks to their oil resources, but notes that from the beginning of Islam, economic factors have been inextricably intertwined with religious factors. For example, pilgrimage, a central pillar in Islam, has attracted a large number of people every year to a very impoverished region: "One of the main goals of pilgrimage was the alleviation of poverty in this dry desert, helping its people break out of their isolation so that their territory becomes, for a specific period of time each year, the gathering place of Muslims from all over the world."[24] Undoubtedly, this argument is valid.

Zakariyya hits the marks when he says that it is indeed a "civilizational paradox" (*mufāraqah ḥaḍāriyyah*) that this same region, which has attracted people from diverse cultures over the centuries, has been blessed with oil, allowing the political elite of the region to become virtual billionaires. Because of the importance of the oil resources to the international economy, the political elites in the Gulf had to modernize the infrastructure of their societies, which in one sense meant implementing sweeping changes in the educational system for both sexes.[25] Furthermore, Zakariyya argues that oil has not been a factor in historically stable agricultural and centralized societies, such as Egypt, but rather in desert societies, which had been under the spell of tribal tradition. As a result, in the oil-rich Gulf States, Islam itself has been tribalized.[26]

Zakariyya spends little time assessing the impact of the modernization program of the Gulf tribal state on society and the clash existing in many Gulf societies between actual modernization programs and the absence of a modernist consciousness. To camouflage the gap between modernization and modernism, Zakariyya asserts that the political elite are taking full advantage of Islam for their own purposes:

> A specific type of Islam has been gathering momentum of late, and the appropriate name that applies to it is "Petro-Islam." The first and foremost objective of this type of Islam has been to protect oil wealth, or, more appropriately, the type of social relations underlying

> those tribal societies that possess the lion's share of this wealth. It is common knowledge that the principle of "the few dominating the largest portion of this wealth" permeates the social structure [of the Gulf region].
>
> Certainly, wise planning and distribution of this immense Arab oil wealth would benefit not just the local petroleum societies, but the larger Arab and Muslim worlds. However, under the present circumstances, oil wealth has not resulted in lasting solutions even in the societies themselves and has remained, more often than not, a privilege in the hands of the few at the expense of the majority and in the hands of the present generations at the expense of future ones.[27]

Although Zakariyya bases his arguments on secular premises, he appears to be concerned about the predicament of Islam and Muslims, as do intellectuals of the Islamic movement. He also revives some of their terminology in his secularist discourse. He bemoans the fact that, in petroleum-dominated countries, "it is in the interest of the ruling elite to preempt Islam and reduce it to shallow formalities so that the problems of poverty, the unequal distribution of wealth, the predominance of the consumption mentality, and the loss of the final opportunity for a thorough revival of the petroleum-based societies, would escape the attention of the masses."[28] The elites' preemption includes the deployment of selected ancient texts and commentaries that have no connection with the fundamental challenges facing contemporary Muslims, but do reinforce an Islamic behavior which is indistinguishable from Islamism. As a result, Islam is held hostage by the Gulf regimes, and a new type of Islam has emerged: "the Islam of the veil, the beard, and the *jilbāb*; the kind of Islam that permits work to be interrupted for prayer, prohibits women from driving automobiles."[29] In the final analysis, Zakariyya reminds us that the current state of affairs is ideal for international and exploitative capitalism:

> Would a country like the United States dream of a better condition than the one dominating the new generations of the petroleum-producing countries who are in perpetual fear of the severe punishment of the grave and its snakes that tear to pieces anyone who dares to question, criticize, or rebel against the prevailing conditions and values? Would the West, including Israel, imagine to dream of a better condition than the one in which the most dynamic and active Islamic movements proclaim that the question of Jerusalem and the problem

with Israel must be postponed until the establishment of the Islamic political system?[30]

Zakariyya argues correctly that there is definitely a strong and an unbreakable bond between Petro-Islam and the interests of modern capitalism: "In a nutshell, this Islam is placed at the service of protecting the interests of the ruling elite and its allies of exploiting foreign countries."[31] Zakariyya is certainly critical of the explicit alliance between the political elite of the Gulf region and the United States. He is critical of US political and economic hegemony in the area, which he considers to be one of the main reasons for the absence of true democracy in the Arab world, and warns the Arab world against adopting American ideas simply because they are American.[32] The ruling elite embraces modernity in the name of protecting the type of Islam of which Zakariyya speaks. All of this is fair enough.

However, Zakariyya fails to mention the Islamic protest movements in the Gulf States against the manifestations of the same. In his brilliant essay, "The Limits of Religious Criticism in the Middle East: Notes on Islamic Public Argument," Talal Asad discusses in detail the Islamic tradition of public criticism in Saudi Arabia and the state's intolerance, especially after the stationing of US troops in the Gulf in 1990. This tradition is represented by a group of young Saudi ulama who criticize the prevalent corruption and nepotism made possible by the country's tremendous oil wealth.[33]

Zakariyya is unwavering in his plea for a rational and progressive Arab secularist movement. He considers the religious solution to have exhausted its limits, at best. He sees no hope in religious ethics. Zakariyya's ideas are embedded in the secular ideal and owe their inspiration to the historical manifestations of secularism in Arab lands at the end of the nineteenth century. Although not nihilist in a Nietzschean sense, Zakariyya substitutes metaphysics for rationalism.[34] To him, the project of secularism, aided by rationalism and ultimately individualism, is a better alternative in contemporary Arab societies than religious ethics. Although he does not declare the "death of God" in his philosophy, he abandons the idea that human ontology should derive its authenticity or essence from Divine Being.[35]

Zakariyya is well aware that the modern period in the Arab world, beginning in the early part of the nineteenth century, posed a fundamental challenge to the classical definition of the self in traditional Muslim societies. These societies were challenged by scientifically superior societies and aggressive modernist views. The result of this challenge has been the breakdown of the traditional expression of the Muslim self and the emergence of multiple centers of self-definition in modern Arab society. From the burgeoning number of modern Arab historical identities, the secularist-individualist identity has commanded the respect of a committed minority of few intellectuals and leaders who see no virtue in the continuation of the classical "Muslim self." Zakariyya considers the "Good" to fall squarely into this modern definition of the "Arab self," which to him cannot be disengaged from the modern world. In other words, the modern "Arab self" cannot be nurtured by historical Islamic tradition, since this tradition has disengaged itself from the "modern self," which had been developing in the West since the Enlightenment. However, it seems to me that Zakariyya fails to consider two additional facts about the multiple expressions of the "self" in the modern period. First, it is true that the nineteenth century was filled with grandiose ideas about progress and human prosperity, which enabled individualism to transcend the boundaries of the classical Western definition of community and self. But one of the main consequences of the modern definition of the "self" has been the colossal destruction seen in World Wars One and Two.[36] Second, under the pressure of the "Other," that is, the West, the traditional Muslim expression of the "self" had to give way to a new reconstruction of the Muslim self in the modern period. The idea of revival in modern Muslim thought does not exclusively denote political revival, but social, moral, and philanthropic revival. Zakariyya, like many secularists in the Arab world, does not ponder the many virtues of such a revival in times of severe social crises and change in many Arab countries. The Islamic ethos of generosity, patience, compassion, and kindness has been revived as a result of the encounter with the West. Zakariyya ends his argument on secularism as follows:

> The glaring mistakes surrounding the concept of secularism are a clear expression of the decline of Arab thought in the past two decades. This decline is not confined to this concept alone but to others as well, which have resonated with a large number of people, especially adherents of the Islamist movements. These conceptual errors are rampant, not just among the common people but among thinkers as well. All approach, without real understanding, such concepts as European "materialistic" science and "materialistic" philosophy as ways of thinking that make Western man mere instinct and completely dismiss the spiritual components … one reader to another except in the age of intellectual decline, which is characterized by biased missionaries *(du'āh)* and ignorant writers who do not read. If the contemporary

> Islamist movement was truly open-minded, enlightened, and desired achieving independence from foreign thought, it would expend every effort to understand its enemies correctly, form a realistic image of them, and plant the seeds of research and criticism in the minds of its followers instead of drowning them in the darkness of past clichés.
>
> I have tried to dispel the most frequently held myths regarding secularism in the contemporary Arab world and, most importantly, raise the reader's critical consciousness, a consciousness that is almost absent in the discussions of contemporary Islamists. I hope that the reader is now in a position to understand secularism in its current historical phase in Arab societies. Secularism is not a "comprehensive" project or ideology in the full sense of that word; neither is it a political program adaptable to a political party or to a reform movement. In our current state, secularism is an attempt to thwart a dark current of thought sweeping through our countries, and aided by strong internal and external forces. In a wide framework, secularism contains a variety of ideological and political positions. It can include conservative, leftist, liberal, Marxist, and even religious secularists. In that sense, secularism does not show us the path we should follow; however, it clearly points out the path to be avoided ... In the above sense, secularism is a civilizational requirement. When we consider present conditions in the Muslim world, how it is submerged in the darkness of extremism, anger, and narrow-mindedness, and hear about bloody demonstrations against a vulgar author [Salman Rushdie] who intended with his foolish work to expose the dominant narrow-mindedness in the Muslim world, or when we hear threats against a man of letters [Najīb Maḥfūz], the first Muslim since Tagore to receive the Nobel Prize in literature, we then realize that the contemporary Muslim world still displays the backwardness of the Middle Ages, and that the need for secularism and enlightenment is as urgent in our present context as it was in Europe during its exit of the Medieval period.

Arab secular political philosophy, such as Zakariyya's, rejects any divine intervention in the historical and political process. Political philosophy, as advanced by Arab secularists, is based on the notion that the best context for political action is that democracy. Arab secularists argue that only secularism and not Islamic resurgence can ensure a smooth transition in the Arab world from "the closed society" to "the open society." One can find similarities between Arab secularist theory and Karl Popper's famous notion of what constitutes an open, progressive, and future-oriented society. For instance, Popper claims that its organic ties, tribal and collectivist mentality, lack of individuality, and religious rigidity are the main characteristics of "closed society." The open (secular) society, on the other hand, is marked by individuality, freedom of expression, rationalism, social mobility, and a critical appraisal of social reality.[37] In other words, secularists assume that Arab society must be able to maintain a degree of tolerance and openness to outside influences, and that a transition from "the closed society" to an open one signals a total breakdown of tribalism and religious rigidity. Then, to the minds of secularists, any reaction against liberalism in the modern Arab world, especially in the form of Islamism or tribalism is in fact a reaction against socio-economic progress, and the scientific culture of modernity.

The above begs, once more, the question of the so-called "Arab enlightenment movement" (*al-ḥarakah al-tanwīriyyah*), a dominant trend in contemporary Arab thought and culture.[38] According to Egyptian thinker Galāl Amīn, the contemporary Arab enlightenment movement has lately reached its limits for two reasons: first, its move into the orbit of gradual Israeli domination of the Middle East and, second, its propensity to attack *any* form of religiosity as being terrorist. That the "tanwīrī trend" in modern Arab culture has been exhausted indeed is clear from its history in the Arab world. The main "tanwīrī" representatives in Arab thought, from Ṭāha Ḥussain and Salāma Mūsa in the first half of the twentieth century, to Jābir 'Aṣfūr and Zakī Najīb Maḥmūd[39] in the second half, are united on an ambitious project of secularization, unfettered criticism—especially of tradition and the sacred, pragmatism and doubt.[40] Most secularist Arab thinkers tenaciously hold to the proposition that the "universalization of modernity" and its acceptance by Arab society and the Arab mind in the nineteenth century was inevitable, and that an appeal to traditionalism in the form of authenticity is just an escape from new conditions created by modernity.[41] Furthermore, this trend has attached its fate to the survival of dictatorial regimes in the Arab world. Its best defense line is that "modernizing elite" have failed to modernize society.

In addition, contemporary Arab tanwīrī thought has intensified its attack on religious thought by ascribing to it fanaticism and extremism because of its doctrinal belief in metaphysics. Galāl Amīn contends that attacking religious thought as the only source of fanaticism in society is just plain wrong. There are many other sources of fanaticism in Arab society. In addition, this trend has not been questioned, not even slightly, by America's gross violations of the rights of the nations of the Third World to political and economic independence.

The main goal of the first generation of Arab enlightenment was to catch up with the West, whereas the Enlightenment in the West represented the economic and political aspirations of the bourgeoisie to make a clean break with feudalism.[42] Progress and freedom in this sense were synonymous with bourgeois progress and freedom, and this is what thinkers of the Arab enlightenment missed.[43] They followed the West's project blindly, without considering the Arab context. Arab enlightenment took root in the inferiority Arab intellectuals felt *vis-à-vis* intellectuals of the West. Furthermore, during the Cold War, there were two tanwīrī camps in Arab thought. One was socialist and the other capitalist but what bound them together were the ideas of progress, rationalism, and hatred of religious thought.

According to Amīn, with the eclipse of the socialist camp enters a new phase, which he terms the "Israeli age." In this phase, it is "Islamic fundamentalism" or "fanaticism" or "extremism," which has been defined as the main enemy of Israel, America, progress and enlightenment. With the spread of non-governmental organizations (NGOs) and Western-inspired human rights organizations in the Arab world, the enemy has been well defined: religious fanaticism and Islam.[44]

Secularization, which refers to broad cultural, social, and political processes in the Arab world, has been inevitable since the advent of colonialism. In the absence of political democracy in the Arab world, the rise of political Islam, and the predicament of the Arab secularist movement, what is the best alternative?

At present, it is important to choose a specifically Arab secular vision in order to guide the different transformations currently under way in the Arab world. The progress of the Arab world in the past century has been inconsistent. However, what has been astonishing about almost every Arab country has been the military hegemony exercised by the ruling elite over the masses. In an important article on secularism in contemporary Indian society, Amartya Sen identifies three challenges to secularism: communal fascism, sectarian nationalism, and militant obscurantism.[45] These challenges present themselves to Arab secularism as well, but we must also add a fourth: the military suffocation of civil society. With its centralized power, the army in many Arab countries has blocked the formation of healthy civil associations. The Arab secularist movement has been living in crisis due to the general crisis affecting the Arab world. A large part of the secular movement takes the side of the ruling elite against the "religious masses." To gather momentum, the secularist movement must distance itself from the ruling elite and present a critical discourse that reflects the feelings and concerns of the masses.

Furthermore, the secularist movement must rethink its position on religion, which should be accommodative rather than confrontational.

It is time to move from political control to democracy and from religious extremism to religious tolerance and pluralism. Religious tolerance should be preached with this secularist vision as one of the major cornerstones of Arab societies. Religious tolerance is not new to the Arab and Muslim world, as Bernard Lewis argues.[46] It must be resurrected in the contemporary era.[47] In addition, there must be a clear-cut separation between Sharī'ah and politics to safeguard both religious tolerance and freedom. To leave Sharī'ah to the whims of the ruling elite only complicates matters since some modern rulers have tended to exploit religious feeling for their own political ends. Muslims can practice Islam perfectly well without implementing Sharī'ah from the top down. To argue, as many conservative Muslim thinkers have over the years, that a separation between state and religion is harmful to Islam is contentious at best. This separation has been a fact in Muslim history since the very beginning. I think it is crucial to develop a secularist vision that is protective of religious belief, that is, the theistic dimension of religion. Without such an approach, it is difficult to safeguard Islam and protect it from political manipulation.

It is far from true to argue that an Arab secularist vision should be antithetical to religion. On the contrary, religious identity should be protected as one among many in the Arab world. It is easy to argue, as did Charles Taylor in his magisterial work, *Sources of the Self: The Making of the Modern Identity*,[48] that the modern period of the Arab world has been inundated with new patterns of identity. The religious identity has redefined itself in the midst of the epochal transformations befalling the Arab world in the past two centuries. However, the ruling elite and their intellectual supporters in the Arab world cannot tolerate free expression of the religious identity as an equal among many patterns of identities.[49] In other words, the Arab elite is ready to ascribe the word "terrorism" to any Islamist activity, however innocent, that falls outside of the state's control. Any healthy debate about secularism in the Arab world must start with the premise of "intellectual and religious pluralism." Because most institutions in the Arab world are secular, a public expression of the religious must not diminish this reality. A plurality of religious and secular voices must coexist in order to improve the status of civil society in the contemporary Arab world. Religious people must be allowed to express their identities in public. Increased oppression naturally leads to religious extremism and fanaticism. Undoubtedly, this is a frightening aspect of the current situation in the Arab world. However, one must acknowledge that only a minority of disgruntled religious intellectuals and practitioners express religious fanaticism. Most who define themselves as religious are anxious to implement change by peaceful and democratic means. Also, in spite of the oppressive nature of the contemporary state, there has been a marked resurgence in religious life in Arab society. One must admit that the public expression of religion is one of the most central facts in contemporary Arab society.

FOUAD ZAKARIYYA'S BIOGRAPHY[50]

Fouad Zakariyya was born in Port Said in Egypt in 1927. After graduating from high school in Cairo he went to the University of Cairo where he obtained a BA in philosophy in 1949. In 1952, he obtained an MA degree in philosophy from 'Ayn Shams University and in 1956 he received his PhD from the same univerity. Afterwards, Zakariyya taught philosophy at 'Ayn Shams University until 1974. Between 1974 and 1991, he taught at the Department of Philosophy at Kuwait University. In 1998, his students and admirers at Kuwait University published a *Festschrift* in his honor.[51] Currently, Zakariyya lives in retirement in Cairo.

Zakariyya was one of the few leading Arab intellectuals to stand against the Iraqi occupation of Kuwait in the summer of 1990. He could not fathom how most Arab thinkers applauded the Iraqi occupation event although it overrode United Nations resolutions. He wrote critically of such leading Arab thinkers as Muḥammad Ḥassanayn Haykal, Muḥammad 'Ābid al-Jābirī and Ḥassan Ḥanafī, who more or less supported the Iraqi occupation of Kuwait. In his criticism of these thinkers, he singled out Haykal, the most famous contemporary Arab journalist and a pillar of Nasserism between 1952 and 1970. Zakariyya argued that Haykal's problem was that he never broke away from the mental atmosphere of authoritarianism. The contemporary Arab intellectual has fallen prey to this mentality and political victories will be achieved the moment this dictatorial mentality is gotten rid of.[52]

Throughout his academic career, Zakariyya published a great number of books in Arabic on Western philosophy and rationalism in general. Here is a summary of his main publications: 1) *Nietzsche: silsalat nawābigh al-fikr al-gharbī* [*Nietzsche: The Series of Western Genius Thinkers*] (Cairo: Dār al-Ma'ārif, 1956); *Spinoza* (Cairo: Dār al-Nahḍah al-'Arabiyyah, 1963); *Ārā' naqdiyyah fī mushkilāt al-fikr wa'l thaqāfah* [*Critical Considerations of Cultural and Intellectual Problems*] (Cairo: al-Hay'ah al-'Āmmah li'l Kitāb, 1975); *al-Tafkīr al-'ilmī* [*Scientific Thinking*] (Kuwait: Silsilat 'Ālam al-Ma'rifah, 1978); *Khiṭāb ilā al-'aql al-'Arabī* [*Addressing Arab Reason*] (Kuwait: Kitāb al-'Arabī, 1978); *al-Ṣaḥwah al-islāmiyyah fī mīzān al-'aql* [*Islamic Revivalism in the Scale of Reason*] (Beirut: Dār al-Tanwīr, 1985); *al-Thaqāfah al-'arabiyyah wa azmati al-khalīj* [*Arab Culture and the Gulf Crisis*] (Cairo: Maṭābi' al-Ahrām, 1991); and *Āfāq al-falsafah* [*Horizons of Philosophy*] (Beirut: Dār al-Tanwīr, 1988).

NOTES

1. See Richard Mitchell, *The Society of the Muslim Brothers*, new edition (Oxford: Oxford University Press, 1993).
2. See Montasser al-Zayyat, *The Road to al-Qaeda: The Story of Bin Laden's Right Hand Man*, tr. Ahmed Fekry and ed. Sara Nimis (London: Pluto Press, 2004), and John Cooley, *Unholy War: America, Afghanistan, and International Terrorism* (London: Pluto Press, 2000).
3. A recent *Festschrift* has been devoted to Fouad Zakariyya by his students from Kuwait University. See 'Abdallah al-'Umar, ed., *al-Duktūr Fouad Zakariyya Bāhithan wā muthaqaffan wā nāqidan: kitāb tidhkārī* [*Dr Fouad Zakariyya: Festschrift*] (Kuwait: University of Kuwait Press, 1998).
4. Yāssīn al-Ḥāfiz, *al-Hazīmah wa'l idiolojiyyah al-mahzūmah* (Beirut: Dār al-Ṭalī'ah, 1979).
5. Sādiq Jalāl al-'Azm, *al-Naqd al-Dhātī ba 'da al-hazīmah* (Beirut: Dār al-Ṭalī'ah, 1969).
6. Sādiq Jalāl al-'Azm, *Naqd al-fikr al-dīnī* (Beirut: Dār al-Ṭalī'ah, 1969).
7. Abdallah Laroui, *L'idéologie arabe contemporain*e (Paris: Maspero, 1970).
8. Yūsuf al-Qaraḍāwī, *al-Ḥall al-islāmī: Farīḍa wa ḍarūrah* (Beirut: Mu'assassat al-Risālah, 1979).
9. Costantine Zurayk, *Ma'nah al-nakbah mujadaddan*, in *al-A'māl al-Kāmilah lī Qustantine Zurayk*, volume 2 (Beirut: Markaz Dirāsāt al-Wiḥdah al-'Arabiyyah, 1994).
10. For more on that, see Muḥammad al-Rumayḥī, "Fouad Zakariyya: rajul al-istināra," in 'Abdallah al-'Umar, ed., *al-Duktūr Fouad Zakariyya Bāhithan wā muthaqaffan wā nāqidan: kitāb tidhkārī*, 669–81.
11. On Sadat and the Islamists, see Mohamed Heikal, *Autumn of Fury: The Assassination of Sadat* (New York: Random House, 1983), especially part 3, chapter 4.
12. Zakariyya, *al-Sahwah al-islāmiyyah fī mīzān al-'aql* (Cairo: Dār al-fikr li'l Dirāsāt wa'l Nashr, 1989), 73. Ḥassan Ḥanafī of Cairo University more or less argues the same point: "In essence, Islam is a secular religion. What this means in effect is that there is no room in Islam for an additional kind of secularism, especially the Western one," Ḥassan Ḥanafī, *al-Dīn wa'l thawrah fī miṣr*, volume 8 (Cairo: Madbūlī, 1989), 105.
13. "Nous autres musulmans avons grand besoin de quelqu'un qui nous dise, comme les philosophes de la Renaissance: 'Si vous avez devant vous la nature et les problèmes des hommes, pourquoi faut-il que toujours vous reveniez aux textes des ancêstres? Pourquoi faites-vous de la pensée héritee une autorité inniscutable? Pourquoi ne pas affronter les situations nouvelles avec vôtre raison? Selon moi, cette incapacité du monde arabe a historiciser sa relation au passé constitué la cause première de

sonsous-développement intellectuel,'" Fouad Zakariyya, *Laïcité ou Islamisme* (Paris: Sindbad, 1989), 38. Quoted by Massimo Campanini, "Egypt," in Seyyed Hossein Nasr and Oliver Leaman, eds, *History of Islamic Philosophy*, volume 2 (London: Routledge, 1996), 1120.

14. Fouad Zakariyya, *al-Ḥaqīqah wa'l khayāl fī'l harakah al-islāmiyyah al-mu'āṣirah* (Cairo: Dār Sīna, 1988). Zakariyya has this to say about secularism: "The European secular movement was not a reaction against religion but against a method of thinking. Europeans were advancing in science and industrialization. They aimed to expand and dominate the entire world. The biggest obstacle to these advances was the closed religious thinking of the Church. The secularists opposed intellectual rigidity while remaining committed to their own faith," quoted by Nancy E. Gallagher, "Islam v. Secularism in Cairo: An Account of the Dār al-Hikma Debate," *Middle Eastern Studies*, vol. 25(2), April 1989, 210.
15. Richard Hofstadter, *Anti-Intellectualism in American Life* (New York: Alfred A. Knopf, 1963), 25.
16. Fouad Zakariyya, *al-Ḥaqīqah wa'l khayāl fī'l ḥarakah al-islāmiyyah al-mu'āṣirah*, 7.
17. Fouad Zakariyya, *Khitāb ila al-'aql al-'arabī* (Cairo: Maktabat Miṣr, 1990), 21.
18. See Muhammad Arkoun, *Essais sur la pensée islamique* (Paris: Editions Maisonneuve et Larose, 1984) and *Pour une critique de la raison islamique* (Paris: Editions Maisonneuve et Larose, 1984). See also Naṣr Ḥāmid Abū Zayd, *Mafhūm al-nass: dirāsah fī 'ulūm al-Qur'ān* (Cairo: al-Hay'ah al-Miṣriyyah, 1990).
19. Zakariyya, *al-Ḥaqīqah wa'l khayāl*, 10.
20. Ibid., 11.
21. Ibid., 15. Elsewhere Zakariyya comments on extremism: "The true reason surrounding these extreme phenomena is, in my view, the political use made of Islam. The young extremists are part of a huge bureaucracy, which continues to grow and swell since the early seventies. Its aim is to exploit Islam in order to achieve political goals. Like any small part of a huge bureaucracy, it knows its aim well and marches to execute its mission relentlessly. Since these youngsters were taught that the commandments of religion bid them to lead society and since they heard from their counselors that society will not be set right unless it places itself under their tutelage, they, therefore, allow themselves to take the law into their own hands according to their law and methods ... Just imagine how society could attain perfection if every individual within it has the right to be a lawgiver, judge and a policeman at one and the same time," Fouad Zakariyya, *al-Ahrām*, March 1988, translated and quoted by David Sagiv, "Judge Ashmawi and Militant Islam in Egypt," *Middle Eastern Studies*, vol. 28(3), July 1992, 541.
22. Zakariyya, *al-Ḥaqīqah*, 17.
23. Ibid., 19.
24. Ibid., 22.
25. Ibid., 22.
26. Samir Amīn proposes the same argument. See Samir Amīn, *The Arab Nation: Nationalism and Class Struggle* (London: Zed Press, 1987).
27. Ibid., p. 23. See also Fouad Zakariyya, "People Direct Islam in any Direction they Wish," *Middle East Times*, May 28–June 3, 1991, 15.
28. Ibid., 24.
29. Ibid.
30. Ibid., 25.

31. Ibid., 25–6.
32. For more details, see Fouad Zakariyya, *al-'Arab wa'l namudhaj al-amerīkī* (Cairo: Maktabat Misr, 1990).
33. "The religious criticism described in his chapter is undeniably a vigorous expression of political opposition to the Saudi ruling elite. That criticism is not merely a one-sided assault, it invites argumentative exchange," Talal Asad, *Genealogies of Religion: Discipline and Reasons of Power in Christianity and Islam* (Baltimore, MD: Johns Hopkins University Press, 1993), 232. On protest movements in Saudia Arabia, see Mamoun Fandy, *Saudi Arabia and the Politics of Dissent* (London: Palgrave, 1999). On the larger context of the alliance between Wahabiyyah and the state in Saudi Arabia, see Alexei Vassiliev, *The History of Saudi Arabia* (New York: New York University Press, 2000).
34. Nihilism is summarized by the "death of God" thesis extolled by Nietzsche; in that sense, nihilism means the devaluation of the highest value, the highest value being God. For more detail, see G. Vattimo, *The End of Modernity: Nihilism and Hermeneutics in Postmodern Culture* (Baltimore, MD: Johns Hopkins University Press, 1988), especially chapter 1.
35. "Ultimate Concern is the abstract translation of the great commandment: 'The Lord, our God, the Lord is one; and you shall love the Lord your God with all your heart, and with all your soul and with all your mind, and with all your strength'," Paul Tillich, *Systematic Theology*, Volume 1 (Chicago: University of Chicago Press, 1953), 12.
36. Charles Taylor, *The Ethics of Authenticity* (Cambrdige, MA: Harvard University Press, 1991).
37. Karl Popper, *The Open Society and Its Enemies*, two vols (Princeton, NJ: Princeton University Press, 1962).
38. See Galāl Amīn, "Ḥawla mafhūm al-tanwīr: nadhrah naqdiyyah lī tayyār assāssī min tayyārāt al-thaqāfah al-'arabiyyah al-mu'ūṣirah," *Al-Mustaqbal al-'Arabī*, volume 20(7), 1997, 35–51. In an insightful article on the "secularism debate in contemporary Egypt," Fauzi Najjar mentions that the *tanwīrī* movement in Egypt is supported in the main by the Egyptian Ministry of Culture and that their books are printed by the General Egyptian Book Organization, which is a government organ. See the following by Fauzi M. Najjar, "The Debate on Islam and Secularism in Egypt," *Arab Studies Quarterly*, volume 18(2), Spring 1996: 1–22, and "Book Banning in Contemporary Egypt," *The Muslim World*, volume 91(3 and 4), Fall 2001: 399–424.
39. See al-Bukhārī Hamānī, "Makānat Zakī Najīb Mahmūd fī'l falsafah al-'arabiyyah al-mu'āsirah," *Al-Mustaqbal al-'Arabī*, volume 20(8), 1997, 48–55, and Salāh Qunsuwwa, "al-'Aql al-'Arabī wa'l thaqāfah al-'arabiyyah: hiwār ma' Zakī Najīb Mahmūd," *Al-Mustaqbal al-'Arabī*, volume 11(8), 1988, 121–33.
40. Galāl Amīn, *al-Tanwīr al-zā'if* (Cairo: Dār al-Ma'ārif, 1999), 28.
41. This thesis is highlighted mainly by Burhān Ghalyūn in *Ightiyāl al-'aql: mihnat al-thaqāfah al-'arabiyya bayna al-salafī yya wa'l taba'iyyah* (Cairo: Madbūlī, 1990).
42. See Peter Gay, *The Enlightenment: An Interpretation* (London: Weidenfeld and Nicolson, 1966).
43. Amīn, *al-Tanwīr al-zā'if*, 45.
44. Ibid., 56–7.
45. Amartya Sen, "The Threats to Secular India," *New York Review of Books*, volume XL(7), April 8, 1993, 28.
46. Bernard Lewis, *The Jews of Islam* (Princeton, NJ: Princeton University Press, 1987), 3.

47. For an interesting view, see Nurcholis Madjid, "Islamic Roots of Modern Pluralism: Indonesian Experiences," *Studia Islamika: Indonesian Journal for Islamic Studies*, volume 1(1), 1994: 55–77.
48. Charles Taylor, *Sources of the Self: The Making of the Modern Identity* (Cambridge, MA: Harvard University Press, 1989).
49. Jamāl al-Ghīṭānī, one of the best-known novelists in contemporary Egypt, makes the point that "In the battle between a religious extremism and terrorism seeking to bring down a corrupt and basically repressive government, the choice for many of us, lamentable though it may be, is to side with the army and regime," quoted by Edward Said, "The Other Arab Muslims," in his *The Politics of Dispossession* (New York: Vintage Books, 1994), 400.
50. The biography of the author was provided by Dr Fouad Zakariyya to the translator in an interview in Cairo in January 2004.
51. See Abdullah al-Omar, ed., *Dr. Fouad Zakaria: Festschrift* (Kuwait: Kuwait University Press, 1998).
52. See Fouad Zakariyya, *al-Thaqāfah al-'arabiyyah wa azmat al-khalīj* (Cairo: Matābi' al-Ahrām, 1991).

Part One

Secularism, the Gulf States, and Islam

1
The Contemporary Muslim and the Search for Certitude

When the Iranian Islamic Revolution erupted in 1979 and succeeded in destroying one of the most tyrannical regimes humanity has ever known, it established a completely Islamic political system in a country endowed with the vital qualities needed for growth and progress: an immense and dynamic population, tremendous natural resources, most notably petroleum, and a noble civilization dating from time immemorial. At that time, my own assessment of the revolution was that it would serve as a critical test for all contemporary Islamist movements. If the Iranian Revolution succeeded in establishing a society based on justice, freedom, and progress, these movements would benefit from an enormous motivational energy, which no one in the Muslim world, complaining as it does of backwardness and the burden of oppressive governments, could stop. If the revolution failed, however, its failure would silence for a long time those voices calling for the establishment of Islamic rule and the implementation of Sharī'ah. The Iranian Revolution therefore faced a critical test because it took place in a Muslim country of great importance, one that possesses both an ancient past and a potentially bright future.

Despite the fact that the Islamic Revolution suffered setbacks year after year, proponents of Islamic government in the Arab and Muslim worlds ignored the reverberations that issued from them. These Islamists were not moved by the fact that the revolution and the state ended up firmly in the hands of the clergy; on the contrary, they reiterated their claim that Islamic rule does not necessarily mean that the clergy must be in control. Furthermore, these same Islamists were silent when the Islamic government eradicated all opposition parties so that no one except the clergy remained in the political arena. Nor did they protest the hasty and ostentatious trials presided over by the Iranian Justice Minister Khilkhālī, who speedily issued orders of execution and imposed rigid curricula on both public and university educational systems, thereby spreading depression among the people.

Only a few years passed before another Islamist experiment was implemented, this time in the Sudan, the Arab country closest to

Egypt, albeit under markedly different conditions. There, one ruler, Ja'far Numairi, who vacillated between different political systems and orientations, applied Sharī'ah. Initially, people considered Numairi a man of the left supported by progressive forces; he ended up, however, securing only the support of his country's most ignorant and reactionary quarters. Despite the oppressive conduct of this dictator, proponents of Sharī'ah praised him, and asked his opponents to let him undertake his project, while ignoring such issues as starvation, capital punishment, the continuous and scandalous hemorrhage of the country's natural resources, and the open theft of the people's wealth by their rulers. They placed the latter problems on one side of a scale, and the hasty implementation of Sharī'ah, as well as the prohibition of prostitution, the consumption of alcohol, and theft, on the other. In their view, the scale tipped in favor of Sharī'ah at the expense of rectifying the other gross injustices.

Iran and the Sudan are the two countries to have most recently experimented with the implementation of Sharī'ah, and one must consider them in the context of a long series of past attempts in such countries as Saudi Arabia and Pakistan, and partial attempts made in Indonesia and Libya. All of these led to one unmistakable result: systems of governments disconnected from freedom, justice, equality, and other values that both religions and philosophers have always advocated. Even so, the proponents of Sharī'ah in Muslim countries paid no attention to the stark failure of the preceding attempts. On the contrary, they became more vocal in their support for the implementation of Sharī'ah in the Sudan, Egypt's eternal neighbor and co-partner in that vein of life, the River Nile, and watched it become an international scandal.

What does this complete failure to take into account reality, recent history, and concrete models of progress signify? Why does a Muslim society agree to entrust its affairs to leaders who have turned a blind eye to other countries' experiments with Islamic government and who make no effort to learn from the lessons before them or examine their objectives in the light of reality?

The prefabricated response the supporters of these groups give when defending the failure of these experiments is that they were not "Islam" and that Numairi's and Ziyaul Haq's errors have been those of persons alone, and not of Islam itself. In a sense, the supporters' answer is correct: certainly, any attempt at implementing Sharī'ah can potentially deviate from the essence of Sharī'ah itself. In the cases of Iran and the Sudan, it is not fair to burden Sharī'ah with the costs of its faulty implementation. No one can argue this fact.

Nevertheless, the supporters' response contains grave errors, since any other attempt to implement Sharī'ah, let us say in Egyptian society, will be merely another failed implementation. Are we confident that this new implementation of Sharī'ah will avoid previous mistakes and accurately reflect the "essence of Islam"? What guarantee of this do we have? From where do we derive certitude that this, indeed, will happen? How do we know that this new implementation will not repeat the errors of the Saudis or the crimes committed by Numairi and Ziyaul Haq? Have our Islamist movements, which advocate Sharī'ah, exerted any effort to guarantee, in a decisive manner, an implementation devoid of these deficiencies? Although we hear that those two leaders deviated from the "essence of Islam," have we already forgotten that each of them affirmed and still affirms that his experience is the true reflection of that "essence," and is able to find among the clergy, intellectuals, and media people who will marshal the strongest proofs in his favor? Who can ensure that this will not happen in our own [Egyptian] experience? On what basis do we hope that we will be capable of avoiding the problems arising from implementation and realize the "essence of Islam"?

Indeed, the utter neglect of history's lessons is a distinguishing feature of Islamist movements, not just *vis-à-vis* contemporary attempts to implement Sharī'ah, but also in past ones throughout Islamic history. The portrayal of Islamic history by Islamist movements derives primarily from religious texts. When, for example, Islamists speak about Islam's position on social justice, their discussion is saturated with Qur'anic verses and Hadīths [sayings of the Prophet] that advocate social justice. Islamist movements stop with a reading of the texts, imagining that they have proved their case, that is, Islam calls for social justice, and that Islam, more than any other religion, has realized social justice. Does mere reference to religious texts, however, suffice to prove this? Let us take an example familiar to us all: most of the Third World's constitutions are filled with fascinating texts that advocate the realization of justice, equality, and the preservation of freedoms and respect of human rights. Can we claim that in Latin America, a continent plagued by bloody military dictatorships, justice and freedom reign because the constitution guarantees social and economic justice and essential human rights? Isn't it clear that invoking texts alone does not allow us to judge accurately conditions in a certain society or civilization?

This simple example exposes the mistake committed by proponents of Sharī'ah implementation, especially when they posit texts alone as the foundation for their judgment of humanity's central problems. By doing this, they neglect what really happened in Islamic history.

Throughout most of Islamic history, rulers have possessed Qur'anic and Hadīth texts that could have been utilized to promote lofty principles and high moral values. This, however, did not prevent most of these rulers from taking complete control of power, exercising absolute rule, committing folly with the Muslim soul, considering their wealth fair gain, and confiscating people's freedoms. Thus, looking to texts alone clearly cannot compensate for a critical examination of historical events. Undoubtedly, the picture would have been totally different had these lofty texts been actualized throughout Islamic history.

Islamists will argue, once again, that the inadequacy of Sharī'ah implementation has nothing to do with the "essence" of Islam. If this "essence" had never been implemented throughout Islamic history, however, doesn't it lead us to doubt the possibility of its implementation in modern times? Does that not lead us to suspect the ability of this "essence" to influence Muslims generally, when the dominant pattern of their behavior throughout history has been distant from it?

Briefly, proponents of Sharī'ah implementation commit a grave error when they focus their efforts on textual Islam and neglect Islam's historical experience, that is to say, when they are satisfied with Islam as text but neglect Islam as reality. This error becomes even graver when one realizes that Islamists focus their arguments on questions of government, politics, and Sharī'ah. All of these issues have practical aspects that cannot be considered from the perspective of texts alone. We must learn from experience in these matters; they are not simply theoretical or philosophical problematics but questions intimately connected to the kernel of humanity's practical problems. To neglect, therefore, historical events or contemporary attempts to realize Islamic rule is an unforgivable error.

Proponents of Sharī'ah implementation invoke verbal expressions that tend to have a great emotional impact on the masses. Because of this emotional impact, no one debates the expressions themselves, and they become stable and absolute truths in people's minds. Under the microscope of rational analysis, however, these expressions are full of confusion and darkness.

It suffices to give two examples of these claims: first, divine rule as compared to human rule and, second, the viability of Sharī'ah implementation at all times and under all circumstances. As for the first expression, I acknowledge my failure to grasp the meaning of divine rule, referring judgment to God's Sharī'ah, divine governorship, and such similar expressions. My guess is that the reader will find enough evidence in this book to prove that governance is first and foremost a human process, and that invoking divine texts does not preclude the possibility of human intervention in choosing appropriate texts and interpreting them in ways that support the status quo, as has historically been the case. Talking about "divine rule" was only justifiable during the age of prophecies. In historical eras, after the end of the age of messengers and prophets, however, the task of governance became human and it remains human, even if the stipulations invoked are of divine origin. Let us refer once again to the example of a constitution: the loftiest constitutional principles will not bar the emergence of an oppressive ruler who might persecute his subjects and spread fear and oppression among them. In the same vein, the loftiest of heavenly injunctions do not bar and, as a matter of fact, have not barred the emergence of oppressive rulers who manipulate these injunctions in any way they choose, interpreting them according to their whims.

We can only derive a simple lesson from the above—that the implementation of Sharīʻah is not in itself a guarantee of better rule than those governments that have repressed us throughout history. What are more significant and essential, to my mind, are those guarantees that stand between the ruler and deviation from justice (as understood universally). The concept of guarantees is a human creation, one that has evolved during the course of history and has been subject to trial and error until humanity was able to nurture it after many bitter experiences, most of which ended in failure. Humans, however, are still learning and benefiting from each experience.

What is important is that the expression "divine rule" is self-contradictory, since humans have always ruled and have always converted any divine rule into a human experiment, which can either succeed or err depending on how rule is practiced.

The viability of Sharīʻah at all times and under all circumstances is the second expression that has proved controversial. I doubt that there is a direct religious text that denotes the eternal viability of Sharīʻah! I think that deep contemplation of this expression (that is, that Sharīʻah is eternally viable) leads to two essential contradictions: first, the human species changes, and therefore it is essential that the rules that organize human life should change as well. No human who possesses any measure of self-respect and intelligence can deny the fact of human change. This fact stipulates that the rules governing change must change themselves. Simple human reason contradicts the notion that rules of human affairs can be applicable at all times and under all circumstances, especially when humanity has faced fundamental changes from the Stone Age to the Space Age.

Human reason, after deep reflection and experience, has discovered that the essence of human life is subject to change, and is not the creation of the devil. Those who support the idea of viability of Sharī'ah, in its simplest meaning, must acknowledge another fact that stands in sharp contradistinction to their claim: change in human life is inevitable. No one can escape this reality.

The second contradiction, which is inextricably linked to the first, stems from Islamists' understanding of human action. They believe that God has predetermined certain laws for humans that they must eternally follow. The most humans can do is to interpret the religious text anew, though the general outlines of human progress have been predetermined.

The contradiction of this position lies in the fact that God has chosen man as his viceregent and given him priority over all other creatures. How could this notion of the election of man be consistent with the idea that laws are predetermined, even if man were to change? Does a father who cares about raising his children properly and nurturing them emotionally and mentally resort to establishing fixed rules and maintaining specific orders from which the children cannot deviate?

The question of the applicability of Sharī'ah to all times and places needs a careful and comprehensive re-examination in light of the fact that from the standpoints of science and reason, everything in the human arena is subject to change. It is important to draw a clear-cut distinction between Sharī'ah rules and their implementation. Some Muslim legal scholars have pointed out that the principle of *ijtihād* (reasoning) must be used in order to meet the changing conditions of the age. No doubt, this is correct; however, we need to pay close attention to its results. Whenever complexity sets in, especially as economic, social, technological, and scientific transformations take place, the role of *ijtihād* increases. Most of our efforts to conduct our daily affairs are human endeavor, since we must depend on our reason and thinking to run the affairs of our lives. The more distant we are, both in matters of time and civilization, from the Age of Revelation (*'aṣr al-waḥy*), the more important human intellectual effort becomes. Anyone of a realistic inclination who does not blindly follow unclear rhetorical expressions will undoubtedly recognize the importance of stressing the role of human beings in directing their futures. It is only in this context of the increasing importance of human reason that one must examine the assertion of "the viability of Sharī'ah at all times and under all circumstances."

The call to implement Sharī'ah, which is often heard nowadays, is undoubtedly based on great popular appeal. Many Sharī'ah proponents take this mass support as evidence of its correctness. To my mind, the strength of a mass movement that calls for the implementation of a certain principle is not a criterion for the success of such a movement except in one case: when the masses have achieved high levels of consciousness. Many concrete historical examples have proven that the loss and falsification of consciousness may lead to a popular rallying around meaningless issues. For example, the decline of the popular artistic consciousness in Egypt, since the 1970s at least, led millions to embrace unethical songs, foolish movies, and cheap plays. No person of reason can claim that the popularity of these low-level artistic works is proof of their value.

From my personal perspective, I can say with all confidence that the current proliferation of Islamist trends is a stark expression of the lack of consciousness among the masses. The proliferation of such trends is inevitable, after a quarter-century of oppression, the banishment of reason, and the hegemony of a political authority intolerant of discussion. And, after a quarter-century of vacillating, chaotic policies toward religious trends—that is, a complete ban on religious activism and inhuman oppression on the one hand, and support on the other—it is natural that millions of people begin to search for religious alternatives that are least demanding in terms of thinking and mental labor.

The reader must pay special attention to the expression I used in the preceding paragraph: "the current proliferation of Islamist trends." The basic weakness of these trends resides in their superficial understanding of religion; therefore, the attraction of the masses to these religious trends is not a health sign. The Islamists focus on religious rites, sexual taboos, and forms of dress, and imagine that the primary and most important side of Sharīʻah implementation resides in the implementation of rules about alcohol, theft, and prostitution, thus completely overlooking the political and economic problems of modern life and their unending complications. This situation is definitely abnormal, which Egypt has known only under continuous authoritarian regimes and when people are susceptible to the infiltration of backward thought coming from petroleum-based societies that use religion as a tool to preserve their national interests and propagate their deformed ideology internationally.

If any community chooses to be truly Islamic, it must give preference not to the return of legislations of the past, but to removing the rust these legislations have accumulated during the dictatorial past of the Muslim world. A Muslim society must be able to review its laws so that it will be able to cure present problems and face future challenges with a view toward rejecting any oppressive, unjust, and externally imposed rule. What, however, dominates the thinking of contemporary Islamist movements is a backward-looking view that focuses on a return to the past and obscures any futuristic and pragmatic perspectives.

The dangers and challenges of the future face us all, notwithstanding the differences among Islamist, nationalist, and progressive forces. Therefore, it is surely a huge mistake for people like us, critics of contemporary Islamist movements, to consider the proponents of these movements as our enemies. We are all in the same boat, but that boat becomes less and less seaworthy by the day. It is truly unfair to consider the tens of thousands of serious young people who show a keen desire to achieve reform as a deviant group or a lost community that must be fought. To my mind, their biggest problem is that they do not take full advantage of their minds and very often subject themselves to complete intellectual paralysis. No form of oppression or antagonism will solve this problem. Only dialogue leads to the clarification of concepts and positions and the removal of the blind spots that result from adhering to one position all of the time.

To be an extreme partisan of a single religious perspective or to support a specific trend or community within this perspective will, no doubt, lead to dangerous mental deformities, the least of which is intellectual closed-mindedness, wherein one feels that he possesses the whole truth while others follow the wrong way. This feeling of extreme certainty does indeed jeopardize the formation of human reason, especially if such a person falls prey to this feeling while young. Unfortunately, this type of position is not confined to religious questions only, but is apt to extend to other aspects of human life. A person inclined to this position does not believe in a plurality of ways to reach the truth, but feels comfortable with a single opinion and a final answer that needs no further questioning. When this position becomes an enshrined mental habit, it ultimately leads to the disappearance of the spirit of criticism, thus destroying one's creative ability. As a consequence, reform is considered a disease that must be avoided and creativity an innovation that must be resisted.

My guess is that a nation that thinks in such a manner will ultimately face a calamitous end. I also think that the enemies of our Arab and Muslim people (that is, those enemies who refuse to emancipate themselves from the shackles of the past, and who reject creativity and constant renewal in their lives) will be happy to see us founder in our concept of truth and certainty.

In my opinion, the most unfounded myth common in contemporary life is the one propagated by the proponents of the Islamist movement: that imperialism in general and the United States and Zionism in particular are afraid of the Islamist movement and are busy fighting against it. In Egypt, for example, Sadat gave much assistance to the Islamist movement while at the same time adopting a position overtly favorable to the US. As for Saudi Arabia, one can clearly detect a strong alliance between Islamic extremism, which sponsors, both morally and financially, most Islamist movements in the Arab and Muslim worlds, and American interests. In the Sudan, the Muslim Brotherhood Movement (Ikhwān) allied itself with the Numairi regime until he implemented a shallow form of Sharī'ah, Islamic in name only, while becoming an active member of the American camp in the Arab world. In the Occupied Territories, Israel supports the position of Islamist students in Palestinian universities against those students who belong to progressive and nationalist wings. One must not be surprised at these phenomena. It is my firm belief that the direction of contemporary Islamist movements only causes minor and meaningless damage to the interests of the West and those of the United States. The programs of the Islamist movements do not touch, not even in a remote sense, the real interests of the West in the Muslim world. I am certain that the Islamist movements' priority to fight against what they call "communist atheism" renders a great service to the United States. In exchange for this great service, the United States can tolerate much yelling and cursing as long as its true interests benefit.

I repeat once again that any mental attitude that follows a limited path and fails to understand relative truth and the plurality of ways of reaching the truth will ultimately lead its proponents, without their knowledge, to dangerous consequences. As a result, the followers of this path end up formulating undisputed axioms that lead them to think that doubt is a sin, criticism is a crime, and questioning is evil.

It is my sincere hope that the thousands of proponents of the Islamist movements will exit, for however brief a time, the cages into which their spiritual guides have squeezed them, and contemplate what would have happened to humanity since the beginning of civilization had the certainty of reason been the guide. The ages of "certainty" in the life of humanity were ages of decline. In the primitive age, myths were not subject to suspicion. In the Middle Ages in Europe, "certainty" was the dominant state of mind, the certainty of religious truth as understood and practiced by the Church.

Contrary to all of this, the ages of doubt and questioning have been those of progress, renaissance and breakthrough. This was the case with the ancient Greek age, the golden age of Muslim scientists and thinkers, the age of the European Renaissance, and, I might add, the ages of renaissance across the globe.

I seek the permission of our Islamist youth to raise the following motto, which is necessary for our contemporary life: a little bit of skepticism sets reason on the path of righteousness. Skepticism is not always destructive and does not always lead to denial. On the contrary, it is questioning that leads to new intellectual and civilizational positions. It is truly a huge mistake to drive a wedge between skepticism and reality and imagine that they are mutually exclusive. In truth, there is an organic connection between them. In this case, both the negative and positive are intertwined. Humanity reaches a positive form of reality based on conclusive proof only after experiencing precedents based on skepticism, questioning, and criticism. Undoubtedly, both destruction and construction are two sides of the same coin.

The biggest problem facing those thousands of men and women who have sworn allegiance to the contemporary Islamist movement is that they imagine that reaching complete certainty with ready-made answers is the beginning of one's righteous path. To my mind, this attitude lacks any individual or social benefit. In our world marked by constant creativity, innovation, change, and even severe competition, the wheel of progress crushes anyone who searches prematurely for complete certainty and final truth. Certainly, if such certainty were to materialize, it should do so at the end. From the beginning through the long journey of life, the spirit of criticism and questioning is necessary for those who desire to live their lives without self-deception or burying their heads in the sand.

2
Secularism: A Civilizational Requirement

The concept of "secularism" has had a powerful presence in the contemporary Arab world, especially during the past two decades. That is not to say that the Arab world only became familiar with this term in the 1970s, since it had a prior history going back to the beginning of the twentieth century. However, in the last two decades, "secularism" has become the most important current term, used not only in Arab cultural circles but also in political circles, religious platforms, and social and economic symposia. The term appears in almost every book dealing with any aspect of life in the contemporary Arab and Muslim worlds. It rarely happens that a daily or a journal does not devote a section to "secularism."

What is strange about the widespread use of the word "secularism" is that most of its users are incapable of accurately defining it, to the extent that a person may use it several times in conversation before raising the question: "So, what does secularism mean exactly?" I myself have been involved in conversations with Arab intellectuals searching for an accurate definition of the term, as its meaning has become nebulous in their minds and disappeared behind haphazard expressions and false presumptions. All of this may not be surprising, since this term has been permeated by religious, civilizational, historical, and philosophical meanings. What is more dangerous is that the way people use this term has been influenced by their ideological inclinations, to the extent that it has ceased to be a "neutral" term, measurable by both logic and reason. "Partiality" and actively "taking sides" as well as the desire to defend oneself or to hurt antagonists have all influenced the various meanings of this term. As such, it is quite impossible to delineate one specific meaning.

In this chapter, I will try to eliminate some of the ambiguity surrounding the term. I will also point out some factors leading to the confusion in using this term in our contemporary political and cultural lives. I am fully aware that some readers may consider my endeavor to be partial, since I myself am classified as a "secularist," using the language of contemporary political and cultural polemics. However, I hope that in the following pages I will show that this classification itself is part of the problem I would like to clarify, and labeling as "secularist" specific people or currents in our contemporary history is one of the symptoms of the disease that we will try to diagnose.

SECULARISM: BETWEEN SCIENCE AND THE WORLD

A heated debate has arisen in our cultural lives about the meaning of secularism. Is the term connected to "science" (*'ilm*) or to the world (*'ālam*)? If the Arabic term *'ilmāniyyah* was derived from the word *'ilm*, then we would need to use a lower diacritical mark (*kasrah*), and if it is derived from the word *'ālam*, then we need to use an upper diacritical mark (*fatḥah*). What is curious is that both secularist thinkers, such as Zakī Najīb Maḥmūd, and anti-secularists, such as Anwar al-Jindī and most theoreticians of the contemporary Islamist movements, totally reject the derivation of the term *'ilmāniyyah* from *'ilm* ('science') and affirm its derivation from *'ālam* or 'world'.

Undoubtedly, the linkage between *'ilmāniyyah* and *'ālam* is more accurate than that with the latter term *'ilm*. As a matter of fact, if we wish to be accurate, the correct translation of secularism to Arabic is *zamāniyyah* ("temporality" or "of time") since the English expression "secular" is derived from the Latin "*saeculum*," translated as "the times" or "the spirit of the age."

Therefore, the word "secularism" in European languages is linked to temporality or temporal matters, that is, to what happens in this world and on this earth, as compared to spiritual matters that concern the afterworld. However, there is a close link between the interest in the affairs of this world and science, since science in its modern usage appeared at the moment when the transformation to extract the affairs of this life from the institutions dominated by spiritual authority began to take shape. By its nature, science is temporal; it has no claim to eternality and, as a matter of course, science is always disposed to self-correction and to overcome its own deficiencies. Science assumes that our accurate knowledge is solely focused on the world in which we live, and it leaves what is beyond the world to other types of knowledge, religious or mystical.

Scientific discourse is worldly (*'ālaminiyyah*) by nature, focusing on this world in order to understand its laws. Also, scientific discourse is temporal, in the sense that it recognizes that it is constantly evolving and changing and has no place for "eternal truths." Since science is the human proclivity to understand the world, I think that the uproar over the derivation of the term '*ilmāniyyah*' from either '*ālam* or '*ilm* is highly exaggerated, since the meanings are intertwined.

The aforementioned discussion summarizes the linguistic and historical backgrounds of this term, used in the Arabic language as a description of the term '*ilmāniyyah*'. In its origin, the expression "secularism" was a reflection of a civilizational condition appearing in Europe at the dawn of the Renaissance, and it is still what distinguishes the West's position on the affairs of this world and those of religion to this day. In the contemporary Arab world, the term '*ilmāniyyah*' has been misused especially by its opponents. Undoubtedly, the transition of the expression to our contemporary life in the Arab world has given birth to specific problems and added new shades of meaning to the expression.

IS SECULARISM AN INTEGRATED PROJECT?

In order to discern its salient features, we must distinguish between two phases of secularism in the modern Arab world. The first phase appeared during the time of the Arab world's civilizational shock (*ṣadmah ḥaḍāriyyah*) resulting from encountering a superior entity, that is, the West; the second is the contemporary phase of secularism, which occurred during the last quarter of the twentieth century.

At the end of the nineteenth century, European science had reached its acme, and optimism in the triumph of science over the problems and hindrances facing humanity bewildered human minds, even in Europe, and pushed them to conclusions that were somewhat removed from scientific precision itself. It is natural that this enchantment with science is reflected in the thinking of our leaders in the Arab world, who assert that salvation from the backwardness of the Middle Ages, which still remains with us in major aspects of our lives, will take place only by adopting the European secularist model *in toto*. Without embarking upon a detailed analysis of the opinions of such thinkers as Salāma Mūsa, Shiblī Shumayl, and Ismā'īl Mazhar, and without passing judgment on them, the first and oldest movement of Arab secularism was characterized by the following three features.

First, it was positive in the sense that it sought to realize a civilizational objective with well-rounded features, which was the construction of Arab society along the lines of a modern European model.

Second, what distinguishes the preceding characteristic is that it was an integrated project purporting to modernize all parts of life in the Western fashion. In this sense, one may consider Muḥammad 'Alī (an Albanian ruler in Egypt in the nineteenth century) the first real secularist in the modern Arab world and the leader of the first integrated project of renaissance founded on a comprehensive modernization of the European example. However, 'Alī's brand of secularism can be seen in the domain of praxis, that is, in the realms of education, economics, and politics, without being supported by a conscious theoretical discourse. It took the thinkers mentioned above about a century to articulate this discourse.

Third, and paradoxically, the first Arab movement of secularism was primarily directed against Europe. It is well-known that the declared goal of the pioneers of this current was to follow in the footsteps of Europe in order to achieve emancipation from it. Nineteenth-century Arab secularists advocated technological and scientific progress while resolving to eject European colonialism.

In discerning the specific features of the first Arab secularism in its early phase, we can grasp, by way of comparison and antithesis, the distinguishing characteristics of contemporary Arab secularism, that is, the second phase. The historical context in which this second secularism appeared was to a large extent different from the first. Our countries passed through several experiences during these two phases during which they enjoyed some victories and also suffered from cultural, economic, military, and political defeats and setbacks. After independence, the dominant issue was no longer that of seeking liberation from imperialism. The focus shifted to the question of economic development and the capacity of Arab societies to achieve and maintain the minimum levels of a reasonable livelihood. As a result, nationalist, liberal, and leftist movements competed with each other. However, it was the Islamist movement that attracted the larger number of people, excited their imaginations, and offered them the broadest hope. It very quickly broke through the narrow confines into which official authorities planned to squeeze it. Islamists' ambitions went beyond the official line, which subsequently forced the authorities to change course and open new doors to them, giving them moral and financial support. Initially, the authorities in the Arab world planned to use the Islamists in order to silence those voices advocating democracy and social justice. They were voices belonging to a variety of political trends. However, the main objective of the Islamist current matured into a special project, that of constructing its own state. As a result, its own mission became quite popular and competitive. Therefore, it was expected that the Islamist movement would expand its framework from one that intended to augment the role of religion in the life of the individual to one calling for giving religious guidance to the institutions themselves, and the subjection of the social system to the authority of religion. Thus, the Islamist movement showed more ambition, going so far as to put its religious stamp on the politics of the state. The underlying feature of this goal was to construct legislation in the image of Sharī'ah. The same call moved swiftly into the economic domain, advocating the Islamization of economic institutions.

The Islamist movement wedded action to theory by establishing Islamic banks and giant financial corporations. Afterwards, it moved to Islamize cultural and intellectual institutions and flooded the markets with books, journals, and publications with the intent of shaping the minds of a whole generation. It also censored cultural activities, which led to the banning of plays and dance parties, and in certain cases, asked its followers to boycott television and to wear Islamic dress during sports activities. As the Islamist movement became more and more active in the various affairs of society, focusing its efforts on framing the various aspects of life and all social institutions in its own specific image, it naturally had a decisive impact on the meaning of secularism in our contemporary history.

Presently, secularism in the Arab world is on the defensive in every sphere. That is to say, its major goal at present is to resist this torrential Islamist current. It does not purport to construct its project, as was the case with the first secularism of the early part of the twentieth century. It is now a negative secularism, fully aware of the things it rejects. Present-day Arab secularism includes nationalist, leftist, liberal, and non-politicized intellectuals. To the extent that these people differ in their definitions of such terms as progress, reform, and renaissance, and in determining which path they want society to follow, they all reject the general goals promoted by the Islamists and are united in the conviction that the kind of organization advocated by the Islamist current will never solve society's real problems. This organization would lead to the multiplication of problems in society and would, sooner or later, lead to the dominance of bloody conflict over democratic dialogue.

Therefore, the contemporary Arab secularist movement differs from its predecessor at the beginning of the twentieth century in the following features. First, contemporary Arab secularism does not constitute an integrated project capable of competing with other projects of renaissance. Second, far from forming a discourse supported by a homogenous group of people or currents of thought, this secularism is made up of a variety of groups which hold divergent ideological orientations. Third, what unites these divergent groups is their rejection of the Islamist project. That is to say, they cooperate in the negative features to the same extent that they disagree over the positive orientations. This makes contemporary Arab secularism a defensive movement from the start.

We can now clearly grasp the difference between the contemporary Islamist current and the secular one. The antithesis between both currents is not a matter of two projects *per se*. On the one hand, there is an Islamist project, and on the other, defensive attempts to critique and expose the points of deficiencies in this project. Neither is it an antithesis of two ideologies. On the one hand, there is a singular Islamist ideology (with some differences among its subcurrents in the area of detail, but its general orientation and agenda for the future are the same), and on the other, a group of divergent ideologies united only by their rejection of the political solution adopted by the Islamist current.

Undoubtedly, this description of secularism in our contemporary Arab world as more of a "reaction" than an "action" will cause many to raise a justifiable objection, namely that secularism of this nature will accept the current status quo and focus its efforts on arresting "the change" promoted by the Islamist current. While the Islamist movement makes a courageous appeal to its millions of proponents to introduce radical change in the affairs of society (an appeal that includes, implicitly or explicitly, a total rejection of the status quo), it seems that secularism only advocates silencing the voice of this strong call for change; consequently, its own thinking, implicitly or explicitly, includes the acceptance of the current status quo.

However, this objection, as a matter of fact, rests on a superficial understanding of the position of contemporary Arab secularism. Any attempt to fathom such a position will necessarily unveil a radically different image: contemporary Arab secularists of all types in fact desire the continuation of these radical changes in the movement of society, changes that confirm society's vitality, its capacity to renew itself and correct its direction. However, they insist that the conflict between the two opposing groups leading to this change should be "human" in nature. That is, the conflict should take place amongst groups of people; one group should not be able to claim that it speaks in the name of the divine and therefore gain, at the expense of the others, a place it does not deserve. Secularists assert that invoking "heaven" or seeking an association with the divine in order to promote one group against another will distort the real issues by delaying solutions and placing the conflict in a false framework dominated by formalities to the extent that reason, logic and effort will fail to produce successful and realistic solutions. In reality, in spite of its exploitation of sacred texts, the Islamist trend remains human, that is, guided by the perspective of human beings who fight for specific social and historical interests. The simplest proof of this is the great divide that separates many of the Islamist subcurrents, each of which is propagating its own form of Islam. This division would not exist had these voices been divine. What Arab secularists desire is that both sides, religious and secular, face each other as humans who can be either right or wrong, or that this conflict is actually "the survival of the fittest" in an intellectual sense, and "heaven" is not supporting one side against the other.

In other words, contemporary secularism, in its different currents, demands that the right conditions provide structure for any social conflict and that this conflict should take place on a human platform. Furthermore, it demands a healthy atmosphere and correct choices among the existing alternatives, be they conservative reactionary, liberal, leftist, or nationalist. The reliance of one side on a "heavenly pole" in this conflict is but a deception that masks an implicit desire to terminate the conditions of this dialogue in principle.

Since the 1970s, this Arab secularism has waged an unequal battle with the Islamist current. This battle had also taken place in the preceding decades but the features of the current battle between contemporary secularism and the Islamist trend have taken shape since the 1970s, or to be more precise, since the defeat of 1967.

What has made us portray this as an unequal conflict? And which side is more likely to tip the balance? Islamists have persistently claimed that they have been the oppressed side in this conflict and point to the confrontations that sometimes take place between some of them and official authorities, which often lead to arrest, repression, torture, prison sentences, and sometimes execution. In spite of our admission of this fact, the lack of parity between the two sides works in the interest of Islamists and against secularists for a number of reasons.

First, most of the conflicts between the state and Islamists have been principally political and not doctrinal in nature, though it is true that both sides attribute a doctrinal color to these conflicts. On the one hand, the state asserts that it fights against religious extremism because such extremism offers a false interpretation of Islamic teachings; the state counters by recruiting its preachers to refute extremism from a normative or theological Islamic perspective. On the other hand, Islamists criticize the conceptual framework of the state on the premise that it is man-made and secularist, and suggest that such terms as *kāfirah* or *Jāhiliyyah* (infidel or ignorant) are perhaps applicable to the state. However, behind this doctrinal façade hide sharp political differences that are at the heart of most of these conflicts. No sharp conflict would exist had the Islamist movement not mounted a political challenge, in the widest sense, against the state and had it not been extremist at the doctrinal level. One should not consider these sharp conflicts as signs that the state persistently oppresses the Islamist current.

Second, it is possible to argue that, contrary to what is usually thought, the state gave strong moral and material support to Islamists in the mid-1970s. It is now taken for granted that some state organizations lent their support, in terms of money and training, to the Islamist movements in order to overcome democratic and leftist currents, especially on university campuses. That is, secularists suffered some heavy blows from these state organizations, whose intent and efforts were meant to tip the balance toward the Islamists.

It is possible to say that when the phase of direct official support to these groups came to an end (that is, when Islamists proved they were not ready to be forever used as a tool with which the government could hit its real enemies, and when they felt they had the power to chart an independent course of action), the government still supported them, albeit indirectly. At the height of the bloody confrontations between the Egyptian state and the active Islamist organizations, such as al-Takfīr wa'l Hijrah, al-Jihād, and al-Nājūn Mina'l Nār, the state used the mass media to promote a steadily increasing diet of religious programs. It is possible to argue that as the tension between the state and the Islamists heightened, so did the desire of the state to broadcast religious programs. Whenever the intensity of the conflict increased, the state would take care to convince its citizens, through the mass media, that it was fighting *individuals* who misunderstood Islam, and not Islam itself. Naturally, the expansion in broadcasting the religious message to millions of people, though usually implemented at low levels, ended up serving the interests of the Islamist current. This was the case because the published or broadcast topics attacked specific subgroups and ended up broadening the mass base of literalist religiosity from which Islamists recruit their members. Thus the state still unintentionally promoted the religious current. This procession of events serves a model that has been repeated elsewhere.

Third, the state has never denied its Islamic origins. Egypt and the other Arab countries have never known any radical secular movement even remotely connected to how the United States and Europe operate. Therefore, the depiction of the Nasserite era 1952–70, for example, as an extremist radical phase treating Islam with contempt is a myth, lacking either historical or realist bases. In this era, new Islamic institutions such as the Islamic Conference were established and were quite active in the fields of Islamic mission and publication. In addition, Islamic doctrine was highly revered in the domains of general education, media, and official addresses. Of course, what gave rise to this myth was the confrontation taking place between the Muslim Brotherhood Movement and the regime. This myth also flourished among the next generation, which did not witness the events of this period and believed what they read in books and publications.

Individually, no Muslim country has known radical secularism as it is practiced in most countries of the Christian world; and no critical writings, questioning Islam's doctrinal foundations, similar to the type constantly appearing in the West, have ever been known in the Muslim world. Secularist authors are often careful in the choice of their words before they publish their articles, making sure to deny the accusations of unbelief that the ignorant use to threaten any intellectual striving to bring a gleam of light into darkened minds. This is undoubtedly intellectual terrorism, conducted not so much by governments as by public opinion itself. Those doubting this should analyze the content of secularist writings and the discourse secularists use in presenting their perspectives. They will find that secularists are careful to assert their innocence and prove their honesty before they commit even one word to their topic. One will also discover that the arguments of most secularists against the interpretations of Islamists are derived from Islam itself and are presented in a context affirming secularists' desire to declare themselves innocent of an accusation that they know beforehand will be leveled against them.

Undoubtedly, the accusations of extremism leveled against secularists in the Muslim world or of being "a secularist Jihād organization," measured against the famous Islamist organization, come from the mouths of narrow-minded people with limited educations. If they compare the discourse of the most extremist secularists in our country to those in the West, or even to those in our country at the beginning of the twentieth century, they will discover that our country at present does not have any of what is called "extremist secularism," as long as the foundations of Islamic doctrine are protected from harm.

Fourth and finally, the most significant feature of inequality in the current conflict between Islamists and secularists is that the former invoke the support of deeply enshrined Islamic tradition, seek the protection of the religious sacred and derive their arguments from it. It is quite easy for the Islamist side to besiege secularists on the premise that they fall outside tradition or that they challenge it. Thus, Islamists have the complete freedom to present their arguments while accusing their adversaries of unbelief (*kufr*) and forcing them to keep silent and thus denying the opportunity to offer constructive solutions to their people's problems.

The preceding point has special significance at this point in history, which overflows with written and oral polemics between Islamists and secularists. The former claim victory in this ongoing conflict, although they have not waged the war with any special effort. The war has been waged on their behalf by tradition and piety, which are deeply enshrined in the souls of millions of people. This confrontation is akin to those we had as little children: a child, living with his extended family, confronts another from outside the neighborhood. With one shout the first child can bring his whole family to his side, whereas the other child finds himself in a state of isolation, unable to put his capacities to use since he is not familiar with the territory. Afterward, the former child claims victory over the latter.

The conflict in this case does not take place between two equal discourses, but between an ambivalent secularist discourse, strongly restraining itself, and a supercilious authority, in the perfect sense of the word, used by the one side against the other in the absence of rational argument. This side raises a familiar cry: "Be vigilant against the unbeliever!" The intention is to dominate the battlefield with the help of Islamic tradition, which is the heart and soul of the people.

Generally, the conflict between Islamists and secularists remains unequal in spite of the myths about the suppression of Islamic thought and the opening of doors to secularist thought. To convince someone of this, it suffices to compare the number of journals devoted (from cover to cover) to the dissemination of the points of view of the various Islamist movements. One needs to ask: is there even one journal in the Arab world devoted to the spread of secularist ideas? From time to time, some political dailies launch an attack on the Islamist current. However, if these dailies were devoted entirely to secularist thought and specialized in attacking the thought of religious groups, they would expose themselves and their staff to the gravest of dangers.

3
Critiques of Secularism

The meaning of "secularism" lacks clarity in the contemporary Arab discourse. The great variety of secular currents that form this general orientation diverge over a number of issues; however, they agree that the solution offered by the Islamists is not feasible. Either intentionally or unintentionally, Islamists fundamentally misunderstand the meaning of "secularism." However, it is easy to conclude from reading the writings of the different Islamist currents that in describing secularism, the authors have distorted the whole concept to an unfortunate degree. In this chapter, my task is to unveil the nature of this distortion and misunderstanding through a sustained analysis of contemporary Islamist discourse and a careful dissection of the reasons why contemporary Islamists and their sympathizers claim that secularism has no place in a society that believes in Islam.

It is possible to divide the Islamists' critiques of secularism into two major categories. The first consists of propaganda-like criticism devoid of any scientific basis, and the second consists of semi-scientific criticisms. To simplify the task of analysis, I will call the first category "rhetorical criticisms" (*intiqādāt khiṭābiyyah*) and the second "scientific criticisms" (*intiqādāt 'ilmiyyah*), despite the fact that many will be dissatisfied with the use of these two expressions.

RHETORICAL CRITICISM

Undoubtedly, the use of the expression "rhetorical criticism" inherently reflects a measure of underestimation of this orientation and includes an implicit judgment that it does not match the level of criticism that is used in debate. One must not conclude, however, that the rhetorical orientation is less influential than the other; it is, in fact, the most widespread type of criticism in the writings and discourses of contemporary Islamists. The rhetorical nature of this orientation purports to nullify true criticism and evoke an angry emotional response from among the common people. This quality of the rhetorical orientation has become popular among the proponents of the Islamist current because their mental upbringing, which is under the firm control of the contemporary Islamist movements, is based on the planting of the seeds of submission and faith and the elimination of any inclination to accurately research and investigate matters before passing judgment on them. This mental upbringing is based on a contemporary form of *'an'anah*, that is, someone reporting on the authority of someone else without seeking verification or accuracy. So, for example, A conveys an idea from B, and B from C, and so on, while making sure that the ideas forming this *'an'anah* support their claim. Thus, the primary error spreads and very quickly changes to a given which is not subject to debate. I can say without any bias that this brand of rhetorical polemic, which capitalizes more on vulgar emotionalism than on the deliberate use of reason, determines the position of most contemporary Islamist movements toward the question of secularism.

SECULARISM IS IRRELIGION

There is a consensus among contemporary Islamist thinkers that links secularism with irreligion (*lā dīniyyah*). This is their strongest and most influential weapon. When the secularist position is predefined as irreligious, the whole question is resolved before any debate takes place. In this case, it does not matter whether the judgment passed by the Islamists is antithetical to both logic and history, since no one exerts any effort to think about it accurately. What is more important is to distort the reputation of the secularists in the minds of a youth devoid of education, maturity, and the capacity to question, and to manipulate their minds for the purpose of winning supporters in the easiest way possible.

Let us consider a group of definitions of secularism offered by contemporary Islamists that were created in order to ensure that their audiences reached the conclusions the Islamists desired:

The Lebanese religious thinker Muḥammad Mahdī Shams al-Dīn defines secularism as "A way of life, which removes any religious orientation or influence from the organization of society, human relations in society, and the values at the heart of these relations. Secularism is a materialist way of life that originated as a result of the growth of non-religious materialistic philosophies."[1] Let us examine the errors contained within this definition, which seems innocent on the surface.

First, the preceding definition defines the secularist method as one that alienates religion from the organization of society, a political truism to which secularists themselves most probably do not object, since they call for a real separation between religion on the one hand and the political organization of society on the other. This definition, however, very soon moves from the political domain to both the ethical and the social, and depicts secularism as removing religion from the domain of human relations in society and the values contained in these relations. The error lies here. For example, any dedicated secularist in Muslim or Western Christian societies does not accept the notion that the political organization of society should be based on religion; nevertheless, they enter their marriage on the basis of a religious contract, and follow the inspiration and guidance of religious principles and values, applying them to most aspects of their personal and social behavior without abandoning their "secularism."

The second error lies in manipulating the expression "irreligion." This word might mean someone who "is outside the domain of religion," or someone who is "anti-religious" or is "a religious rejectionist." Undoubtedly, if it is possible to describe secularism as irreligious, it is the first definition that applies, since it purports to remove religion from the domain of politics by stressing the human nature of politics, where social and economic interests compete with each other without giving one group the right to claim that it represents the perspective of "heaven." As for the second meaning, the rejection of religion, this is not at all the essence of secularism. It is true that some secularists reject religion but certainly many other secularists are religious, and many religious people are secularist, since, in both cases, religion preserves its sacred character by being distinct from changing religious practices, while at the same time organizing important parts of human life, such as the ethical and spiritual.

The third error lies in imposing the word "materialistic" on the definition, such as when the author claims that "Secularism is a materialist way of life that originated as a result of the growth of non-religious materialistic philosophies." Most Islamist writers link the term "materialism" with secularism, a practice devoid of any scientific basis. Most probably, this is an intended fallacy purporting to link secularism to the negative connotations of materialism in the minds of the people. This linkage performs a great role at the psychological level, since it marshals a great discontent and subconscious hatred that is then directed toward secularism and secularists.

If we consider the modern history of Europe, the cradle of secularism which exported, as many say, secularism to us, we will find that its dominant philosophers and intellectuals fell into two opposed camps: materialism and idealism. The idealists was more prevalent and influential than the materialists and yet, in spite of this, all were secularists. Such philosophers as Descartes, father of modern European idealism, Kant, proponent of critical idealism, Hegel, and many other writers and thinkers steeped in idealism, were all secularists. They strongly opposed the intervention of the Church or religion in the political and social organization of the state, while at the same time being arch-enemies of materialism. Although it is true that some secularists followed materialist doctrines, materialism does not necessarily have an organic connection with secularism. Can we assume that the history of secularist Europe was materialist, while a great number of idealists—poets, artists, spiritual thinkers, and philosophers—were waging fierce battles against materialism?

It seems that Islamist thinkers believe that any discourse that does not issue from a religious source must necessarily be materialistic. Our Shaykh, from whom we quoted the preceding definition, describes the scientific curricula as "materialistic," which make man "an instinct" devoid of spirit, reason, will, and ambition. The author summarizes his position: "This philosophy and human knowledge, influenced by its pure materialistic consideration of man, converted itself, in its social and political practice, into what is called 'secularism.' This purely materialistic philosophy is based on a method, which atomizes man and condenses him into a highly complex materialistic mass."

Thus, the whole of Western civilization—the civilization of Shakespeare, Goethe, Bach, Beethoven, Rembrandt, Michelangelo, and Einstein—is reduced to materialism, which cancels out humanity's sublime and spiritual aspects, as though all of these people had no message in their lives except to assert human instinct and bestiality. I am not sure whether this shameful reduction is based on ignorance or is an intended slur directed at people who cannot call the Islamists to account. If we permit ourselves to refer to science, which has flourished since the dawn of secularist European civilization, as materialistic, what do we call other spiritual products, such as poetry, music, literature, philosophy, and historical, social, and political thought? Even science cannot be referred to as materialistic, except from a narrow-minded perspective that overlooks its most important features. Scientific discovery is in fact a spiritual process of the highest order. And it is impossible to portray the scientist, who spends their entire life trying to clarify one ambiguous point, to elevate and expand the authority of human reason, and who practices the highest levels of patience and control of will, as a person who purports to reduce human beings to an "instinct," without a soul, reason or will. If science targets the sphere of matter (and this is not the case with all sciences), it aims to conquer the world of matter, overcome it and control it by means of understanding its laws.

Let us consider another fallacious case offered by Islamist thinkers. In a book devoted to critiquing secularism, Egyptian author Anwar Jundī defines the expression *'ilmāniyyah* as a translation of the Latin word "secular," which, he states, in European languages means "irreligious." One notices first that the word "secular" is not Latin but English derived from a Latin source, and the word does not mean "irreligious" at all, but "temporal." Our great thinker begins his book with a fundamental distortion, followed by more flagrant distortions. For example:

> Secularism did not confine itself to a call of separating religion from society. In the estimation of its proponents, such a call is but the first stage, which prepares both thought and society to a critical step, which is the secularization of the Arab self on the premise that permanently leaves behind anything connecting it to its thought, tradition, religion, and old values themselves. Instead, the Arab self turns to adopting the scientific method.[2]

Here, we face a series of errors, the most important of which is that the secularists' goal is to banish thought, religion, tradition, and all old values. The mere mention of leading Arab secularists such as Ṭāha Hussain, 'Aqqād, Māzinī, and Haykal, original researchers in tradition and firm defenders of the authenticity of Arab identity, refutes such a claim. The second glaring fallacy places scientific method in opposition to tradition, religion, and ancient values. It sounds as if a person who adopts the former, science, will discard the latter, and vice versa. This fallacy is refuted not just by secularists but also by Islamists themselves, who correctly assert that our original Islamic tradition abounds in examples of scientists who followed a pioneering scientific method in both accuracy and discipline.

Still another Egyptian Islamist writer, Dr Muḥammad Yaḥya, equates secularism with irreligion (*lā dīniyyah*). He argues that the general orientation of education and culture in our Arab countries rejects religion:

> The universities and schools, following in the footsteps of Western doctrines, were the first institutions to preach irreligion in the curricula, advocating the elimination of religion from them, and studying religion as a positivist human phenomenon. Irreligion, conveyed by such Western cultural models as the realistic novel, theatre, modern poetry, ballet, and cinema, seeped into the domains of the arts and humanities. These purely positivist domains have not given room to any religious conception and, with these influences, non-religiosity spread to the whole social collectivity.[3]

Thus, all of our teaching has become non-religious. Why? Because "religion was separated from curricula." With this ambiguous phrase, our author has condemned the entire educational system. This system may be deficient in many ways; however, these deficiencies have absolutely nothing to do with what our author says. How can he say that religion is separated from our curricula when all of us, and our children after us, study religion throughout the various stages of our general education, in addition to being exposed to the wide area of religious topics covered by our mass media? Perhaps by the separation of religion from our curricula the author means that we have yet to study in our colleges such "sciences" as Islamic chemistry, Islamic cosmology, and Islamic geology, propagated by the "Islamization of knowledge" school. The doctrine of the "Islamization of knowledge" is strongly advocated in Islamist circles nowadays; this is proven by the great circulation of such modes of thinking as "Islamic medicine." If my interpretation or "reasoning" (*ijtihād*) is correct, my response to the "Islamization of knowledge" doctrine is to refer to the simple fact which stipulates that the science being sought should be the most advanced, and I doubt contemporary science has achieved the best progress in the Muslim world.

As to the reference that religion is being taught in our curricula as a positivist phenomenon, this is clearly a fallacy, since no textbook in any part of the Muslim world would dare touch this area. I wish that our esteemed author had given us even one example of a textbook that presents religion in the light of positivism.

Finally, the preceding quoted text implies the notion of subverting all the arts that cultivate and nurture us, since the author places on them the stamp of non-religiosity. Dr Yaḥya is asking us to give up on literary realism. He is, of course, targeting the famous Egyptian novelist Najīb Maḥfūz, whose blood has recently been made permissible to spill by one of the most famous Islamist leaders. For any artistic work to be accepted it must be based on the Islamic conception. Since it is impossible to envision an Islamic ballet, for example, such arts must be banned or must acquire an Islamic coloring in order to become legitimate.

In light of the preceding opinion, embraced by an Islamist not known for extremist views, one of the crimes of secularism becomes its search for the gleam of light that the arts and literature bring to human life. Thus, the Islamic mission (*da'wah*) expands from the domain of Sharī'ah, which should replace any positivist law, to that of the sciences, which must be disqualified if incompatible with the Islamic framework, and, finally, to the domain of arts and humanities, which must be condemned and prohibited as long as they are based on positivistic human themes.

In sum, anything that illuminates human spirit and reason is condemned as secularist, and as long as it is secularist, it is irreligious.

SECULARISM DEPICTED AS A PLOT

In the ideological and theoretical discourse of contemporary Islamist movements, there is a widespread conspiratorial interpretation of cultural, historical, and sometimes scientific phenomena. Islamists see in these phenomena Orientalist, Masonic, Zionist, imperialist, and crusading conspiracies, lying in wait to cause Islam and Muslims harm. More often than not, Islamist writings imply that these quarters are preoccupied with nothing but Islam and Muslims, and that they expend their effort, wealth, energy, and thought convening conferences and planning activities to confine the vindictive Islamic danger and balance their accounts with this ancient enemy.

The logic that justifies the preceding conspiratorial outlook is that Islam, from the Byzantine Empire to the largest crusading country in medieval Europe, inflicted heavy losses on Western powers. They claim the West still remembers these Islamic victories, and is the reason why the West exerts so much effort in preventing the regrouping of Islamic forces, so that it avoids danger to itself. In confronting this type of logic, it is futile to point out the huge differences between the reasons for the victory of one nation over another in the Middle Ages and their equivalent in the modern period. These victories cannot be realized nowadays except under conditions of extreme complexity in which society's doctrinal, political, social, economic, technological, and scientific forces are marshaled. In these matters, the Muslim world lags behind, which makes it impossible to pose the danger to the West that it did in the past. It is also futile to respond to the proponents of this logic and argue that the main concern of the West at the moment is to consummate its control over the Muslim world, which enjoys huge natural resources and strategic locations. All of these responses will be considered moot, mainly because the myth of the "Golden Age" of Islam, which might suddenly arise and renew its past power, glory, and hegemony, occupies a strong and unshakable place in the minds of contemporary Islamists.

These conspiracy theories appear most directly with regard to contemporary Islamist attitudes toward secularism. There is a consensus among Islamists that secularism is but a plot to destroy Islam, that the source of the plot is foreign, and that the proponents of secularism in the

Muslim world are either willing participants in this plot or naïve tools in foreign hands that conspire against Islam.

Let us look at some examples of this. Anwar al-Jundī claims, "Secularism is an original Talmūdic Jewish product, which has had a lasting effect on Western thought." He also makes on a connection between secularism and the Masons, the Talmūd, the French Revolution, and the Age of Enlightenment. He argues that all the above forces aimed to take the Jews out of the ghettos and grant them citizenship as a prelude to dominating European social and intellectual life. This conspiratorial thesis dominates al-Jundī's book from beginning to end. To him, the center of this conspiracy is the "global octopus" from which world evil emanates, and which he tries to describe by using ambiguous expressions such as "Talmūdic" and "Masonic," concepts that have no purpose except to stir fear and contempt in the minds of the youth, especially with regard to the ramifications of such a plot, notably, secularism. People of modest minds such as ours may show some surprise at implicating the French Revolution in this plot or at the claim that the Talmūd and the Age of Enlightenment shared a common goal, even though the latter aimed at liberating human minds from superstition and supernatural beliefs, Talmūdic or otherwise. We may be even more surprised when we find that al-Jundī, whose writings are read with much piety and reverence by thousands, considers the French Revolution and the Age of Enlightenment to have given Jews more civil rights while turning a blind eye to the social, educational, and scientific impact of the Enlightenment, which was a breakthrough in liberating human reason from superstition and myth. He also ignores the enormous influence the French Revolution, whatever its negative points, had on liberating human beings, both socially and politically: the replacement of a feudal aristocratic class by a much more enlightened one and the paving of the way to emancipate oppressed nations. All of this has no value in the eyes of our author; all he is concerned with is that the Enlightenment and French Revolution granted Jews some civil rights and therefore were part of a global Jewish and Masonic conspiracy to dominate the destinies of people all over the world.

In the mind of Dr Muḥammad Yaḥya:

> The secularist idea is the darling daughter of that major enterprise we have referred to as Westernization and cultural colonialism. By attacking religion and separating it from life, the major intention of this enterprise is to create a doctrinal and conceptual vacuum to be filled thereafter by the philosophies and theories of the West. As a

> matter of fact, Christianity, the doctrine of the West, will fill this vacuum. No wonder, therefore, that secularism is the primary arm of Crusading evangelization (*tabshīr ṣalībī*).[4]

In sum, these authors focus on secularism's conspiratorial role, although the conspiracy takes various forms. The case of the conspiracy to destroy Islam seeks to create a doctrinal vacuum paving the way for Christianity to replace Islam. This is the goal of "that huge enterprise we have referred to as Westernization and cultural colonialism." Let us now turn to a logical analysis of this text, while remaining aware that our critique will concern people whose logical reasoning has been reduced to a minimum after joining any of these Islamist currents.

My first observation is that another colleague of the preceding author, Anwar al-Jundī, more esteemed and established than Yaḥya, portrays secularism as Talmūdic Jewish, whereas Yaḥya portrays it as a crusading evangelical plot aimed at replacing Islam with Christianity. Which interpretation do we trust? Shouldn't Islamist thinkers reach a consensus among themselves in order to understand the source of the secularist conspiracy, whether Jewish Talmūdic or evangelical Christian?

Second, Muḥammad Yaḥya keeps referring to secularism as "irreligion." If this is the case, why does he say that the intention of secularism is to replace one religion with another? Wouldn't it be wiser for him to say that the intention is to replace Islamic doctrine with a human one, or to remove human reason from all religious doctrines and replace them with positivist laws?

Finally, putting logic aside for a moment and considering present reality and historical precedent, how can one say that secularism is the primary arm of Christian evangelization? Secularism emerged, as many recognize, including the author himself, as a reaction to the tyranny of the Church, which tried to hinder social and scientific progress in the West. Will the Church, the sponsor of evangelization, be content to employ an arm that tries to destroy it?

The main goal of selecting and analyzing these texts is not to critique their proponents *per se*, but to show the dominant mode of thinking widespread among contemporary Islamist thinkers. The logical contradictions inherent in this mode of thinking prove that contemporary Islamist writers address audiences deprived of both the critical sense and general education that allow them to see these deficiencies. This level of contemporary Islamist discourse assumes a submissive audience, that reads Islamic books only, and does not believe the writings need exposition or criticism. It is in the best interest of these writers to tame their audience in order to market their superficial writings. So what we end up with is an audience with minimal critical consciousness propagating intellectually superficial writings, which in turn deepen the masses' lack of critical consciousness.

SCIENTIFIC CRITIQUES

The critiques of secularism do not rest solely on rhetorical or propagandist foundations such as the ones we have already highlighted. Other forms of critique can be described as scientific and historical, and contain a degree of integrity and cohesiveness. To our mind, secularism's fate depends to a large extent on the ability of secularists to tackle those critiques that have a rational and scientific underpinning. These critiques revolve around linking the question of the secular with the circumstances of European societies at a particular stage in history.

IS SECULARISM A EUROPEAN REQUIREMENT ONLY?

Critics of secularism assert that it appeared in European societies reflecting an historical requirement, which was organically linked to the unique circumstances of Europe in the process of its transition from the medieval to the modern age. This requirement is specific to these societies, whereas other societies that did not undergo similar conditions to those of Europe must not be forced to embrace secularism; if they were, they would then be emulating Europe in a way that obliterates their own authenticity and betrays their national pride. Secularism forms an indivisible part of European history and is organically connected to it. Therefore, it would be a drastic mistake to extract it from its original ground and plant it in another, one not ready or forced to accept it.

This distinction between Europe, where secularism emerged at the dawn of the Renaissance, and the contemporary Muslim world is based on an historical analysis of the conditions of these two social formations in these different eras. During the Renaissance, Europe was struggling to break free from the scientific and intellectual stagnation which characterized the medieval age, Europe's longest historical and least creative and changing period. The Church was the single biggest obstacle standing in the way of Europe's transition to the modern age. The Catholic Church was a powerful, rigidly hierarchical, institution, exerting a huge influence with tyrannical force. Because the Church had a say in both religious and worldly matters, the new European philosophers were forced to confront its authority, which was proving to be an impediment to progress.

Scientists suffered the most at the hands of the Church; they were victimized by the tyranny of the clergy, as a result of the Church's desire to secure complete hegemony for itself. Thus, the progress of Europe depended on confronting that hegemony; curbing the authority of the clergy was a necessary precondition for the renaissance of art, science, and thought in Europe.

In their efforts to refute secularism, Islamists argue that, while secularism was necessary for European progress, the Muslim world did not suffer those same conditions that made secularism inevitable in European societies. Islam never had an ecclesiastical organization equivalent to that of the Catholic Church, a post equivalent to that of the Pope or clergy forming part of a stratified hierarchy. Also, Islam, the argument proceeds, never oppressed scholars or tried to obstruct scientific research. The conditions that gave rise to secularism have not existed in the past or in contemporary periods of Islamic history. Therefore, the call to emulate the West would simply be a form of enchantment with it.

In brief, these are the broad outlines of the arguments refuting secularism in the contemporary Muslim world and for considering it an exported commodity, foreign to the spirit and originality of our societies. This argument is quite attractive and appears decisive, which, in addition to refuting its opponents, places them in an embarrassing position and makes a mockery of them. Many writers seem to have taken this argument at face value, and here I do not just mean Islamists such as Ghazālī, Qaraḍāwī, Jundī, Shams al-Dīn, and 'Imārah, but others influenced by Western culture such as Ḥassan Ḥanafī, Muḥammad 'Ābid al-Jābirī and 'Iṣmat Sayf al-Dawlah.

NOTES

1. Muḥammad Mahdī Shams al-Dīn, *al-'Ilmaniyyah* (Beirut: al-Mu'assassah al-Jāmi'yyah, 1983), 7.
2. Anwar al-Jundī, *Suqūt al-'Ilmaniyyah* (Cairo: Dār al-Kitāb al-Lubnānī, 1973).
3. Muḥammad Yaḥya, *Waraqah thaqāfiyah fī'l radd 'ala al-'ilmāniyyīn* (Cairo: al-Zaharā' li'l I'lām al-'Arabī, 1988), 13.
4. Ibid., 12.

4
Islam and Religious Hierarchy

The primary feature of comparison between the historical conditions in Europe, which made secularism an inevitable phenomenon, and those in the Muslim world is that in its medieval phase an official religious hierarchy dominated Europe, whereas Islam did not experience such a condition. Nor did Islam have clergy in the European sense of the word. Islam had ulama or men of religion, but their authority did not go beyond their own reasoning (*ijtihād*) in matters of religion.

It is impossible to conduct an exhaustive comparison, especially between medieval Europe and the contemporary Muslim world. Besides the four centuries separating the two eras, there is a huge divergence in the foundations of both societies. We would therefore expect to see clear differences in the position of the religious leadership.

However, the claim that Islam has not experienced a religious hierarchy is baseless. Islam may not have experienced a religious institution comparable to that of the Catholic Church, but a strong religious authority exists in almost every Muslim country, which is represented by men specializing in religious matters; this authority very often influences the executive branch of the state. For example, the Azhar in Cairo is a religious institution, presided over by the Shaykh of the Azhar, who had been, until recently, the most influential religious personality revered throughout the Muslim world. In addition, both the Egyptian Iftā' Council, presided over by the mufti of the country, and the Council of the Leading Ulama represent strong religious authority; they consult over significant matters and no execution may take place without its attestation. In contemporary Shī'ism, there is also a hierarchical organization beginning at the bottom with the Mullah, and going to the Ḥujjat al-Islām and Āyat Allah and Āyat Allah al-'Uzma. Since the Iranian Revolution, this hierarchical institution has gained immense power and exercises control over the different areas of life, surpassing even papal authority in the medieval period.

Religious authority has had a presence throughout Islamic history and has used its weight and prestige to defend the original principles of religion, sometimes causing confrontation with the rulers of state. However, under other circumstances, it has placed itself at the service of the rulers, giving them religious and legal support and justifying their actions even when they were tyrannical. This is the case even today. For example, the Azhar has the right to review books and publications and ban them and any other literary and scientific product if they deem the material incompatible with their own interpretation of religion.

If the application of Sharī'ah were realized, as Islamists advocate, it would be inevitable that some religious institutions would surpass in power other societal institutions. Such religious leaders in Egypt as 'Umar 'Abd al-Raḥmān, Ḥāfiz Salāmeh and al-Samāwī and their supporters would have authority in the new state comparable to that of al-Makāshifī in Sudan and Khilkhālī in Iran.

Contemporary critics of secularism insist on drawing a distinction between Christianity and Islam, saying that the former accepted the polarization of secular and religious authorities, whereas the latter did not. What these critics overlook is that Catholicism in medieval Europe dominated these two realms; the term "Catholicism," etymologically speaking, means comprehensive authority in control of this life and the afterlife. It is only after long conflict that the division between the temporal and divine realms took place. Therefore, the meaning of comprehensiveness (*shumūl*) is not confined to Islam alone, as these critics seem to believe, since Christianity experienced the same issues as well. The dominant belief among critics of secularism in Muslim countries is that Christianity is incapable of organizing life or lacks the religious criteria for such an organization; this is quite simplistic, since the critics try to shape history in their own image. Anyone familiar with the history of the medieval period can clearly see the huge effort the Catholic Church expended in order to secure its religious hegemony over small and large matters of life. The New Testament's expression, "Render unto Caesar what is Caesar's," taken by the critics of secularism as proof that Christianity affirms the religion/world dichotomy, was not interpreted as such in the Middle Ages. Europe was able to liberate itself from the Church's hegemony only after intellectuals and scientists and some clergy waged a bitter conflict over a period of two centuries against the Church's dominant authority.

If the proclivity toward comprehensiveness was an historical fact in the history of Christianity, especially in its first ten centuries at least, the conditions of medieval Christianity did not differ from those of Islam. Naturally, the doctrines differ over many details; however, what they had in common was the general orientation toward comprehensiveness. As a result, the factors leading to the emergence of secularism in Europe can be found in the modern Muslim world as well.

RELIGIOUS AUTHORITY AND SCIENCE

The most famous argument the critics of secularism in the Muslim world marshal in their defense is the one stipulating that secularism was the product of an historical requirement in Europe because of religion's open hostility toward science. In order to allow scientific progress to take place, European society had to confine Church authority and it did so by asserting the principle of secularism. The critics go on to argue that Muslim civilization did not witness religious persecution of science and that there was a relationship of mutual tolerance and understanding between the two in Islam.

That there was a conflict between religion and science in medieval Europe is historically accurate, but I am at a loss to understand how these critics are convinced that no conflict between religion and science has ever taken place in Islamic history. What do they have to say about the trials and tribulations befalling such thinkers as the Mu'tazilītes, Ibn Rushd, Suhruwardī, and al-Hallāj, to take but a few examples? Weren't religious leaders behind such persecution? And is the picture here very different from that in medieval Europe?

It might be said that these conditions were pre-modern and that things have changed in the modern period. But what do we say about the oppression perpetrated by men of religion or the Azhar to such modern thinkers as Ṭāha Ḥussain, 'Alī 'Abd al-Rāziq, Muḥammad Khalaf Allah, and many others? Isn't this sufficient proof that the conflict between the intellectual or the scholar and religious authority is still rife in the modern Muslim world?

It might be said as well that the preceding conflict concerned people who challenged essential religious principles, and therefore the conflict was inevitable. In spite of my rejection of such an argument, we still find men of religion in Islam adopting similar attitudes toward modern scientific and intellectual theories. Most Islamic thinkers, mainly men of religion, remain firm in their blacklisting of Darwin and Freud, whose works are still denounced by people who never actually read them. A mere reference to either of their names, along with the name of Karl Marx, is of course one of the major taboos in those countries that nominally embrace Islamic teachings.

It has also been said that these theories result in great damage to religious values. If this were true, what would we say about neutral scientific discoveries that have nothing to do with religion, such as genetic engineering and test-tube babies? In order to find a legitimate place in contemporary Muslim societies, such discoveries must secure the blessing of high religious authorities. We still remember that some religious committees expressed opinions prohibiting the idea of test-tube babies; however, these committees changed their minds after receiving guarantees that blood relationships would be protected in the process.

What matters to us in all of this is that there is indeed a religious authority in the Muslim world that interferes in scientific affairs, and renders opinions on scientific and technological discoveries to the point of prohibiting them. I am not in a position to assess this intervention in this book; what I intend to prove is that the argument of the critics of secularism—that Europe resorted to secularism as a way out of the intrusion in scientific affairs by the official Church and that Islam has no religious institution or ever interfered in science—is a myth we embraced in order to eliminate secularism from our midst. In reality, the reasons that led to the emergence of secularism in Europe also exist in the contemporary Muslim world, with one major difference, which is that the Church was very hostile to science at the dawn of the Renaissance, when science was still in its infancy and ignorance still rampant in society. What is our justification for fighting science in the name of religion after four centuries of miraculous scientific discoveries? How do we permit ourselves to claim that religious authorities in the Muslim world do not impede the progress of science?

ISLAM AND THE MEDIEVAL MENTALITY

The third feature of the argument that links the appearance of secularism with the unique conditions of Europe at the end of the Middle Ages draws a distinction between medieval Europe and Islamic history. Since the Islamic Middle Ages represent the "golden" phase in Islamic history, this argument goes, then adopting secularism is pure emulation of Europe by a society that has had its own unique historical process.

This argument makes a connection between the appearance of an intellectual doctrine and its origin, as though the doctrine must be interconnected with its origin indefinitely. If secularism was the product of the Renaissance, what prohibits it, in principle, from being applied elsewhere? Often, new doctrines making breakthroughs in human history are linked to a specific origin but soon become universal. To confine secularism only to Europe is equivalent to rejecting the application of democratic principles in the Muslim world on the premise that "democracy" is originally a Greek word belonging to the heart of Western civilization. Undoubtedly, the injuries suffered by modern Muslim societies as a result of tyranny and absolute rule should convince us that such a great principle as "democracy" must not be confined to its point of origin, and its ability to serve the foundations of politics and government could be successfully applied, with some modifications, to any human society.

The same is true of secularism. Those who imagine it to be a direct product of the European rebellion against the Catholic Church in the Middle Ages overlook the essence of secularism. European secularism has never rejected religion; this can be easily proven by the fact that religion has not disappeared from Europe after four centuries of complete secularization in all realms of life. Secularism only rejected a certain method of thinking adopted by clergy who used their immense power to enforce it. What is the nature of this method rejected by secularism?

First and foremost, what secularism rejected was the notion of religious authority, which was not based on scientific principles but on using religious texts to prove a certain point. It is clear that such a notion of authority precludes any rational or logical argument since anyone using such a method puts forward no proof or argument, but confronts their audience with the authority of religious text. An audience that does not submit to this authority would be accused of heresy and blasphemy.

This discourse impedes real social, intellectual, and scientific progress. It encourages the belief that some people who possess religious authority control absolute truth and that humanity is divided into those who are on the true path and those who are living a lie. Furthermore, this discourse presumes that reason plays a marginal role, that change in human life is merely a myth, and that to depend on experience and practice is a form of deficiency, since sublime realities ensue from a supreme authority.

Now, let us pose the question: was the medieval period a uniquely European situation or is it applicable to other situations? Our acceptance of secularism, indispensable to us at present, or our rejection of it on the premise that it is not relevant, depends on the answer to this vital question.

Historically speaking, one may say that the Middle Ages belong to a specific civilization and a specific period in history. However, as a mode of thinking, the Middle Ages can recur anywhere, and has many equivalents at present. People who conduct their lives on the basis of possessing the absolute truth, who are not open to debate or who keep quoting the sacred texts possess the medieval mentality even though they live at the dawn of the twenty-first century.

Every society, even in the contemporary period, has its medieval aspects, and every society needs to wrestle with its problems directly by means of rational logic, concrete evidence, and experience. Any contemporary Muslim individual who only debates issues regarding women from the perspective of religious texts or the narratives of the ancestors, without considering the concrete problems and conditions of contemporary women, lives with a medieval mindset and is in need of a comprehensive conceptual revolution. This situation does not only apply to us but to many Third World countries as well. Even many Soviet thinkers, unable until recently to present their views without making reference in large and small matters to the statements of Marx and Lenin, were living with the mentality of the medieval period, even if the subject matter was as modern as space travel. Therefore, Gorbachev's *Perestroika* represented a movement of intellectual reform, in addition to being a social and political movement, and in this it was equivalent to the role of secularism at the end of the medieval period.

The dominant method of contemporary Islamists measures any new situation against a sacred text or searches for a similar case in old legal writings; if not, they use *ijtihād*. Anyone familiar with European civilization knows that Europeans first rebelled against this method of *qiyās* or measurement in an attempt to shake off medieval authority.

Don't we, in the Muslim world, need someone to say to us (as the leading thinkers of the Renaissance said to their contemporaries): if nature and the problems of the world and human beings face you head on, why do you refer everything to the religious texts? Why do you consider inherited thought an authority that is not subject to debate? And why do you not use your minds, which cannot be weaker than those of the ancients, to tackle new situations?

The preceding analysis results in two points. First, besides being an historical phase, the medieval period is a state of mind and manner of thinking that can be repeated in different times and under different circumstances. Second, the salient features of this (medieval) mental situation are still present in contemporary Muslim societies, at the apex of which is the method of religious thinking and the belief that there is one absolute truth, which belongs to Muslims alone. This means that the conditions that led Europe to embrace secularism do currently exist in the Muslim world, and the argument that secularism was a product of specific European conditions which cannot be recreated elsewhere is baseless.

Secularism becomes necessary in any society where autonomous thinking has been replaced by an incapacitated thinking that depends on external sources and that cannot face problems on its own. In this sense, secularism is not a principle imported from the West, but an original principle that all human societies need to consider when finding themselves face to face with authoritarian thinking.

All of this leads to a result that may appear strange at first. We must reverse the above relationship between secularism and the authoritarian mentality. It is quite common for Islamists to portray secularists as imitators of Western civilization, whereas they refer to themselves as authentic and independent in thinking since they reject imported ideologies and adhere to their historical and religious tradition. To my mind, if we think about the matter carefully, we will turn this situation upside down. In their inability to tackle the present from their own perspective and their constant attempt to derive their thinking from past principles, traditionalists (or Islamists) reveal their failure to achieve autonomy and declare directly their dependency on past generations, distant from them by several centuries. It is true that these generations are not foreign to us and that they are squarely located within our civilization. However, the mental outlook of a person who relies on ancient texts for solutions to new situations is that of a dependent person afraid of cultivating independent thinking. In comparison, secularists, who advocate facing the problems of the age with both contemporary logic and rationality, undoubtedly portray independence of mind and dependence on the self. The biggest myth, to my mind, is the lie uttered by the opponents of secularism and accepted by their allies, namely, that secularists in the Muslim world follow in the footsteps of Western thought and seek European solutions to their problems, and that, as a result, they are imitators who depend on the "other." Though the secularist method of discourse may share similarities with European method, there is nothing in the secularists' discourse that forces them to imitate Europeans in their own thinking, practices, and methods. The essence of secularist discourse is mental independence rather than dependence.

In sum, the relationship between the traditionalists and the secularists, as to the independence or dependence of each side, is presented to us in a topsy-turvy way. One simple statement summarizes this situation: the traditionalist thinks through someone else, whereas the secularist thinks through him or herself.

SECULARISM AND ISLAMIC TRADITION

The opponents of secularism imagine that they alone are the guardians of tradition and that secularists preach its destruction by deriving their thinking from a foreign civilization. This has resulted in the traditionalists' firm belief that it is only by rejecting secularism that we will be able to preserve our identity and origins. I hope that I have shown in the previous discussion that secularism is but a reflection of a specific discourse of thinking that must not be connected to the West and that secularism reflects a constant intellectual necessity on the part of any society trying to break from authoritarianism and move toward autonomous reason.

Some Islamists argue that the rejection of secularism is a precondition for the preservation of Islamic tradition. In reality, such values as rationality, criticism, logic, and mental independence are not unique to Western civilization, but are found in Islamic civilization as well. Contemporary secularists in the Muslim world need not be carbon copies of modern Western thinkers, but rather an extension of the rational tradition of the Mu'tazilītes, al-Farābī, Ibn Rushd, and Ibn al-Haytham. Certainly, these thinkers fought many battles against the proponents of literal submission to text and religious authority; perhaps they waged these battles under the banner of "reason and imitation" or the attempt to reconcile reason and Sharī'ah. Although these expressions are not used nowadays, the essence of the battle is the same, though the ancient rationalists waged their battles under better conditions than do contemporary secularists.

In reality, no contemporary secularist has ever advocated burning bridges to the past. Though some at the beginning of the twentieth century may have done so, at present, secularist thought does not turn its back on Islamic tradition. Indeed, contemporary Arab secularist writers have penned some of the most important writings on Islamic tradition. This should not be surprising. Anyone who advocates tackling the problems of the contemporary age should face the future with feet deeply rooted in the past.

One example shows that secularism and interest in tradition are not contradictory. When secularism appeared in Europe in response to the stagnation of the Church, it was in the form of humanism, the largest movement for the study of European tradition. Humanists republished the most important works of Greek philosophy and literature, which enabled Europeans to identify closely with the ancient origins of their civilization. Therefore, in principle, secularism must not reject tradition; the alleged rejection is a myth propagated by its opponents.

Secularism will always study tradition in its proper historical context, and does not commit the error of preferring the past to the present. To secularists, the best way to preserve tradition is by a process of criticism and selection. Objectively speaking, to remove tradition from its historical context inevitably leads to that tradition's demise; to the extent that it becomes "fit to every time and place" will rob the past of its vitality and vigor.

SECULARISM AS A SOCIAL AND POLITICAL NECESSITY

After refuting the arguments directed against secularism and concluding that secularism cannot be confined to one particular society or age, we still must prove that secularism is a political and social necessity for our contemporary Muslim societies. I would like to set out the following arguments.

First, in the past two decades, the politicization of Islam has become a major issue. The number of people who oppose such politicization has decreased and many people now accept the principle in general. One common claim is that separating religion from society undermines religion and narrows its scope. One of the so-called moderate Muslim thinkers has gone so far as to coin the term "tourist Islam" (*al-Islām al-Siyāḥī*) when referring to the opponents of political Islam.

Undoubtedly, the forces of political Islam have succeeded in promoting an idea that had been hitherto rejected: the intervention of religion in politics or the organization of politics according to religious principles. Until the 1960s, most politicians, including the religious ones, took the principle of state–religion separation for granted, without intending to underestimate the importance of religion in society.[1] However, the atmosphere of religious terrorism that has existed since the 1970s has forced many to accept the claim that religion dominates all aspects of life, and that anyone who disagress is stifling religious practice.

Second, historical experience has proven that the scope of freedom is greater in a secular rather than in a religious society. Religious rule entices the majority to oppress the minority, rulers exploit the sacred in order to justify their errors and make themselves infallible, and basic human rights such as freedom of religion and expression can be held captive or sacrificed. Some object to this, saying that Muslim civilization has shown a high level of tolerance, especially with respect to religious minorities in Spain and other parts of the classical Muslim world. This does not contradict our position: Islamic rule guaranteed these freedoms as long as it kept its distance from extremism and literalism in interpreting the sacred text, and resorted to reasoning and intellectual freedom in a way comparable to that of the secularists. Arab rule of Spain was not *per se* Islamic. However, most basic freedoms were compromised in those eras when extremism and rigidity were the rule.

Third, secularism does not assert that humans are divine or infallible, and does acknowledge the limitation of human reason and or failure to realize many of our ambitions. However, it does believe that our greatness resides in our incessant endeavor to overcome our weaknesses and deficiencies. Secularism realizes that human consciousness has achieved fascinating results in this domain and is still striving to achieve more. Human civilization can be defined as the attempt to overcome our own deficiencies. This applies to all features of civilization, though what concerns us here are the political and social.

No one claims that human organizations are perfect. However, our imperfections lead us to strive for improvement. In such a process, we acquire more experiences that enable us to mitigate our mistakes and augment our achievements.

In contrast, the opponents of secularism harbor much contempt for the human race, which they do not articulate, perhaps not even to themselves, although it is at the heart of their teachings. The worst sin to their minds is that political authority derives its legitimacy from the people in the domains of political and social organizations. To them, whatever hails from the people is subject to failure, uncertainty, and change. They use the term "positivist" to refer to human rules in a pejorative way. Most Islamist movements despise the word "democracy" for it means the rule of the people; this attitude is often framed in a traditionalist rationale, claiming that the term is Greek by origin and does not reflect Muslim authenticity. This contempt for people and democracy takes another form when the word "*shūrah*" is offered as an alternative to the word "democracy"; then the discussion will be confined to whether or not *shūrah* is obligatory to the ruler. In the process, people forget that the starting point of *shūrah* is the ruler, whereas that of democracy is the people. They further forget that if the principle of *shūrah* is applied in such a way that it is compatible with the conditions of the age, it will end up as a form of democracy and will have to follow democratic criteria and rules if it is to overcome the authoritarian framework.

Undoubtedly, the concept of "divine sovereignty" (*ḥākimiyat Allah*), introduced by the late Egyptian Islamist, Sayyid Quṭb [d. 1966] and embraced by many other Islamist groups, reflects a basic mistrust of humanity and of the ability of people to properly manage their own affairs. As I argued previously, the principle of "divine sovereignty" can only exist through human beings, which makes it easy for "divine sovereignty" to become "human sovereignty." Also, the principle of "divine sovereignty," which claims to contain a heavenly message, is far more dangerous than human rule, since the latter is subject to error whereas the former grants the ruler infallibility.

Fourth, if international relations are not based on secularist principles, it will be quite difficult for the nation to manage its external affairs. If the principle were religious, then the allegiance of people would follow religious and sectarian lines. For example, the allegiance of the Philippine Muslims would go to Indonesia and the Lebanese Christians to France, etc. Also, the progress of history and civilization has made the adherents of the same religion, who are dispersed in different countries, feature different economic, social, and political characteristics. The substitution of national allegiance with a religious one will lead to problems within societies. Therefore, in international relations, states must define their interests according to their national, not religious, interests. Some Muslim countries take the sides of the Christians in the Turkish–Greek conflict in Cyprus or the side of India against Muslim Pakistan. It is important to point out that any international alliance established on the basis of Islam would translate to an equivalent alliance based on Christianity, which would lead to international conflict between nations not unlike the Crusades and the sectarian conflicts of yesteryear.

Those countries that base their policies on religious and not secular principles do not apply the same logic to their foreign policies. In fact, the moment these countries renounce secularism, they become less independent and more submissive to foreign influences. It suffices to compare Sukarno's Indonesia to Suharto's Indonesia, Bhutto's Pakistan to Ziyaul Haq's Pakistan or democratic Sudan to Numairi's Sudan. Thus, secularism becomes a necessity in international relations, whereas the return to religious bases would cause much harmful disruption in the international arena.

CONCLUSION

The various problems surrounding the concept of secularism in contemporary Arab society clearly reflect the decline of Arab thought in the past two decades. A feature of this decline is the fact that a large number of Arab people, including the Islamists, blindly embrace wrong ideas without first engaging in much contemplation or thought. This is the case with the common Arab understanding of European science and civilization. For example, some Arab authors equate Western science and philosophy with materialism and thus dismiss the spiritual features of Western civilization. Others think that Europeans live in a state of continuous ethical decline, are completely preoccupied with sex and lack any sense of morality. Furthermore, some believe that European legislation is utterly preoccupied with enacting legislation to protect homosexuals and prostitution, etc. These myths, which reflect a false image of contemporary Europe, constitute the only intellectual diet of millions of people in the Arab and Muslim worlds. It would be impossible for these myths to be conveyed from one writer to another, one preacher to another, or one reader to another except in this age of intellectual decline, characterized by biased missionaries (*du'āh*) and ignorant writers who do not read. If the contemporary Islamist movement were truly open-minded, enlightened, and desirous of achieving independence from alien thought, it would expend every effort to correctly understand its enemies, form a realistic image of them, and plant the seeds of research and criticism in the minds of its followers instead of drowning them in the darkness of worn-out clichés.

I have tried to dispel the most frequently held myths regarding secularism in the contemporary Arab world and, most importantly, raise the reader's critical consciousness, a consciousness that is almost absent in the discussions of contemporary Islamists. I hope that the reader is now in a position to understand secularism in its current historical phase in Arab societies. Secularism is not a "comprehensive" project or ideology in the fullest sense of that word, and neither is it a political program adaptable to a political party or to a reform movement. In our current state, secularism is an attempt to thwart a dark current of thought which is sweeping through our countries, aided by powerful internal and external forces. In a wide framework, secularism contains a variety of ideological and political positions. It can include conservative, leftist, liberal, Marxist, and even religious secularists. In that sense, secularism does not show us the path we should follow; however, it clearly points out the path to be avoided.

Contrary to the claims of its critics, secularism is not the product of a particular society in a specific phase of its evolution, but is a necessary requirement for any society threatened by the oppression of tyrannical and authoritarian modes of thinking, in which millions of people are subjected to a systematic campaign to rob them of their ability to question, criticize, and think about the future. The Middle Ages threaten us at the foundation of contemporary life, and the danger of the medieval mentality is not confined to Europe in the first millennium of its Christian history. If the Islamists permit themselves to extract the notion "*Jāhiliyyah*" from its pre-Islamic historical context and consider it applicable to any contemporary society that does not apply divine law, we can also permit ourselves, according to this logic, to extract the concepts of "the Middle Ages" and "secularism" from their European historical contexts and apply them to any society passing through similar social and political conditions as those of Europe in the medieval period.

In the above sense, secularism is a civilizational requirement. When we ponder present conditions in the Muslim world, how it is submerged in the darkness of extremism, anger, and narrow-mindedness, and hear about bloody demonstrations against a vulgar author (Salman Rushdie) who intended with his foolish work to betray the dominant narrow-mindedness in the Muslim world, or when we hear threats against a man of letters (Najīb Maḥfūz), the first Muslim since Tagore to receive the Nobel Prize for literature, we then realize that the contemporary Muslim world still displays the backwardness of the Middle Ages, and that the need for secularism and enlightenment is as urgent in our present context as it was in Europe during its exit from the medieval period.

NOTE

1. In a meeting with Indian leader Nehru in 1954, Egyptian politician Naḥḥās Pasha hoped that the newly-declared Egyptian Republic would be secular in orientation. It was well known that Naḥḥās Pasha was the most religious of Egyptian politicians.

5
Petro-Islam

When Islam appeared fourteen hundred years ago, its birthplace, the Arabian Peninsula, was in dire poverty and the land of the Prophets was barren and dry. As told by the sacred texts, the Prophets spent a great deal of their lives struggling with the basic survival issues of finding food, drink, shelter, and grazing for their animals. When the father of the Prophets, Abraham, said, "O our Lord! I have made some of my offspring to dwell in a valley without cultivation,"[1] this reflected the situation in which the Prophets found themselves and functioned in order to fulfill their mission.

As one of the pillars of Islam, the main objective of pilgrimage was to improve and strengthen religious feeling by establishing bridges among the different generations of Muslims and connecting them to the spiritual milieu that witnessed the rise of their doctrine. Pilgrimage further underscored the connection among Muslims by providing them one center, which is the Ka'bah in Mecca. However, it is undoubtedly clear that economic factors played a leading role in the formation of the Islamic doctrine itself: the most important objective of the pilgrimage was to alleviate the poverty of the inhabitants of this barren desert and enable them to break out of their seclusion when their territory annually became the meeting place of Muslims from all over the world.

It is taken for granted that poverty was the most powerful incentive leading to the emigration of Arabs from the Arabian Peninsula, who carried with them nomadic, austere, and tough values. With the fervor of their new religious message, Arabs were able to stand up to and defeat the most ancient and tyrannical empires. They were thus able to establish a strong and overextended state and build a young and blooming civilization in a surprisingly short time.

However, this formula, based on rigidity, austerity, and poverty in the birthplace of Islam, completely changed in the twentieth century. This change is credited to an accident of nature: the birthplace of Islam suddenly became the home of the greatest of treasures deposited in the recesses of the barren land itself. This accident of nature has led to civilizational paradox (*mufāraqah ḥaḍāriyyah*): from the land which gave rise to the religions of the poor burst forth gold, in the form of oil, from the inside of the earth like an unstoppable torrential rain. This civilizational paradox has radically changed many factors in the world.

The oil of the Middle East did not appear in agricultural societies like Egypt, that had been centralized for thousands of years; nor did it appear in dynamic, active, and mercantile societies such as those in Syria and Lebanon. Oil appeared instead in the lands of tribal societies strongly dominated by inherited traditions, including Islam itself. That is to say, oil appeared in those regions where conservative or traditional Islam exerts the most influence.

In this scenario, one of two things could happen: either that oil wealth could be used in the service of Islam, or Islam could be used in the service of oil wealth. The contemporary reality proves the indisputable fact that the latter probability has materialized. Instead of preserving Islamic purity and using the immense wealth accrued from oil to strengthen its pillars, disseminate it, and realize a complete renaissance throughout the huge Muslim world, contemporary Arab history has followed the opposite direction.

A specific type of Islam has been gathering momentum of late, and appropriately labeled "Petro-Islam." Its first and foremost objective has been to protect oil wealth, or, more appropriately, the type of social relations underlying those tribal societies that possess the lion's share of this wealth. It is common knowledge that the principle of "the few dominating the largest portion of this wealth" permeates the social structure of the Gulf region.

Certainly, wise planning and distribution of this immense Arab oil wealth would benefit not just the local petroleum-based societies, but the larger Arab and Muslim worlds as well. However, that wealth has not been used to resolve the main problems of these societies (such as social and economic inequality) and has remained, more often than not, in the hands of the few at the expense of the majority and in the hands of the present generation at the expense of future ones.

To preserve this unjust state of affairs, it has been quite simple to exploit the religious feeling of the masses in order to spread a form of Islam previously unknown in the history of the Muslim people: the Islam of the veiled woman and bearded man, of the interruption of work for prayer time and the ban on women drivers. In this type of Islam, the struggle focuses on preventing social interaction between men and women; sexual taboos and fears play major roles, having been exaggerated beyond their importance in real life. The fulfillment of religious rites becomes an objective itself, without giving credence to the implied social, ethical, and behavioral contents of such performance.

In essence, this "Petro-Islam" drives a wedge between religion and active human life or between the realm of belief and that of the problems of the individual and society.

Has the appearance of this type of Islam in the land of petroleum and its spread to the rest of the Arab world been a mere accident? Is it a form of intellectual retardation or are there other hidden and more permanent factors we have to account for its spread? What exactly has been the role of petroleum in its appearance?

As we well know, petroleum production has two sides. On one side are the oil-producing countries. Although "oil-producing countries" is a common expression, it does not reflect reality, since most of the so-called oil-producing countries do not produce oil themselves but have foreign companies produce oil for them. On the other side are the oil-consuming countries. It is in the interest of both sides to encourage the appearance of "Petro-Islam." In those countries where oil is produced, the dominant regimes prefer to reduce Islam to mere formalities so that the problems of poverty, unequal distribution of wealth, dominance of the consumption mode of economy, and the loss of the last opportunity to completely revive the oil societies will disappear from people's thinking.

The oil-consuming countries are confident that the flow of this precious commodity will remain safe as long as the minds of the people in the oil countries are occupied by formalities and the texts of the ancient exegetes, interpreters, and jurists. A country like the United States dreams of no better condition than the one prevalent in oil-producing countries, where the new generations are in constant fear of the grave and its severe punishment, especially of those who keep raising critical questions, or dare to rebel against the prevailing conditions and values. Would the West, including Israel, dream of a better condition than the one in which the most dynamic and active Islamist movements proclaim that the question of Jerusalem and the problem with Israel must be postponed until the establishment of the Islamic political system? Can both producers and consumers of oil dream of a better condition in which those Islamist movements that dominate the young generations have never uttered a critical word against the unequal distribution of wealth and the madness of consumption in their countries?

The connection between this "Petro-Islam" and the interests of the oil-consuming countries is indisputably stark, especially when we realize that the avarice of the Muslim oil societies to obtain the commodities of the industrial countries increases day by day.

Thus, the threads of the conspiracy become clear: "Petro-Islam" distracts the minds of its adherents from the external and internal problems of Muslim societies while at the same time deflecting them from posing any threat whatsoever to the oil interests of the big capitalist states. This brand of Islam invites people to be ascetic in this life and to be mindful of their fate after death without impacting their consuming proclivities, which can sometimes become low. This "Petro-Islam" sees no conflict between its encouragements to spread at all levels the rites of Islam and its privileged possession of oil wealth. In brief, this Islam is placed at the service of the oil interests of the ruling elite and their exploitative foreign supporters.

In opposition to the above-described brand of Islam, we can imagine another one that shoulders the responsibility of using oil wealth in order to realize the lofty principles expressed by religious doctrines such as justice, equality, and cooperation. This form of Islam does indeed challenge contemporary Muslim minds and imaginations. Muslims face a new situation they have not met before, namely a situation where doctrine and wealth are intertwined. Therefore, the real challenge facing Muslims is how to make use of wealth in order to preserve the purity of their doctrine and bring about radical improvement in the welfare of the people.

However, that this challenge would be met is a mere dream. Reality testifies that the biggest hurdles facing a real renaissance of the people are those who own the most important wealth in the contemporary world, which is "Petro-Islam." Whenever we hear the preachers and callers (*du'ās*) warn us, almost daily, of the Christian/Western conspiracy against Islam, we must say to them that the closest thing to the West's heart, a West that is oppressive and exploitative before it is Christian, is to make sure that "Petro-Islam" becomes the most dominant doctrine in the whole contemporary Muslim world. The most obnoxious occurence in the eyes of this West would be for the Muslim world to rebel against "Petro-Islam" and make use of this huge wealth to elevate Muslim lives as well as realize the purity of Islamic doctrine.

NOTE

1. Qur'ān, 14: 37.

6
The Contemporary World According to Shaykh Sha'rāwī

This chapter swims against the current. The current about which I speak is both deep and erosive; it washes away all boundaries and dams in its way. This is the religious current, which since the 1970s has evolved to exert huge power in social and cultural milieus, and legislative councils, as well as in the world of economy and finance. I have chosen to swim against not just the worldview of this current, but also against its strongest, most popular, and widespread representative: Shaykh Muḥammad Mutawallī Sha'rāwī [d. 1998]. A number of readers may remember what happened to prominent thinker and philosopher Zakī Najīb Maḥmūd [d. 1989] and the famous man of letters, Yūsuf Idrīs [d. 1991], when both turned their critical attention to him, albeit in the most polite of ways. These two men were severely attacked by the mass of people who make up the Shaykh's disciples and admirers, and both have suffered in the most degrading fashion. This has been the case since Shaykh Sha'rāwī became the Imam of the age; the word "awed" does not accurately convey the relationship between the masses and the Shaykh. In spite of the fact that Islam does not recognize saintly monks, I would say that the masses consider the Shaykh to be in this category.

Shaykh Sha'rāwī spent a great deal of his life humbly teaching with an influence that did not go beyond the circle of his closest disciples. He spent most of his teaching career in both Egypt and Saudi Arabia. In the 1970s, when the Egyptian president Anwar al-Sadat defeated his political enemies and took hold of power, the Shaykh returned to Egypt. Sadat began to lay the groundwork for a dramatic shift in policy, which was predicated on many factors. However, two important factors stand out: first was Egypt's *rapprochement* with the wealthy oil countries and second was the reconstruction of the Islamist movements that had been severely oppressed under the Nasser regime. Sadat intended to use these movements as pillars of support for his new policies and as a counterweight to democratic, leftist, and progressive trends, on the one hand, and the Nasserite trend, on the other.

At this crucial moment in history, Shaykh Sha'rāwī returned to Egypt; his star began to shine the moment he set foot on Egyptian soil. The astute television personality Aḥmad Farāj, who specialized in both liberal artistic programs and serene religious broadcasting and who held a prominent position in the Council of the Arab Broadcasting Corporations in Saudi Arabia in the 1980s, hosted the Shaykh in his program *Light Upon Light*. This program featured a number of artists who later became prominent ministers and others holding prominent jobs.

After being hosted by this program, Shaykh Sha'rāwī's fame shot through the skies like a rocket. It is true that the objective political and social conditions we have already clarified helped a great deal to propel him in a specific period in the contemporary history of Egypt and the Arab world, but the Shaykh's charismatic personality ensured that his television program became the most famous in the Arab world in a short period of time. The Shaykh possesses an attractive personality and an enormous dynamism that accompanies his words and, more importantly, his knowledge of traditional Islamic sciences such as Qur'anic exegesis, Hadīth, and jurisprudence. He is also distinguished by sharp intelligence and deep intuition.

Shaykh Sha'rāwī's sermons have been printed and videotaped and have sold tens of thousands of copies throughout the Arab world. A huge mass of people flock to the places where he preaches in order to listen to his attractive sermons. Because of this, it has been difficult for the Shaykh to resist the temptation of dealing with subjects in which he has no expertise and this is exactly what he began to do after his fame skyrocketed. More often than not, the Shaykh confines himself not just to being an exegete and attractive orator, but takes on the authority of astronomer, ethicist, politician, and economist. It becomes the right if not the obligation of any sound person to challenge the Shaykh on a deep level when he ventures beyond his field of expertise by dealing with controversial issues about which he has no knowledge.

I will just give a number of examples taken from his television programs broadcast during the month of Ramadan. In one of these discussions, the Shaykh offers his thoughts on woman's morality and the type of dress she must wear. He proposes that the woman must be veiled so that men do not suspect the legitimacy of her children. In essence, the Shaykh decrees that the covered or veiled woman is the only kind who gives birth to legitimate children, and if the woman does not conform to this, suspicion will hang over the legitimacy of her children.

When Shaykh Sha'rāwī offers such unfounded ethical theories, it is difficult not to feel both pain and sadness. In this type of thinking, what is implicit is that women are a source of evil and a deviation from what is right, a situation that can only be corrected if women are hidden from the public. According to this thinking, if a woman remains unveiled, her inherent evil and her straying from the right path would lead her to cohabit with men other than her husband. Thus, woman is totally reduced to body and sexuality. This view overlooks the working and educated woman who works hard alongside men without letting her sexuality interfere with her work. The Shaykh's image of women appears to be a call to preserve women's safety and purity. However, in reality, this view reduces woman to the sphere of man's sexual desire. The natural extension of this view from proponents of contemporary Islamist movements prohibits men and women shaking hands, as though this gesture is not simply a social behavior whose function is to facilitate human and social interaction. Such a prohibition is definitely contemptible to human nature and this view of human beings is both bestial and barbaric.

One notices that in the field of sciences, Shaykh Sha'rāwī expresses his opinions freely. I will cite only one example, which centers on his personal explanation of the Qur'anic verses dealing with the cosmos. The Shaykh gave a detailed explanation of his conception of the cosmos in which he determined the connection between the first heaven with the second, the third, etc., and the kind of people who inhabit the different heavens. The Shaykh was addressing a subject matter that the science of cosmology thoroughly covered a long time ago. However, he persists in offering his viewers a medieval view of this science.

What is important about these discussions is the Shaykh's insistence on belittling human reason and science and his infatuation with the perspective that scientific theories are both weak and trivial. This tragicomic situation reaches its apogee when the Shaykh says with utter certainty, while his audience applauds him, that the sciences of technology and cosmology are worthless and that the invention of Kleenex tissue paper or the match is much more useful than the invention of a rocket that reaches the moon.

One cannot avoid raising the question: who benefits from such a discussion in a country that is struggling to catch up in the domains of science and technology and to take a leading position in a world that is governed daily by scientific knowledge? What can the impact of this discussion be on the youth, many of whom live in families infatuated with the Shaykh and who blindly accept whatever he says without criticism? Doesn't the Shaykh realize that our future is linked to science? That we must explore alternative sources of energy before oil runs out and invent new methods of producing food so that we can be self-sufficient and protect our children from starvation, as well as discover affordable economic methods in order to facilitate constructing homes, highways, and cities?

Accusing human reason of deficiency has been one of the most distinguishing characteristics of contemporary Islamist movements. Clearly, a great number of preachers believe that divine revelation can only take its proper place in the human psyche at the expense of human reason: they downplay reason so that people start to believe in revelation. To my mind, this is one of the worst methods of preaching, especially in this age when no creature of sound mind should deny the achievements of science and human reason. Hasn't the Shaykh achieved fame due to scientific achievement, namely, print technology and the mass media? Undoubtedly, human reason is far from omniscient and some of its discoveries are self-contradictory or proven to be wrong. However, the greatness of human reason resides in the fact that it always strives, in spite of its weaknesses, to go beyond its limitations. Undoubtedly, it has greatly succeeded in this endeavor: in less than one century, it enabled us to leap from the age of horse power to that of rockets, and from the communication technology of carrier pigeons to that of the media. It is true that human reason is still limited and that as of yet no solution has been found to such phenomena as cancer; however, it continues to strive and after a while it usually succeeds in finding solutions. Therefore, who is the beneficiary of such unsound criticism of science and reason and the derision directed at the great contributions of human reason, contributions we must learn from in order to improve ourselves?

However, as we have read recently, the most significant venture of the Shaykh has been into the domain of politics. On June 12, 1984, the Kuwaiti daily *al-Waṭan* published a major article by the Shaykh entitled "Islam Challenges Both Communism and Capitalism." When I read the title of this article, I was elated: finally the Shaykh was tackling the domains of politics and economics! Whenever he was asked in the past about politics, the Shaykh refused to answer. I remember that an editor of one of the Egyptian weeklies asked him about his opinion on the Camp David Agreement, signed between Israel and Egypt in 1979. His response was that he did not delve into politics. It is my opinion that refusing to deal with political issues, which in the end center on the organization and planning of people's lives, contradicts the Shaykh's mission and that of most contemporary Islamist movements that insist that "Islam is both religion and life" and that Islam does not recognize the state–religion separation. It seems that politics and religion can be separated in the mind of this great Islamic figure when he finds the questions raised embarrassing.

I read the Shaykh's article very carefully and discovered many surprising things, which I would like to share with the reader. I think that these reflect the real objectives of this great Islamic preacher. The first half of the article discusses the difference between the Persians and the Byzantines during the Prophet's age. At the time, the Persians were polytheists whereas the Byzantines were monotheists, although their doctrine was Christian. Consequently, the Byzantines were closer to the heart of the Prophet and his companions; when the Byzantines were defeated by the Persians [in 614], the Prophet and his companions felt great sadness. The reason for this was that the enmity between the people of Islam and the Persian polytheist was insurmountable. But when the Byzantines defeated the Persians at the same time [c. 628] that the Muslims defeated the polytheists in the battle of Badr, "the victory of the People of the Book over the polytheists was a source of immense happiness to the [Muslim] believers." In his article, the Shaykh purports to speak about our contemporary situation by making connections between our age and that of the Prophet and by dealing with the Islamic position on both communism and capitalism by referring to the Persians and Byzantines. The Persian polytheists symbolize the communist camp and the Byzantines, the People of the Book, symbolize the capitalist camp, or, to be more specific, the United States.

In order to prove to the reader that this is not an unfair assessment of the Shayhk's words, let us ponder the proof:

1) The first proof is in the title of the article. It is indeed unreasonable to devote half the article to the challenge of Muslims to Persian and Byzantines while the subject matter of the article is the challenge confronting Islam with respect to both capitalism and communism. There must be a strong connection between the two.
2) But the strongest proof is Shaykh Sha'rāwī's assertion, before he begins his discussion of the Persians and Byzantines, that "Islam was born in a world similar to the one in which we live nowadays. There was a camp that did not believe in God, but in materialism, and another camp were believers in the *rapprochement* between heaven and earth, and Islam faced each camp according to what it deserved. It faced atheism and declared mighty war against it and faced the camp of those believers in God and embraced them with openness, peace, and security." Therefore, the matter is crystal clear in the comparison. Islam came to a world in which two camps were struggling, and the reader should note his use of the term "camp," which denotes the two camps dominating the contemporary world.

By speaking about the Persians and Byzantines, the Shaykh intends to direct us to the proper attitude we must take with respect to the capitalist and communist camps.

3) Further, the Shaykh repeatedly emphasized in a manner that caught one's attention that Islam's enmity toward the atheist Persian camp (that is to say, the Soviet camp today) was stronger than its enmity toward the Byzantine camp, the People of the Book (that is to say, modern-day Americans). He says afterward, "We must respond to the atheist current in our midst that claims that communism is capable of organizing human life whereas Islam is incapable of doing so." He directly links ancient history to current conditions at the end of his talk, as he does at the beginning.

Therefore, the Shaykh's real objective emerges when he alludes to the Persians and Byzantines. The message he wants to deliver to his millions of listeners and adherents throughout the Arab world is this: your relationship to the Soviets should be open enmity and you should vigorously fight them. As for your relationship to the Americans, the "confrontation" should be milder than with the former since they belong to the camp of believers and People of the Book. In any conflict between the Soviets and the Americans in which the former have the upper hand, Muslims should weep as the Prophet and the believers did when the Persians defeated the Byzantines. If the opposite happens, Muslims should feel joy and happiness.

This noble Shaykh invites us to determine our relationship to the world's superpowers on the basis of religious doctrine alone. As long as the communists are atheistic, we must show constant enmity, and as long as the capitalists of the Western camp are believers, our enmity toward them should be mild. Thus, international conflicts are reduced to a mere comparison between religious doctrines, with the Shaykh failing to pay attention to the policies of this or that camp. So the leader of the capitalist camp (that is, the United States), which provides Israel with weapons that kill our children, set our homes on fire, and expropriate our land, must remain closer to our hearts than the Soviets who, as a matter of principle, support us in all international organizations, have no diplomatic relations with Israel, and try to block Israel's initiatives whenever they are able. They supplied us with weapons which enabled us to launch our most successful war against Israel, the conflict of 1973. The Shaykh ignores the fact that questions of belief and atheism do not determine international relations at all, and that the call to elevate enmity toward the Soviets and reduce that toward the Americans must be looked upon with utter suspicion at this critical juncture in the history of the contemporary Arab world. These calls exploit ancient religious traditions in a way that belittles people's thinking ane are unpatriotic, to say the least.

I would like to go a bit further by saying that anyone who invites us to reduce our enmity toward the capitalist camp on the premise that it is the camp of believers and to launch a crusade against the socialist camp consciously serves, and not naïvely, the interests of the West. The Shaykh knows with certainty that imperialism, from which we have suffered terribly for a long time, hailed from the West, and that Israel would not have been established and continued to persevere into the latter part of this century had it not been for the direct support it received from the West, especially from the United States. He also knows that the socialist camp, after committing the mistake of recognizing Israel before its main traits were revealed (that is when Israel began to function as a base of influence for American neo-imperialism), made amends by giving moral and material support to the Arab world against its enemies. Of course, the socialist camp does not act for the sake of the Arab world alone, but simply aims to weaken the capitalist camp all over the world. In this situation, our interests are the same as those of the Soviets, despite our doctrinal differences.

Therefore, does the noble Shyakh have the right to invite his millions of listeners throughout the Arab world to look with favor at the capitalist camp because it is similar to that of the Byzantines? Granted, the communist camp interfered in Afghanistan and this is an unpardonable sin. However, does the Shaykh know how many "Afghanistans" the capitalist West itself has instigated? Has he heard about the millions massacred at the hands of Western imperialists, those descendants of the Byzantines and the People of the Book, in such countries as Congo, Angola, Kenya, and Mozambique? Or does he support these massacres in the same way they were supported by the Christian clergymen who accompanied the imperialist troops and justified their crimes on the premise of converting these atheist nations to Christianity and including them in the People of the Book? Is it enough to say that Carter's or Reagan's Sunday church attendance justifies the assertion that our relationship to Americans should be like that of the Muslims and the Byzantines meanwhile overlooking deadly US interference in such regions as Latin America, the Middle East, Asia and Africa? Are religions, sent down to poor prophets for the sake of poor believers, empty rituals when perfomed by rulers, even as the teachings of these religions are contradicted by the rulers real actions? Is interest-based banking capitalism's main fault, as our noble Shaykh seems to intimate? Does he not realize that usury supports capitalism, which dominates and exploits poor nations, expropriating their natural resources and planting the seeds of constant political unrest?

I cannot forget what I once saw in Mexico, a country well endowed with oil resources: a mother carrying her child, cleaning with her teeth watermelon rinds from the garbage in order to feed her child. What religion accepts what the strong American neighbor and its giant central secret services do to people in the wretched nations of Mexico, Chile, Argentina, and Grenada? What do the "killing squads" do in El Salvador? What religion accepts the burning of crops and the long-term destruction of fertile land with biological weapons in Vietnam? We do not claim that the Soviet camp is made up of angels; they have many faults as well. However, the Shaykh has targeted one camp at the expense of the other and has forgotten that we live in a country that fights for just causes, and that this conditions us to go beyond the perspective of seeing matters as the People of the Book against the atheists in terms of our international relations.

The Shaykh also gets bogged down in a long discussion that has no other objective than to justify capitalism. To quote the Shaykh,

> Islam did not violate wealth, since if it did, the laborer would not excel in performing his job, and people would have lost their ambition and sense of elevation in life. We must not envy the owner of a building that accrues wealth. The owner of such a building did not exploit anyone since he spent a great amount of money for the sake of the poorest classes. He gave salaries to the digger of the foundation and builder of the building. That is to say that the building acquired its final shape only after its price became food that filled the stomachs of the poorest laborers and clothes that covered the bodies of the workers. Society has benefited from the wealthy. Regardless of whether or not he accepts it, the person who builds for himself (that is the beneficiary) ultimately benefits others.

What catches the eye here is the resemblance of arguments between supporters of the Shaykh and those who preach capitalism: that the spender of money (that is, the capitalist) is the one who moves people to work and enables them to make money. What is really strange is the idea that employment is a gain that society earns from the rich. To my mind, the problem is not in the rich paying the workers, especially if the rich cannot do the job themselves, but the problem is how much money the workers should be paid! Does the amount received correspond to the effort invested by the workers, or are they being exploited? What is the relationship between the owner of the building and the renters? What is the rule of Islam with regard to the raising of rents, sometimes doubling them every five years? The Shaykh appears to be a true defender of the spirit of capitalism, applying such ornate terms to it as "permissible wealth." He certainly knows that the most difficult situation is to establish the limits of what is permissible in the domains of commerce and business.

We reach the peak of our surprise when we hear the Shaykh comment on the following Qur'anic verse: "And We raise some of them above others in ranks."[1] The plumber, according to his explanation, is equal to the government minister as long as the latter is in need of the former; in some instances the poor become much more elevated than the rich: "If we scrutinize the domains of the life of the wealthy and those of the poor, we find out that the poor are more elevated than the wealthy in the realms of ethics, knowledge, and wealth." Thus, the Shaykh returns once more to the following philosophy: "How sweet is the life of the peasant, who has a self-contented heart and who embraces the earth with joy while being covered by a blue tent." In general, according to this philosophy, the poor are elevated while the "wretched" rich own only money.

Thus, the Shaykh delves into the domains of sociology, economics, and politics and takes a stand in all of these against the interests of the poor, the interests of nations and the noble cause of his land. He has done all this in the name of Islam. Therefore, we are not surprised that the Shaykh, in his long life, never criticized the inadequate manner in which the Sharī'ah has been implemented in Pakistan or the Sudan. We are not told that he had raised funds from wealthy Arabs, whose lavish spending is rejected by Islam, for Muslims who die in the thousands in such countries as Bangladesh, Pakistan, Nigeria, and Somalia. All we know about the Shaykh is that the wealthy host him every year and he has nothing but praise for them.

However, the most important issue that the Shaykh raises in his writings is that of the general culture of religious leaders in the Muslim world. Let me begin by giving an example. The only theoretical argument behind the Shaykh's understanding of communism in the above-mentioned article is the following:

> The philosophers of communism have postulated that the theory of communism is based on a thesis and antithesis. And the explanation

> of that is that the owners of wealth [capitalists] have oppressed and exploited the workers and taken away their resources. The antithesis of this situation is that the workers are placed in charge, which would lead to the humbling of the capitalists. In this case, oppression would be shifted from one group to another. The Communist Party is the one that defends this theory and its antithesis and is in full control.

So the Shaykh strives to prove his cultural knowledge by advancing his own understanding of the Marxist dialectic. However, when he discusses the Communist Party by saying that it combines this call and its antithesis, he seems to be saying that the party combines the oppression and exploitation of the workers on the one hand and the return of authority and humbling of the capitalists on the other. This reveals terrible intellectual confusion. As for shifting the exploitation from one group to another, Marxist proponents in fact argue that there is no comparison between the exploited millions of workers and peasants who find solace in religion, and the exploitative few who control the people's sources of income and who have traditionally been attacked by the religious.

No one should criticize Shaykh Sha'rāwī's or any other preacher's right to attack Marxism, communism, and even socialism. However, it behoves one to be well acquainted with the enemy's language before attacking. As a matter of fact, understanding the enemy well can be most effective in disproving his arguments. The Shaykh has the right to hate communism; however, he needs a thorough understanding of Marxist literature so that he does not attack it in ignorance, which, in the final analysis, ends up helping communism itself.

Does the Shaykh know, for example, that one of the best sources on Marxism was authored by a French clergyman who was bitterly opposed to it?[2] Both Christian and Jewish clergy in the West are pioneer intellectuals in their countries, and some have become internationally recognized philosophers and thinkers (for example, Martin Buber, a Jew, and Richard Neibuhr and Paul Tillich, both Christians). They are not just pioneering religious intellectuals but also central to intellectual activity internationally. Undoubtedly, the Shaykh's knowledge of Islamic culture is extensive; however, if he decides to shoulder the task of attacking Western intellectual systems, he must at least comprehend these systems so that his criticism will be well founded.

Unfortunately, when attacking Western culture so vehemently, our Islamic preachers resort to certain clichés, reach foregone conclusions, and talk unscientifically. The youth, who put their trust in those preachers, memorize and reiterate their preacher's words on every occasion and imagine that they have a real grasp of the subject matter at hand. That is why we hear immaturely conceived judgments, for example, about the theory of evolution in which a number of authors claim that Darwin was Jewish, although he was a devout Christian, and that the trio of Darwin, Freud, and Marx are at the bottom of an international Jewish conspiracy that tirelessly works to spread atheism and promiscuity in the world. With great confidence but little understanding, these preachers reduce these monumental theories, which have shaken the entire world, to a statement or two. Do criticize these theories as you wish, dear sirs, as they have indeed been subject to much criticism from different quarters. However, your criticism must be based on sound understanding, knowledge, and depth, and not on ignorance, superficiality, and insubstantialities.

But how can knowledge attain a high status under an oppressive system that allows such religious messages to be disseminated in our wretched age? Ponder, for a moment, the fashion in which the Shaykh delivers his ideas! It is a one-way message. He speaks while his audience listens in utter silence, and if they respond it is only with praise and awe. Why don't these talks take the shape of dialogue and discussion, criticism and response? Why don't both the Shaykh's supporters and opponents debate him and have him respond to their questions? If the Shaykh were to engage his audience, he would only do so by raising brief questions and expecting the audience to nod and applaud. If he were to talk about the Sacred Book of the Muslims, he would say, "What Book?" to which the audience would respond, "This is the Book of the Muslims." This style of lecturing degrades people and brainwashes them, since the speaker demands the audience repeat his words as children do. Instead of engaging them intellectually, he only asks them to repeat his words ensuring that his net of control is spread both wide and deep—they have nothing to say to him except "Amen." If someone were even to try to make critical comments, that person would not have much opportunity since the Shaykh fires off his words and statements so quickly that people have no chance to think or respond.

Profound ignorance, so widespread among the supporters of contemporary Islamist movements, can cause irreparable damage. Worse yet, the proponents of these movements mistake this ignorance for boundless knowledge with which to respond to all questions and dilute all suspicions. This ignorance appears in the lack of general education, the failure to understand those systems of thought Islamists oppose, and the handing-down of memorized statements and clichés from one generation to another and one level of education to another until they become undisputable facts. Only by following a different method can the Islamist movement break away from the prison of this ignorance, when preaching ceases to be a one-way process and becomes a process of critical dialogue based on enlightened thinking, knowledge, and education.

We must give careful consideration to the thought processes of these preachers, so highly regarded by their followers, who issue rulings in all sorts of domains. We must be wary of following their honey-laced words since great damage can come from such ideas, especially if we are to believe Shaykh Sha'rāwī's recommendation to perceive the two contemporary competing international camps in the same way that the Prophet and his companions perceived the Persians and Byzantines.

NOTES

1. Qur'ān: 43: 32.
2. Michel Henry, *Marx* (Paris: Gallimard, 1976).

Part Two

In Debate with Ḥassan Ḥanafī

7
The Future of Islamic Fundamentalism: A Critical Study in Light of Ḥassan Ḥanafī's Approach

A common mode of thinking, one to which many of our contemporary generation subscribe, is to underestimate the past experiences of the [Egyptian] people in order to defend a new experience currently being propagated. During the time of the July 23 Revolution [1952], intellectuals who offered their services to defend the regime, or those who wholeheartedly supported its orientation, kept repeating a statement that came to be accepted by the people as an uncontested premise: that the Egyptian Liberal Party had failed, that the [Egyptian] Left does not represent Egypt since its ideas were inspired from "outside", and that the Right purported to continue its exploitation by keeping the masses in a state of ignorance. What remains therefore is the thought that the Revolution (regardless of whether it takes the form of liberation, national unity, or socialist endeavor) is the only viable and acceptable formula. In the ten years of the "correction" (*taṣḥīḥ*), new modifications were introduced to this formula; however, its general framework, seeking to destroy previous experiences for the sake of one viable perspective, was still valid. This style of thinking became so dominant that even opponents of the regime found it necessary to raze the framework previous experiences to the ground so that the only construction remaining standing would be theirs. That is to say, these opponents embraced the doctrine of the "only truth," which did not accept pluralism or change and which erased other ideas and positions it considered false and slanderous.

It is against the above orientation that Dr Ḥassan Ḥanafī, a prominent professor of Arabic and Islamic philosophy at Cairo University, begins a long series of articles on the contemporary Islamist movement, based on a complete year of research (as the publishers say), discussing investigation proceedings with members of the Jihād Movement, who were accused of assassinating the former president of Egypt, Anwar al-Sadat. Ḥanafī's starting point is the criticism leveled at past liberal experiences, repeating the same arguments embraced by the propagandist authors of the July

23 Revolution, and without attempting in a scientific or logical way to test the accuracy of these arguments. He also leveled similar criticisms at leftists, secularists, and liberals in order to prove that the trend, in which he believes and which he calls "Islamic fundamentalism," is the only one capable of offering a viable solution.

Undoubtedly, it is possible to imagine another starting point in assessing previous political experiences, especially from the beginning of modern Egyptian history, by seeing them as currents that in various ways fed the stream of popular consciousness. Over the past decades, these experiences have resulted in multiple influences that have accumulated and interacted in Egyptian society. A nation's consciousness cannot be fashioned by a process of elimination and accusation whose final goal is to preserve only one current or orientation of thought and practice. Consciousness consists of varying strata of enriching experiences. We can therefore offer a vision of history based on "integration" and not "elimination." However, it seems that many followers of the school of thought produced by the July 23 Revolution can only view history through the lens of "one truth" and have found it necessary to destroy everything before erecting their own unique structure. Ḥassan Ḥanafī's articles did something similar while trying to defend what he calls "Islamic fundamentalism."

The danger of such articles lies in the general perspective they present, which dismisses experiences that contributed both positively and negatively to the formation of a solid popular consciousness over the modern period of history. This narrow perspective has influenced a whole generation and is not the sole responsibility of one author. It was indeed the general milieu, which made the "one and only truth" an inevitable phenomenon. But the real danger of these articles lies in the fact that they purport to offer a treatment of the most sensitive movement in the contemporary Arab world, the most extremist religious movement, and imagine it to be the future of the Arab world. In addition, these articles use modern methods of analysis in order to place the stamp of authenticity, patriotism, and freedom on this movement. Even Western scholars, and Americans in particular, give credence to Islamic fundamentalism by applying the same analytical method as Ḥanafī's. As a result, these articles are important because they raise a critical issue: have all the options in the Arab world failed to the extent that the only one remaining is the Islamist alternative as presented by extremist groups? Is this alternative the only road to salvation?

It is necessary to examine these articles both critically and carefully in order to uncover their methodological and objective errors, their radical and numerous inner contradictions, and their general orientation, which in our opinion adds intellectual confusion and ambivalence to a subject that is already ambiguous and complex. The taboo surrounding such a topic makes it quite impossible from the beginning to conduct a free and honest debate.

Despite the fact that the analysis and criticism we embark upon are not directed against the author of these articles as much as they are to their implicit principles and ideas, it is natural to portray the negative aspects of such articles before beginning a general discussion of the problems they raise. Thus, the reader can detect two primary objectives behind our discussion: first, to show the mistakes and contradictions inherent in these articles, and second, to express our opinion on the sensitive subjects they raise.

I must admit at the beginning that because of the mistakes and contradictions I discovered in these articles, my tone will sometimes be sharp and biting. I have two primary justifications for such sharp criticism. The first is linked to the subject matter itself, which includes Ḥanafī's huge volume of contradictions and erroneous analyses which we will unravel shortly; the second concerns the general principle that any ill-guided approach to those issues that concern the future of whole generations, particularly in a society that already suffers from the aggression of exploiters, oppressors, and usurpers, does not tolerate slight criticism or flattery. We must be mature enough to confront the person who commits errors, especially when he claims to guide minds, particularly those of the youth, in a nation that has long suffered from conceptual delusion disguised as calls for social reform.

JURISTS AND THE CONTEMPORARY ISLAMIST GROUPS

A good number of contemporary Islamist movements, headed by the Jihād Movement, unabashedly declare their adoption of the opinions defended by conservative jurists, especially Ibn Taymiyyah and Ibn Ḥazm [of the medieval period]; the subject of jurists occupies much space in Ḥanafī's articles, especially as he considers himself a modern-day extension of the legacy of the jurists. However, it is difficult for one to discover, on the basis of these articles, a specific position adopted by the author on the jurists or a clear-cut opinion on the influence these jurists have exerted on contemporary Islamist movements.

The author discusses the antagonistic position jurists took toward traditional Islamic sciences such as religion, jurisprudence, wisdom, and mysticism. In Ḥanafī's assessment, this antagonism was a form of

> ... defense of Islamic doctrine against innovation. The jurists upheld the idea of authenticity as opposed to relativism, and the raw or pure text rather than various rationalizations and interpretations. They served as guardians of the original doctrine deflecting the attempts of those who would modernize it in a manner that would erase its uniqueness, origin, and effectiveness. Consequently, the jurists, in spite of being characterized as rigid, extremist, and narrow in horizon, do reflect Islamic authenticity, and this is the reason why contemporary Islamist movements have attached themselves to this old juristic tradition.

The author goes on to say that proponents of Islamist movements, which are influenced by this tradition,

> ... shoulder the task of defending the original against the foreign, defending Islamic doctrine against atheism and preserving the raw and undiluted text against interpretation. Such proponents, like the jurists, are people of unquestioning emulation and not of reason. The religious edicts (*fatāwa*) of these [old] jurists do contain original Islamic answers to the problems of the contemporary age and form religious paradigms that reflect the ability of Islam to accept the contemporary challenge. In this sense, the compendium of Ibn Taymiyyah's *Fatāwa* is a large encyclopedic work that applies original Islamic solutions to the problems of the age.

These articles illustrate the author's sympathy with and appreciation of the ancient jurists and offer justification for the connection between contemporary Islamist movements and their juristic tradition; it is important to object to the contradictions and reactionary attitudes contained in them. First, a glaring contradiction exists between the thesis that the jurists are people of blind imitation and not of reason and that they defend the raw text against diluted interpretations, and between another which stipulates that they are capable of offering Islamic answers to modern problems and prove the ability of Islam to handle contemporary challenges. Anyone who follows a literal understanding of the raw text and prefers imitation to reasoning will not be able to face contemporary challenges or even want to do so. To be able to face the challenges of the present, it is necessary to interpret and modernize the text and, according to Ḥanafī, this is not acceptable.

Second, the author's expressions fall short of showing that he understands the meaning of "Islamic fundamentalism." In this case, authenticity is linked to the prohibition placed on interpretation and exegesis, and any attempt to understand the text becomes a form of innovation—its modernization becomes a form of alienation from the source. The only guiding principle would be to preserve the raw text (to use his expression), that is, to accept its literal meaning as though it had been sealed in a vacuum. It is quite strange that the author describes those jurists who fulfill this task as "guardians" of Islamic doctrine, whereas what they are doing in reality is safeguarding this sealed vacuum; they are, to be more precise, "prison guards" who incarcerate Islamic doctrine in the caves of backwardness and veil it from the light of reason. Even if the author were presenting the attitude of Islamist movements, his use of such terms as "the guardian of doctrine," the preservation of "Islamic authenticity," or the "defense of doctrine against innovation" would lead the reader to conclude that the author supports these positions wholeheartedly. I am at a loss to understand why a contemporary author like Ḥassan Ḥanafī accepts such expressions as "people of blind imitation and not of reason" and states that they "preserve the doctrine against its rationalization and modernization," without offering a critical analysis. He seems to know that millions of young people are subject to the danger of banishing their reason, a process that will undoubtedly jeopardize the future of the Arab nations. In spite of this, he approvingly presents these expressions as he invites youths to embrace them.

Third, it is indeed strange that the author characterizes this reactionary position as a patriotic position which safeguards the nation from its enemies. Elsewhere, he writes, "[The jurists] were foremost in confronting the enemies of the people, both inside and outside." He justifies their connection to contemporary Muslims on the premise that "Names have changed, whereas conditions and enemies have not," and "The jurists shared one objective throughout history, which was to defend the interests of the people nationally and internationally and to safeguard Muslim territories." In the face of this torrent of praise, one cannot help raise the following question: is sticking to the literalist meaning of the text, rejecting reason, modernity, and science, the best way to defend the interests of the people, nationally and internationally? Does this rigid attitude really serve any nation or is it the fastest way to destroy this nation, even if done in the name of authenticity and resisting innovation?

The author's uneven attitude is completely revealed when he writes, "The jurists were people of reformation and change, the guardians of the Sharī'ah, and the protectors of the ummah's interests." How would they advocate change while serving as the "guardians" of the Sharī'ah, protecting its literal text against rationalization and modernization? I am afraid I am incapable of solving this puzzle and it is only the author who can do so.

Fourth, before we recover from our surprise at the author's preceding contradictory position, we come face to face with another contradiction, which is much worse than the former. The author becomes a critic of the jurists' conservative position, after we have just seen him heap praise upon them in the preceding pages. In one article, he discusses the failure of nineteenth-century reform movements: "The reform movement culminated in religious conservatism, liberalism culminated in individual authoritarianism, and the scientific current reverted to superstition and a return to religion." Here we find that religious conservatism, praised earlier as a pedestal of Islamic doctrine and a form of protection against innovation, becomes a vice. Also, what strikes us deeply is the author's assertion that "the scientific current reverted to superstition and a return to religion" since it links the revival of belief with superstition contradicting everything the author wrote earlier. This puzzles the reader: what is the author's exact position on the question of conservatism and modernization, literal reading as opposed to interpretive discourse, and authenticity as opposed to modernity? The reader's confusion intensifies when the author adopts a radical critical position toward the contemporary Muslim Brotherhood Movement, putting forth the same reasons he used to praise Muslim jurists. According to Ḥanafī, the first negative aspect of the contemporary Islamist movement is "Giving priority to belief over reason which takes belief for granted and without any discussion. As a result, emotionalism and extremism were on the rise, which ended up in rigidity, narrowness of horizons and lack of dialogue."

In his evaluation of ʻAbd al-Sallām Faraj's book *The Neglected Duty*,[1] the first pitfall Ḥanafī points out is itself the first virtue the jurists possessed, as noted by him previously. This pitfall is based on

> … the authority of the raw text, either from the Qur'ān or Hadīth or the Muslim jurists, especially Ibn Taymiyyah. This proves that the contemporary Islamist movement is isolated from its present reality and is on the lookout for an alternative in the old tradition and in the reality of the ancients, which made them discount the factor of history from their calculation.

Thus, the raw texts become a sign of backwardness, even though they were just considered a protection of the doctrine and a defense of the ummah's authenticity.

Fifth, in order to dispel the remaining ounce of intelligence in the reader's mind, Ḥanafī in his later articles praises once again the attitude of the jurists in preserving the raw text and its role in pushing history forward. He again discusses Faraj's book *The Neglected Duty*, saying that it contains the raw text exemplified in the texts of the jurists, which are

> … the cream of tradition and its first yeast and the most effective texts in people's lives. Philosophical texts influence only an elitist minority of intellectuals, and doctrinal texts influence only those scholars who are specialists in religion, whereas the jurists' texts function nowadays as political publications, and declaration of political parties and press conferences of the leaders. Therefore, these texts have directly influenced the Islamic movement and its attitude toward the conditions of the contemporary era.

So, after establishing the links between conservatism, backwardness, superstition, and narrow-mindedness and criticizing the book *The Neglected Duty* for its immersion in the raw texts, he re-elevates the role of conservative juristic texts to revolutionary political tracts, which can alone inspire the masses to action, as opposed to doctrinal and philosophical texts.

Finally, before I conclude this discussion, I would like to point out the huge contradiction between Ḥanafī's position in these articles and his well-known general positions enumerated in his books and other publications. Here I would like to single out his latest book, *Tradition and Renewal*, in which he strongly advocates the conversion of religious text into a living contemporary reality. Also, he forcefully criticizes freezing religious text and imprisoning it in past phases of history. His extravagance in interpretation reaches the level of using such an expression as "God is both freedom and land." He also says that the term "Allah" or "God" is self-contradictory, the term "Islam" has lost its original meaning, and the term '*dīn*' or religion does not convey the original intended meaning on the premise that "any language, even if it was ancient, cannot be used anew if it is rejected by modernity." He also calls for a transition from the ancient era, which "centers around God" to the modern age, which "centers around man." He issues a number of judgments: "Islamic Tradition has a common source, the Qur'ān and Hadīth. This is a mere description of a reality and does reach the level of sanctifying them or tradition," and "atheism in Western civilization can be equated to belief in our tradition. In this sense, atheism means the desire to clarify the pragmatic consequences of ideas and is a response to self-sufficient and stagnant belief." In another section, he writes that "atheism is the original meaning of belief and not its opposite. Transmitted custom detracted belief from its original meaning." Also, he writes, "Doctrines do not possess inner veracity; on the contrary, their veracity is based on their influence on pragmatic life and their potential to change reality. Doctrines solely guide and inspire behavior and do not translate into material reality such as historical events, or personalities or institutions in real life." He also writes, "The main objective of revelation is not to prove the existence of a self-sufficient and absolute being in need of no one, but to develop reality in a certain historical period." Also, "secularism functions as the foundation of revelation. Revelation is secular in nature and religiosity is an accidental phenomenon created by history; it appears in times of societal backwardness and loss of evolution." These quotations, taken from the author's most recent writings, offer us a perspective on his intellectual views. It is not my intention here to discuss such ideas; however, I would like to raise the following important question: how can an author in one book criticize the extreme interpretation of religious concepts and doctrines while sympathizing with conservative jurists of the raw text, who attack any simple interpretation or exegesis? Let us suppose that a future historian decides to tackle Ḥanafī's position on this issue; would this historian be able to keep his mental faculties intact after dancing with our author in his mad circle of contradictions?

THE DIRECT SOURCE: THE MUSLIM BROTHERS

The worldview of the Jihād Movement and other extremist Islamist movements in contemporary Egypt owes its origins to the Muslim Brotherhood Movement, founded by Ḥassan al-Banna [d. 1949] in 1928 and known as the Ikhwān. Because of this fact, Ḥanafī discusses in detail the Muslim Brotherhood, taking into account their positive and negative characteristics. However, he commits a great number of historical and methodological errors and, as usual, his discussion of the subject is full of contradictory statements.

He initiates his discussion of the Muslim Brotherhood by linking Ḥassan al-Banna with the modern Egyptian nationalist movement. Such linkage does not concern me here; however, I would like to highlight the reason the author offers for this linkage: "Ḥassan al-Banna began his movement in the city of Ismā'iliyyah on the Suez Canal while being cognizant of the presence of occupation troops. As a result, from the beginning his movement had a strong link with the nationalist movement." The least mature student in logic is able to see the breakdown of such an argument, which links the foundation of the Muslim Brotherhood Movement to nationalist struggle. The author forgets that besides seeing British troops, al-Banna was seeing on a daily basis merchants and workers, some of whom worked for the British. The author fails to mention the historical suspicions raised by some scholars about the secret contacts between the Muslim Brotherhood and the British embassy, and especially the role of Mr Smart, Secretary of Oriental Affairs in the embassy, in supporting the Ikhwān, and the common interest both shared in removing their bitter enemy, the Wafd Party, from power. The author does not discuss these matters or respond to them. All he can do is to link al-Banna with nationalism as long as al-Banna saw British troops in Ismā'iliyyah.

The author discusses the unofficial relationship between the Ikhwān on the one hand, and the Egyptian Council of Workers and Students in 1947 (though 1946 is the actual date), on the other. He criticizes the Ikhwān because it rejected making this relationship official. In spite of his criticism, he concludes that "British imperialism considered the Ikhwān as its main foe in the region." How does the author make such a judgment without responding to the suspicions, mentioned previously, which a number of famous historians raise? Undoubtedly, the Ikhwān played a significant role in fighting against the Egyptian Council of Workers and Students, and the proof of this is their agreement to a truce, inside and outside the university walls, with the government of Ismāil Ṣidqī, which came to power in the 1940s with the intention of eliminating the strong nationalist movement. Anybody who lived in this era certainly remembers the speech given by the leader of the Ikhwān's students, Hassan Dawh, who referred to Ismā'il as "the righteous," in spite of the fact that Ismā'il's dark history was enough to steer away any patriotic person from his path. The author's comments say nothing about the famous enmity between the Ikhwān and the Palace, an enmity supported only by the assassination of Ḥassan al-Banna. Al-Banna's assassination came on the heels of contradictions resulting from the conflict in the 1940s between the Ikhwān and minority parties supported by the Palace. As for the years before that, the relationship between the Palace and the Ikhwān was fairly cordial, since the Ikhwān furnished the Palace with an effective means with which to fight the Wafd Party; this was the heartfelt wish of the King and his supporters.

Ḥanafī commits a grave historical error by stating that "The elections of the student councils in Egyptian universities used to give the Ikhwān candidates 95 percent of the votes." The documents and testimonies of this period prove otherwise. The Ikhwān were totally incapable of controlling the student councils and most of the votes went to the Wafd and other democratic parties. Furthermore, the author exaggerates in his assessment when he writes, "Every nationalist leader was in contact with the Ikhwān Movement either by becoming a member or attending its symposia and lectures." This statement contains a false generalization since it applies only to the Free Officers, including Nasser, and to Ḥanafī himself; however, this is far from true when it comes to the Wafdist and leftist leadership, leadership that played a crucial role in the nationalist movement before 1952.

The author heaps praise on the Ikhwān, flirting with their patriotism, nationalism, and socialism:

> For most of the 1952 Revolution years, the Ikhwān were incarcerated in prisons, and were distant from the construction of Egypt and the construction of the most ambitious nationalist project since Muḥammad 'Alī's days. They were distant from all of this in spite of the fact that before the Revolution, they were the main proponents of such a project and had left their indelible mark on it. In spite of fighting against the British in the 1951 Suez war, due to their incarceration, they did not witness the nationalization of the Suez Canal. In spite of calling for comprehensive Arab unity, they were not in a position to fight against the 1956 tripartite attack on Egypt; they also were not witness to the socialist construction of Egypt between 1961 and 1964 although they were the first proponents for social justice and socialism. In spite of defending the independence of Egypt against military alliances and the relationship between Egypt and the West, they did not witness the battles waged by Egypt against the Western-inspired Islamic pact in 1956.

On the same page where the author sings the praises of the Ikhwān and gently admonishes those behind the Nasser Revolution for imprisoning them and distancing them from the project of construction, he discusses their release from prison by the Sadat regime: "Sadat released them while knowing that they posed no threat to him because of their enshrined enmity to Nasser. In light of their intellectual backwardness, enmity to socialism, Arab nationalism, the Soviet Union, their traditional pro-Western positions, and their concern about ritual Islam, there was a common denominator between them and Sadat." Thus, in the author's writing, the Ikhwān move swiftly from the camps of socialism, nationalism, and enmity of the West to its exact opposite.

THE ROLE OF NASSERISM AND THE CONFLICT WITH THE REVOLUTION

Ḥanafī shares the opinion of many an historian that the oppression and torture of the Ikhwān in Nasser's prisons was the direct cause of some of their extremism, violence, and thirst for revenge. This is the foundation of the formation of extremist groups in Egypt in the 1970s. On the basis of such analysis, one can say that the main reason for the emergence of these extremist groups was the conflict between the Revolution, that is, the Nasserites who carried out the 1952 Revolution, and the Ikhwān.

Before we discuss Ḥanafī's opinion on this important subject, I would like to point out the way in which he uses the term "Nasserism" in his writings. Sometimes, he considers Nasserism to be an extension of the religious reform movement that appeared in the nineteenth century. He also discusses Arab nationalism, of which he considers Islam to be a component, and takes Nasserism as a continuation of Arab nationalism, "seen by the Arab and Muslim peoples as a continuation of the religious reform movement in spite of its secularist appearance." However, he exaggerates the role of Nasserism in the 1970s, making it solely responsible for student activism and the only movement behind the popular uprising of January 18 and 19, since it was "the poor Nasserite masses who staged the uprising." He must have understood that his judgment was far off the mark: the January rebellion was much wider in scope than that, and he afterward expanded his definition of Nasserites to include socialists, progressives, nationalists, and Marxists. This is quite an odd definition of Nasserism; no one has ever equated Nasserism with all of these trends, especially with Marxism and its multiple subcurrents, and with nationalism. However, what is more significant is that this definition makes Nasserism a secularist current of thought, which then makes it impossible for Arab and Muslim nations to consider it a resumption of the Islamic reform movement of the nineteenth century, as the author mentioned before. The author's confusion makes a complete circle when he discusses in his last article what he calls "populist Nasserism," which he defines as the "repressed popular desire of the last decades; it is impossible to stop the populist Nasserite current in the near future since the Egyptian revolutionary choice of 1952 is still its primary choice nowadays." In spite of this, Ḥanafī, in the first lines of the same article, presents an opposite alternative as Egypt's primary revolutionary choice, Islamic fundamentalism, which he hails as "Egypt's irreplaceable alternative in spite of the political and social achievements of the secular revolutionary ideologies. Islamic fundamentalism is the only future alternative."

After this long detour into the author's contradictory and confusing ideas, let us revisit our original topic, which is the relationship between the Ikhwān and the 1952 Revolution, a tragic relationship that led to the punishment of the Ikhwān by the Revolution, and to the Ikhwān and its extremist offshoots taking revenge from the Revolution.

The author offers a detailed analysis of the conflict between the Ikhwān and the 1952 Revolution, and how members of the Ikhwān were severely tortured and sometimes killed by the Revolution, a situation that deteriorated to the level of "revenge that cannot be erased except by blood." He also considers the Manaṣṣah event (when Sadat was assassinated) to be the most powerful Islamist act of revenge and anger at the Revolution. However, this explanation completely collapses when the author discusses the alliances that were forged between Islamists and the Sadat regime in the 1970s against Nasserism, and other enemies of the regime such as nationalists and progressives. He affirms that when Sadat released the Ikhwān from prison, they expressed their (relative) gratitude, which means that the revenge that could not be erased "except by blood" never existed during most of Sadat's regime. Sadat showed them respect, revived their efforts, and adopted them as his allies.

In fact, the insinuation that there was a "revenge relationship" between the Ikhwān and their offshoots, on the one hand, and the Revolution on the other, would lead us to believe that there was only one line at the heart of the relationship between both over thirty years. To my mind, the relationship had a different form than that presented by Ḥanafī: both tried to exploit the other in order to further their own interests. The move to violence happened only when the gap between both interests was huge. In the first two years of the Revolution, the Ikhwān imagined they would exploit the Revolution to their advantage and the Revolution thought it would exploit the Ikhwān to fight the political parties and therefore a temporary alliance ensued. Conflict was inevitable when the pact to withdraw British troops from the Suez Canal was signed. The Revolution found it necessary to prove that it was the only uncontested power in Egyptian society. The same pattern repeated itself after a period of reconciliation in 1965. During Sadat's reign, the period of reconciliation between the Ikhwān and the regime was much deeper and longer than the earlier one. This time it lasted from 1970 to 1979. The reconciliation with the regime was still intact in spite of the popular movement, the students' revolution and the January rebellion against the regime. Most Islamist movements were easily used as tools by the government against any progressive or democratic trends.

Why did Islamist groups vent their anger on Sadat in particular, though his punishment of them, compared to Nasser's, was much lighter? The claim that there was an old vengeance that required reprisal is a major simplification of the issue at hand. In reality, Sadat was murdered because he was very close to Islamists, as they had thought through all the years of reconciliation. The Ikhwān had pinned so much hope on the fact that Sadat was very close to them and he himself encouraged them to believe that he was working toward many of their objectives. He also gave them the opportunity to expand their membership and they responded by anticipating that their Islamist state was on the verge of realization. However, Sadat, who had his own calculations and projects, thwarted their hopes in the last two years of his rule. He began to distance himself from them after taking into account his relationship with the West and the need to protect the millions of Christian citizens in Egypt. However, this alienation moved to the level of violence when the power of Islamist groups went beyond the boundaries set by the regime. Islamist groups also began to distance themselves from the regime once they began to realize that the possibility of the complete application of Sharī'ah was receding. That is why they were more violent with Sadat than with Nasser, who had tortured and imprisoned them. After pretending to be close to them, they discovered that Sadat was deceiving them and was not prepared to accede to all their demands.

Therefore, it is impossible to speak about one straight line of connection between the 1952 Revolution and the Ikhwān over a period of thirty years. The relationship was far more complex than that, based as it was on mutual exploitation, which usually ended up in conflict, and repeated several times. However, what we must note is that no conflict between the Revolution and the religion of Islam itself ever took place. In spite of the violent conflict between the state and religious groups (mostly Islamic and a few Christian), the Revolution from the beginning encouraged the people's religious feelings, even at the height of the worst campaigns against religious groups. It is true that this encouragement reached its apogee during Sadat's reign; however, it had always been there. The Revolution in Egypt did show some concern about religion; it was never like the Atatürk Revolution in Turkey and it was never secularist in the Western sense of the term. The Revolution never wavered in its commitment to religion and its rites, and it never stopped using religion as a weapon in support of its goals. In its perspective, Islam was used to justify socialism and Arab nationalism; later it was used to justify a free-market economy and making peace with Israel.

NOTE

1. 'Abd al-Sallām Faraj, *The Neglected Duty*, tr. Johannes Jansen (New York: Macmillan, 1986).

8
Evaluating the Discourse of Contemporary Islamist Movements

The Islamist movements [of the 1970s] are offshoots of the "Mother Organization," that is, the Muslim Brotherhood Movement. Ḥanafī's criticism of these movements applies to the Mother Organization as well. To him, these movements grew in size in the 1970s. As with the case of the Muslim Brotherhood Movement, Ḥanafī criticized their premise that they "focused on the priority of belief at the expense of reason, which made these movements more religious than rational, taking belief as an undisputed premise." As we can see, this criticism contradicts what Ḥanafī wrote in previous articles, since he now considers the non-rational underpinning of the movement to be a fundamental error, although the principle is the foundation of this organization; this appeared clearly in the groups spawned by the Ikhwān. Ḥanafī also criticizes the primacy of the concepts of *ḥākimiyyah* (God's sovereignty) and the belief that ruling regimes, regardless of their application of the Sharī'ah, are infidel.

In addition, he says, the Ikhwān Movement calls for the immediate application of the Sharī'ah, "without considering the damage that such an application might produce in contemporary societies. To the Ikhwān, the application of the Sharī'ah means the application of penalty rules and the call for Muslims to fulfill their duties before they receive their rights." The author criticizes the Ikhwān and its offshoot organizations for calling for social change by means of a political coup without first waiting for the spread of their message in society, so that it would be a popular demand. He bemoans the Ikhwān's desire to use violence to institute political change via paramilitary organizations: "In this case the Egyptian nation would be the only loser, since no Islamic state would be established, no security would be guaranteed, the Islamic message would not be established and its members would not be righteous citizens." What draws our attention in the last statement is that the author uses such terms as "stability," "security," "good citizenship," etc., which are the same expressions used by the state in its campaign against the Islamist groups. In addition these terms contradict his flirtation with revolutionary Islamist discourse, described by him earlier as a solution and way to salvation. He also faults Islamist movements for the lack of gradualism in their practice, their refusal to cooperate with other nationalist groups, their absolute obedience to the personality of the leader, and their support of the capitalist system and their hatred of the Soviet Union and Marxism without any appreciation of some of the positive aspects of these systems.

These criticisms are directed at the core worldview of the Islamist movements. One must agree with the author in his assessments, especially since these negatives multiplied within these groups in the 1970s. He who levels these criticisms is alleged to have a negative attitude toward Islamist groups, be wary of the dangers of their discourse or worldview and not to be a party to them. In spite of all of this, the pages of the articles cited are replete with expressions of praise, support, and applause, not just for the practices of the Jihād movements but for their worldview, as well.

Let us proceed to outline the negatives that one may derive from Ḥanafī's sayings, either implicitly or explicitly, and ponder the results.

First, according to the author, one can trace the origin of contemporary Islamist movements to the oppression and torture that befell members of these groups in detention camps, especially in 1965 under the Nasser regime. That is to say, their origin was in an unhealthy, diseased situation that could only foster feelings of revenge. Ḥanafī draws nothing from this fact, however, and does not question its negative intellectual and psychological ramifications.

Second, after the 1967 defeat by Israel, the Egyptian state embarked on "a propaganda campaign exploiting religion to justify the defeat. The Islamist movements provided virgin territory for such propaganda. The defeat is preordained by God and there is no escape from this destiny, and the submission to divine destiny is the only thing that prevents people from rebellion." Furthermore, "A natural religious orientation appeared in the wake of the defeat with the emergence of religious movements advocating return to religion. Israel won its victory while being committed to its religion and we were defeated because of our distance from religion."

Third, when Sadat became president in 1970, he released Islamists from the prisons in order to legitimize his rule, since "in backward nations, religion provides a source of legitimization. He also used them to destroy the remnants of Nasserism ... Thus the Islamist movements flourished in the universities and a great number of students joined them in the absence of any real alternative." This statement contains within it an admission that the power of the Islamist groups was acquired with state support, albeit indirectly. The university walls were plastered with "articles that were oblivious to any nationalist and political consciousness." This is certainly a meaningful evaluation, to which we will return later.

Fourth, after the groups' power increased, they "refused to have a dialogue with the nationalist forces ... They also had the audacity to threaten the professors and deans and were engaged in every form of violence on the university campus." Off campus, Islamist groups cooperated with government candidates in defeating leftist and Nasserite candidates on the basis of the groups' enmity to Nasserism: "Its members took on the role of cops and guards on the streets to apply the Sharī'ah." In addition to bringing in exceptional laws against individual freedoms, the government exploited religion to meet its objectives on the basis that "In backward societies, religion is the most effective means that can be used by the ruler to defend the political status quo." Thus:

> the manifestations of the return to Islam began to have a strong show in public life in defense of the status quo, as was the case after the 1967 defeat ... And Islam was used in the fight against socialism, Marxism, and communism and the destructive atheistic theories that supposedly posed a threat to both doctrine and belief. In actuality, those theories were posing a serious threat to political and social systems ... this is why Saudi Arabia embarked on supporting the Muslim Brothers in Egypt, and the different sub-organizations, that is to say, the Islamist groups, financially and morally, and in financing their form of mission.

These then are the conditions that produced the Islamist movements in the 1970s: oppression and torture, which ultimately led to a sick and vengeful mentality; military defeat which led to a fatalistic attitude, encouraged by the government; the new ruler's desire to erase the influence of the previous one; the use of the Islamist groups to legitimize the new ruler's reign; allowing the groups to practice oppression, gangsterism, and superstition on university campuses; a political alliance struck between them and the government, and the financial support of the world's richest reactionary Arab country, namely, Saudi Arabia. Aren't these conditions sufficient to raise doubts about the orientation of the whole Islamist movement? Can't an intelligent writer derive the appropriate conclusions on the basis of these origins, which produced and encouraged the movement in the 1970s? Let us wait before answering these questions and see how Ḥanafī continues his assessment of the discourse of the Islamist movements!

Ḥanafī treads lightly on the dangerous and frightening ideas expressed in *The Neglected Duty* (by Egyptian Islamist ʻAbd al-Sallām Faraj); actually, he presents them without much criticism. It behoves us to point out two examples. The author of *The Neglected Duty* maintains that a country ruled by Muslims who ignore the Sharīʻah or who do not apply divine rule is "a territory of disbelief." Under this category, the author classifies "the whole history of Islam after the Rightly-Guided Caliphate phase, when Muslim rulers, not applying Qur'anic rule, were in power." In effect, this means that whatever was burgeoning throughout Islamic history, such as the sciences, philosophies, the arts, and a sublime civilization that served to lead and teach the whole world of its time, all appeared in the context of "the Abode of Disbelief." Ḥanafī fails to comment on this dangerous statement in order to correct the misguided and wake from their slumber those youth leaning toward this dangerous worldview and whose numbers increase daily.

The second example pertains to the methods of warfare advocated by the author of *The Neglected Duty*, including "the attack by night on the infidels, even if their women and children were to suffer from such an attack, since the rule that applies to them is the same as that applying to their fathers. This is on the basis of a hadīth from the Muslim author who advocates the killing of infidel women and children." Ḥanafī makes no comment on this terrible and inhumane judgment. One senses that in the general context of approval and support given to the movement, the author supports these ideas.

Ḥanafī admits that the Islamist movements fell into the trap of sectarianism, which was enacted by the state in order to realize its own interests. In particular, he points to the special issue of *Daʻwah* magazine of August 1981, which issued "a warning to the Copts of Egypt as though it was a declaration of war from the Muslims against the Copts." He agrees that "the Jamāʻah Islāmiyyah purported to ignite the flames of sectarian war as an excuse to rebel against the political system and to defend Islam before the Muslim masses." The author also points to the *fatwa* that the Jamāʻah Islāmiyyah issued: "The wealth of the Christians is a permissible target as long as conflict exists between Muslims and Christians, and that the Copts constitute a part of the Christians, and the Christians constitute a part of the crusaders." Of course, the last expression is a clear mistake; the author must mean the opposite.

Also, Ḥanafī cites the *fatwa* issued by the leader of the Jamāʻah Islāmiyyah, Shaykh Omar ʻAbd al-Raḥmān [currently imprisoned in the United States], endorsing the fight against Christians and taking control of their wealth. To him, present-day Muslim rulers are no different from the Tatars, who "accept the obedience of the infidels without imposing a tax on them … They commit a huge error against Islam when they approve of religious brotherhoods and that Muslims and Christians are People of the Book." Ḥanafī does not approve of this vying over religion and instead advocates vying over allegiance to the homeland:

> Sectarianism reached the level where Jews and Christians are viewed as infidels who must be defeated and their wealth appropriated. Sectarianism has led to citizens' disloyalty to each other and the homeland. It seems as though the battle is between the citizens of the same nation and not between the homeland and its enemies.

Thus, Ḥanafī agrees that igniting the flame of sectarianism is dangerous indeed in a country like Egypt, where there is a large Coptic community that has coexisted with the majority Muslim population for the past fourteen centuries. Anyone following the literature of the extremist Islamist groups will discover that this enmity to the Copts is not accidental, and that any literal application of the teachings of these extremist groups will render coexistence between Muslims and Christians quite impossible. It is sufficient to point out the extreme worries expressed by the Coptic community concerning the application of just one rule of the Sharī'ah, namely the rule of apostasy. What would happen if all the laws of Sharī'ah were applied?

Even more significantly, Ḥanafī is conscious that igniting the fire of sectarianism would incite a national political struggle that will distract us from facing our external, true, enemies.

The literature and speeches of leaders of the Jihād Movement ignore the real enemies facing us in the Arab and Muslim worlds. They are not just silent about the major problems that affect the Muslim world, as with their position toward the United States and Israel; they demand the postponement of the battle with Zionism until the Islamic state has been established. Elegance and acumen, as one of their authors says, stipulate that Muslims should not consider the liberation of a certain territory, such as Jerusalem, as the radical solution, since "fighting the enemy close at hand is preferable to fighting the distant one." Also, the sacrifices that will be made in this battle

> … would not serve the interests of the Islamic state, which is yet to be established, but the interests of the unbelieving rulers and the consolidation of the foundations of their state, which deviate from divine legislation. Therefore, the domain of *jihād* does not lie in

> liberating the Occupied Territories or Jerusalem but in replacing the unbelieving leaderships with the Islamic system; it is only from here that we begin.

Translated into everyday language this means, simply, leave Israel to rampage (‘*arbad*) through Arab lands, and let the United States spread its influence and establish its military presence unchecked. Focus first on establishing an Islamic state, and then we will be able to expel all our enemies. What is implicit in this invitation is in essence a betrayal of nationalist aspirations. If an opportunity to fight the Zionists and recover nationalist rights under the present rulers presented itself, Muslims should not participate, since it would strengthen the position of the rulers who deviate from Islamic legislation.

It is true that this time Ḥanafī could not keep silent. He commented negatively on some of these ideas, although his comments are light-hearted and do not match the gravity of the challenge presented by the preceding texts. However, in his final conclusions, the author turns a blind eye to these traitorous ideas, especially when he sings the praises of the Jihād Movement's patriotism and its concern for the future of the Muslim ummah:

> The final salvation of Egypt and the termination of the rule of collaboration and treason happen only in the name of Islam and under its banner. Islam provides a protective shield for the nation and the appropriate crucible for its patriotic feelings. People will commit themselves more and more to Islam after seeing the concrete proof that Islam is capable of saving them from oppression and tyranny. Islam can set the country back on the right path of fighting against imperialism and Zionism.

The author's crazy contradiction needs no further comment.

THE REASONS BEHIND THE ASSASSINATION OF SADAT

Here, we reach the height of the tragedy and the Jihād Movement's baptism by fire, that is, the reasons behind the assassination of President Sadat. For the first time in modern Egyptian history, the Movement was able to kill an absolutist ruler at a time when that ruler was considered to be at the apogee of his power and in a place he considered to be the most secure and fortified, among people he considered loyal to him.

Before we discuss the reasons behind the assassination in detail, we must answer the following question, one that came to the minds of many after this tragedy: was this assassination an individual act or was it part of a "total revolution"?

Much of Ḥanafī's comments imply that he believes in the doctrine of "total revolution" preached by the main strategist of the Movement, 'Abbūd al-Zumr. Ḥanafī writes, "The main objective behind this assassination attempt was to establish the Islamic state by means of eradicating once and for all the whole system and personnel of the state." In the same vein, he points to many quotations stating that the main intention was to exploit the opportunity presented by such a large gathering of state leaders to eliminate them as a prelude to the foundation of the Islamic state, in addition to his repeated emphasis that "the final salvation of Egypt" was carried out by Islamist groups.[1]

However, elsewhere the author affirms that the main objective of the Movement was to assassinate only Sadat: "Khālid and his comrades were after the President's head alone. Their major intention was to save the country from the oppressor so that he would serve as an example and a warning to the future rulers of Egypt. In that sense, the charge that they intended to assassinate the president and all the state leaders does not hold water." Ḥanafī repeats 'Aṭṭa Ṭāyil's testimony: "We intended to kill him alone."

Here, the reader is at a loss to discern the author's position—he does not try to explain the contradiction between the above two positions. However, despite others being killed or wounded, it appears that Sadat was the primary target. This is supported by a statement attributed to Khālid wherein he reportedly told Ḥusnī Mubārak or Abū Ghazālah, "You keep away; I want to kill this dog." If this statement were true, then the intent was not "total revolution," the establishment of Islamic rule or regime change. Khālid and his comrades could have easily eradicated most of the regime's leaders that day, but chose to focus on Sadat, their aim being not to establish an Islamic state, but to teach the regime a lesson.

Our main goal in discussing this issue is not just to point out the author's contradictions in pinning down the party or parties responsible for Sadat's assassination. We also aim to shed light on the question raised by Ḥanafī about the party behind this assassination: was it the United States, the army, or the Jamā'ah al-Islāmiyyah? The author ruled out American intervention on the premise that Sadat's regime had offered the United States the best of services and on the premise that "It is quite difficult to prove any connection between the Jamā'ah al-Islāmiyyah and the CIA."

Those who say that the United States was behind this assassination, while acknowledging that the Sadat regime was a strong ally of the US, at the same time point to a great number of examples where the US had eliminated its most loyal collaborators, such as Syngman Rhee in South Korea, Diem in Vietnam and the Shah of Iran, when they were revealed as collaborators and thus rendered useless. As for establishing the connection between the CIA and the Jamā'ah al-Islāmiyyah, this remains very difficult. In these cases, the CIA pulls the strings from afar, so that the actual executioners believe that they act with complete freedom and without outside interference. Undoubtedly, the intention of the group to assassinate only Sadat and their warning to the leaders around him does strengthen the theory that the United States was behind this attempt.

If we were to analyze this question rationally, we would conclude that no organization would have better served American interests, indirectly but effectively, than the Jihād group, for the following reasons.

First, the Jihād group had the upper hand in eradicating the left in Egyptian universities and fighting the democratic and progressive currents in Egypt, generally speaking.

Second, investigations of the Jamā'ah al-Islāmiyyah revealed that it never took a position against Saudi Arabia, the US's staunchest ally in the area. It was somewhat odd and notable that the group was focusing on their rulers' deviation from divine law while keeping silent about the dictatorial pattern of rule in Saudi Arabia. As a matter of fact, the Jamā'ah al-Islāmiyyah supported this type of rule, as we shall see later. The relationship between the Saudi monarch and the Jamā'ah becomes clear once we know that the latter's authority in this respect is Ibn Taymiyyah and that Saudi Arabia, in turn, considers Ibn Taymiyyah to be its major religious figure.

Third, the Jamā'ah did not advocate a social revolution, never issuing any declaration of discontent with respect to social oppression and class differences in Egyptian society.

Fourth, the struggle against Israel was never one of the Jamā'ah's principal goals. No doubt, the United States warmly welcomes any group or organization that leaves Israel chipping away at Arab land, with the excuse that the Jamā'ah is too busy establishing an Islamic state. Even if the group succeeded in establishing such a state, it would be too late unless a miracle were to happen and Israel was defeated with the help of the "military strategy" of Shaykh Faraj.

Fifth, intellectual stupefication, blind obedience, and religious fervor are the ideal conditions for the United States to spread its hegemony over the entire Muslim world.

What were the reasons behind the assassination of Sadat? In Ḥanafī's opinion, the gulf between Islamist groups and the state began to widen when Sadat started his peace initiative with Israel in 1977, which led to the Camp David Agreement of 1979. Here he establishes a link between these groups' increasing animosity towards the government and the government's renunciation of its nationalist strategy after 1977, and Egypt's alliance with both Israel and the United States, its legislation for limiting individual freedoms, and its reception of the deposed Shah of Iran in 1979. Thus, the Jamā'ah Islāmiyyah "began to move from religious rites to general Islamic activity and, in particular, to social and political criticism. The Jamā'ah began to criticize corruption in the state bureaucracy, which did finally lead to the termination of the *rapprochement* phase between the group and the state, and a new phase of conflict, which reached its climax with the killing of Sadat in 1981, began to take shape."

One must pay careful attention to this type of analysis since it discusses the "conversion" of the Jamā'ah from *rapprochement* to confrontation and links all of this to Sadat's political initiatives *vis-à-vis* the state of Israel. However, 'Abd al-Sallām Faraj, author of the book *The Neglected Duty* which was the latest manifestation of the Jamā'ah's discourse and the main ideological engine behind Sadat's assassination, refutes the theory of "conversion" offered by Ḥanafī. In addition, records of the investigation of the members of the Jamā'ah indicate that the group had complete control of their individual members' by virtue of religious rites and their own profound lack of healthy nationalist and political consciousness.

What is truly surprising is that Ḥanafī himself takes an opposite perspective, after discussing some demonstrations staged by the Jamā'ah after its supposed "conversion":

> The Jamā'ah decided to follow a different route after being bogged down by traditional backwardness. It took doctrinal purity, and not actual revolution and its realization, as the foundation of its action. This placed it in a position to distinguish its mission and future revolution from the Islamic revolution in Iran. After publishing Imam Khomaini's book, *The Islamic Government*, in Egypt, Islamist groups refused to distribute the book because it contained doctrinal difference with the Sunnites.

This "traditional backwardness" returned to the Jamā'ah Islāmiyyah, then, after the triumph of the Iranian Revolution, that is, after February 1979, the same year that Ḥanafī mentions that the Jamā'ah went through dramatic social and political changes. This contradiction does not require comment. However, it is possible that personal factors might have been at play in this campaign launched by Ḥanafī against the Jamā'ah. These factors have something to do with the publication of Khomaini's book, *The Islamic Government*, published by Ḥassan Ḥanafī himself.

He repeats this theme in his discussion of *The Neglected Duty*, appearing at a time when the government declared that the October 1973 war was the last and that peace was the key to abundance and luxury: "The idea of *jihād* was revived in the three years after the peace treaty and alliance with imperialism." Therefore, the author considers the nationalist motive to be principal in this movement.

The author also makes a connection between the movement of the Jihād group against Sadat and corruption in the state: "The Jihād movement was capitalizing on the fact that, psychologically, Muslim youth were torn between the dream of a "Golden Age" of Sharī'ah and disappointing reality. Where the books of the ancestors called for *takfīr*, that is, declaring a ruler an infidel for not implementing divine legislation, the modern-day Jihād movement called for *takfīr* in response to state corruption and religious hypocrisy."

In discussing the aftermath of the assassination, Ḥanafī's level of admiration reaches a high point, and the reader can sense the intoxication of victory in his words. The assassination appears as though it was a noble social, political, and nationalist objective, sought after by the liberation movement in Egypt all these years, until the Jihād group realized "the final salvation of Egypt and the end of the regime of collaboration, treason, and theft." on October 6, 1981. He also concludes that

> the absence of the Muslim Brotherhood Movement from the Egyptian political scene over a period of a quarter of a century harmed the prospects of the Islamist movement as a pioneer in the struggle of the ummah and the leader of its nationalist movement. However, the Islamist Movement reinvents itself anew in order to challenge the oppressive ruler after opposition groups failed to do that.

Ḥanafī's glorification of the Jihād group reaches its apex when he claims:

> In the wake of the October 1981 explosion, Egypt's spirit was revived and people began to feel more secure than before and the terrible nightmare came to an end. Furthermore, people began to feel an awakened nationalist consciousness, and their feelings of commitment and responsibility for the primary problems of Egyptian society were renewed. They worked to put an end to corruption, treason, and collaboration as a legitimate policy for the country. Also, people began to show more seriousness about and confidence in the future of the country—the days of luxury and lavish expenditures came to an end … Being the main thrust of opposition in the country, the Islamist movement paved the way for Egypt to retrieve its nationalist unity, and Islam appeared as a primary melting pot absorbing the diverse political orientations. It was only a matter of time before the Islamist movement would be crowned by the masses; it had carried on its struggle through Egypt's darkest historical period, rescuing the nation from tyranny and from what its corrupt rulers had intended it to become, a mere cadaver avidly devoured by wild beasts.

This sublime assessment, which turned Sadat's assassination into the high point of Egyptian nationalist activity and a victorious symbol of the people's struggle against tyranny and imperialism, and which places the Islamist Movement at the top of the Egyptian movements of nationalist struggle, may appear to some as passionate hyperbole on Ḥanafī's part, forced upon him by the event of Sadat's assassination and his high hopes of maintaining public support for the Jihād Movement after the assassination. To others, this looks like an emotional response from someone who had been personally hurt when the Sadat regime incarcerated hundreds of Egyptian intellectuals and opposition leaders in September 1981. However, in my opinion, this is not the case. The author's opinions are not mere fleeting enthusiasm, since he writes in the introduction to these articles that he had spent an entire year studying the Jihād Movement. Therefore, he must have at some point overcome his initial enthusiasm and hopes that materialized after the event, and subsequently expressed his opinion and judgment after a period of deep reflection. In our view, these judgments are baseless and do not reflect the real reasons that led the Jihād group to assassinate Sadat.

In proving my claim, I rely on what Ḥassan Ḥanafī himself wrote. I am happy to say that I could not find in either his articles or the court records, as published by the daily *al-Waṭan*, even one line proving that the Jihād organization had planned to assassinate Sadat for reasons relevant to social injustice, betrayal of nationalist objectives, or the loss of individual freedoms because of the discretionary new laws. The author has imposed his personal worldview on the Jihād organization and portrayed it in the image he envisioned, which reflects neither the movement's nor society's reality.

The general framework for the justification of the assassination was to apply the *fatāwa* issued by Ibn Taymiyyah against the Tatars to Sadat. This represents a deeply inconsistent justification for making a decision to assassinate a ruler living at the end of the twentieth century. Furthermore, this framework turns a blind eye to hundreds of years of evolution and change, and utterly neglects the fundamental differences between the two situations. The mere enthusiasm of some youth, to assassinate Sadat because of their conviction that he was a repeat of the Tatar phenomenon and that Ibn Taymiyyah's judgment is valid in all ages, is by itself clear proof of the unfortunate decline in the level of their thinking.

Sadat's refusal to apply the Sharī'ah, according to the understanding of the members of the Islamist organization, was directly responsible for his assassination. This is the opinion of 'Aṭṭa Ṭāyil, its most important member: "I have carried out this task, which is to fight all those rulers who do not apply God's commands, and Khālid told me that he had been preparing a plan to eradicate this ruler who does not rule according to divine commands." On the other hand, Karam Zuhdī (another defendant in the case) says: "The primary question here is revenge for God's religion." A third defendant, al-Ashūḥ says: "The reason for killing the president is that he does not apply divine rule and texts to society." Faraj's book *The Neglected Duty* contains detailed examples of cases in which the ruler does not apply divine legislation; these apply to all rulers in the contemporary age, and not just Sadat.

This worldview, confining religion to Sharī'ah rules and penal codes and ignoring the religious message to bring about justice among all people and to liberate them from tyranny and oppression, has made the Jamā'ah stipulate very odd criteria according to which a ruler is declared an apostate or forgiven. One of the pillars of the Jamā'ah, Karam Zuhdī, says: "It is not permissible to rebel against a ruler, however evil, as long as he promotes Sharī'ah. Ultimately, he alone will be accountable to God for his own actions." Following on from this, Zuhdī offers two hadīths, the first to "the rulers who apply the penal codes of the Sharī'ah irrespective of the vices they commit. The second stipulates that the believer must "offer resistance to the the ruler who oppresses and mocks Islam, abandons divine rules for positivist ones, and prevents the spread of the Islamic mission; that is, the ruler who stands against Islam and the Sharī'ah."

What draws our attention (though not Ḥanafī's) is the odd case where the defendant cites the "ruler who does not fight against Islam irrespective of the vices he commits." According to Islamic teachings, wouldn't any ruler who commits such vices indeed shame Islam? Isn't Islam action informed by doctrine, or is it just the empty rituals of fasting and praying? Clearly the criterion used by the defendant has no relevance, since it is not permissible for a ruler to lead a sinful life but remain a Muslim. The second issue where we must disagree with the Jamā'ah is its contention that believers must not wage *jihād* against a ruler who upholds Islam even while filling the land with vices. The Jamā'ah believes this acceptable because the ruler will be held responsible for any reprehensible acts when he meets God on the Day of Judgment. On the other hand, the Jamā'ah believes that it is legitimate to rebel against the ruler who does not apply the Sharī'ah, even if he brings justice to the land.

A third point results from this type of thinking. A ruler like Ziyaul Haq of Pakistan who applies the Sharī'ah and Islamic penal codes is, according to these criteria and irrespective of the vices he has committed, more righteous and closer to religion than someone like Sa'd Zaghlūl or Musṭafa al-Naḥḥās, because they have chosen to apply secular and not Islamic rules. Are we then surprised when the author points out that "Saudi Arabia embarked on supporting the Muslim Brothers in Egypt, and the different sub-organizations, that is to say, the Islamist groups, financially and morally, and in financing their form of mission." The staunch Saudi support given to these groups and that determines their notions of *jihād* and restricts the concept to the arena of rites and not action is somewhat understandable. However, what is not understandable is that Ḥanafī turns a blind eye to these clear orientations and does not derive the necessary lessons from such a religiosity and the forces behind these groups.

When members of the organization cite corruption as a reason for killing, none of them raises the issue of the immense wealth the "Fat Cats" sucked from the people's blood, or the enormous gap between shameless, vulgar luxury and degrading poverty, or the systematic and intentional pillaging of Egyptian economic resources. All they talk about is "moral corruption." Ḥanafī reiterates 'Abd al-Ḥamīd 'Abd al-Salām's words, a man who has been described as "the person most conscious of the reasons behind the assassination": "The state is corrupt in its encouragement of tourism, alcohol consumption and usury; it favors the evil-doers to the righteous, making mockery of the Muslim ulama, and harassing the bearded ones." Ḥussain 'Abbās confirms that he harbored malice against Sadat because the latter fought against the ulama, arresting and cursing them in the mosques, and giving bearded men a bad image.

It is interesting that Sadat's policies toward Israel were not among the reasons the Jamā'ah give for his assassination and were mentioned only a few times by the leaders of the organization. As discussed above, the author of *The Neglected Duty* considers the fight against an external enemy a postponed affair that must not distract Muslims from their primary purpose, which is to defeat the enemy within. In the few times they spoke about this, they raised the issues of "Jews" and the non-permissibility of striking a peaceful deal with them. The focus of this discussion was on the treacherous behavior of the Jews with regard to the Prophet and the non-permissibility of leaving the holy places (that is, Jerusalem) in their hands. That is to say, this question assumes a religious dimension while its political features are erased. In spite of this, Faraj concludes on the basis of these slight references that Islamist groups possess "a political consciousness coupled with religious consciousness," a conclusion not supported by the evidence we have presented.

The assassination team said nothing about Sadat's undermining of democracy, but instead attacked Sadat's democratic claims, not because these claims were untrue, but because the Movement views the tenets of democracy as antithetical to Islam. 'Aṭṭa Ṭāyil says in this regard:

> Even if Sadat claimed to follow democracy, this concept has no Islamic basis at all. Democracy is defined as people's rule, and in this case, the People's Assembly in Egypt can issue rules with which the majority agrees without consulting the Book of God. The greatest example of democracy is in Britain where their Parliament legalized homosexuality. This is their idea of democracy. In Sweden, for example, the parliament legalized polygamy, this time for women, in the name of democracy. Here in Egypt, the People's Assembly legalized dancing, vulgar movies, and alcohol consumption, and is well aware of prostitution and other vices in society. Muslims reject this expression of democracy, and the Book of God is the only guidance we have, "There is no authority but God's."

The preceding statement unveils a number of important issues. First, the Islamist Movement's objection to democracy is not merely the disapproval of a concept not recognized by Islam, as the expressions of the text imply; it is primarily an objection to the essence and content of democracy. As a concept and principle, democracy is rejected, based on the belief that democracy is people's rule by and for themselves, whereas what is required is for authority to be governed by the Qur'ān. If the will of the majority is at odds with a passage in God's Book, then we must still give precedence to the authority of the texts. As for the principle of people's will, this concept does not carry any weight in Islam. Certainly, no one has ever raised the question: "Why does the Book of God contain something that is at odds with people's will or interests?"

Second, Islamists have only considered the ethical dimension of the great democratic experiences, which achieved major historical success and became role models for most nations on earth, such as the British experience, which has lasted a millennium, and the Swedish experiment, which elevated its society to the highest level in the world. They have not considered the social and political features of such democratic experiences, and their actual knowledge of these experiences is almost nil. Even in their ethical considerations, they choose false examples, such as the legalization of polygamy in Sweden, and marginal examples, such as the legalization of homosexuality in Britain, as well as some unconnected with democracy, such as alcohol consumption, dancing, and prostitution. The examples chosen reflect the brand of consciousness raising offered to the youth in these Islamist groups in order to tarnish the image of these great historical experiences. They choose provocative moral examples to disgust the youth and encourage their rejection of democracy. They even choose false or distorted examples—what is important is the end result, which is to alienate youth from the democratic experience, leaving them with the Islamic model as understood by such groups as the Jamā'ah. Certainly, no one has ever raised the issue of the spread of homosexuality in those countries that function under the banner of this particular Islamic mission, or the dominance of sexual and ethical deviations in the heart of the lands that claim to apply the Sharī'ah. For them, it is enough that these phenomena appear in Western democratic societies, which is, to their minds, a radical justification to reject all the achievements of these societies, including the principles of democracy themselves.

Third, since the Islamists' major goal has been the full application of Sharī'ah, their main reason for assassinating Sadat was that he led them very close to actually applying Sharī'ah but then retreated from that goal at the last minute. Many of them had expressed high hopes, which were primarily revived thanks to the promises of Dr Ṣūfī Abū Ṭālib, chairman of the People's Assembly; then demoralization set in when these hopes failed to materialize. As an example of this, let us see what 'Abd al-Ḥamīd 'Abd al-Salām had to say: "Our hope lay with Ṣūfī Abū Ṭālib when he became chairman of the People's Assembly, and when the decisions were issued to codify the Sharī'ah; however nothing has happened as of yet."

Consider with me the level of consciousness of these youths, especially when their hopes are linked to Ṣūfī Abū Ṭālib, chosen by the July Revolution to be, and it is a mockery indeed, an expression as well as a symbol of the people. Look carefully at the bitter reality of the Revolution choosing, over a gradual period of time, men disowned by the people, such as Ḥāfiz Badawī or Ṣūfī Abū Ṭālib or even Anwar al-Sadat at one time, in order to install them as presidents of the Assembly, which is supposed to reflect the free will of the people. Look with me at the extent to which the people are disdained and despised in these choices.

Also, consider the low level of consciousness of the youth belonging to this organization when they ignore the vileness of these leaders and instead place all their hopes in them. If Ṣūfī Abū Ṭālib made some progress in the codification of the Sharī'ah with the same method of religious hypocrisy that was dominant in that era, he would have in their view become an historical hero.

Finally, consider for a minute the naïvety of an author who reads such expressions without drawing the necessary conclusions from them. Also lament with me the lack of depth of analysis when Ḥanafī writes: "The investigations show the deep level of religious and political consciousness that members of the movement possess. Their first and primary commitment has been to Islam and Egypt."

Members of the Islamist Movement continually raised the question of religion–state separation when discussing the reasons for Sadat's assassination. It is sufficient to point to Ḥussain 'Abbās' words: "He deviated from the religion of God in one sentence he uttered: 'Religion and politics do not mix.'" The same appears in the words of 'Aṭṭa Ṭāyil: "He even went so far as to request the separation of politics from religion. Islam is nothing like that. When politics are secluded from religion, what method does the leader follow?"

In reality, the claim that "Islam is both religion and state," advocated by these groups and which is at the heart of their conflict with the ruling regimes in the Arab world, is at sharp odds with the practices of these groups themselves. When these practices reached maturity and took their final shape, they were not above assassinating a ruler for superficial reasons, or engaging members of other religious communities in heated battles for the sake of mosques or churches, or creating unrest on university campuses in order to ban male–female mixing and music. Those who advocate the principle that Islam is both religion and state, and that Islam should be a role model to others, should offer concrete examples that prove the integrity of their mission, that is, they should express their clear Islamic opinion about the affairs of the state, the phenomena of tyranny, and domestic and foreign policies. Their current practices prove that Islam, as understood by them, is quite distant from the managing of the state's complex affairs. If the state they call for were established, the most they would achieve would be to build mosques and legislate prayer everywhere, and to protect women from "the wolves' eyes," who are "Muslim wolves," in reality. They would also freely promote the ideas of wearing the *ḥijāb* and *jilbāb* and men growing beards, while leaving other issues without solution. This is what is going on in those Islamic states that claim to have applied the Sharī'ah. The scenario is even worse in the oil-producing countries because their wealth is a factor that encourages corruption. In other words, the proponents of the slogan "Islam is both religion and state" cannot give this motto real meaning unless they develop the capability to manage affairs of state, in the modern meaning of the term, and take an interest in all aspects of life. However, in their present situation, the real meaning of their slogan is that Islam is both religion and state, and the state has no other function except to practice the rites of religion.

Having said this, it is important to point out that the principle of state–religion separation followed by Egypt since the beginning of our modern renaissance in the nineteenth century and strongly defended by religious leaders such as Musṭafa al-Naḥḥās, was in the Islamists' view Sadat's gravest crime. Sadat deserved to be killed because he followed the same route trod by progressive humanity since it left behind the darkness of the medieval period and the tyranny and domination of men of religion. This raises a fundamental question: "Why was Sadat specifically chosen to be killed for this reason, when most world rulers, including those of the Muslim world, adopt the principle of the separation of state and religion?" I think that Sadat was killed because he intentionally toyed with the hopes of these groups. He teased the groups with the idea of the imminent realization of their goals. He then retreated due to the pressures of reality, a reality of which he had been aware from the beginning: the increasing power of the Islamist groups. That is to say, he was assassinated because he was the only one among the leaders separating religion from state who dared to play the risky game of offering huge promises to Islamist groups. He imagined that he could safely withdraw from this game, and this was his fatal error.

Finally, a fundamental reason behind the assassination, and reiterated by the Jamā'ah's leaders, related to the position of women in society, that is, Sadat's position on the issue of the veil and his modification of family laws. ʻAbd al-Ḥamīd ʻAbd al-Salām spoke disapprovingly about Sadat's mockery of the veil, imposed by God on Muslim women. Also, ʻAṭṭa Ṭāyil disapproved of the opposition shown by the president of the republic "to the orders of God that women stay in their homes and leave only when it becomes necessary, and his mockery of the veil rule, which is a divine rule stipulated in a legislative text in the Qur'ān." Also, Ḥussain ʻAbbās mentioned that the president "made fun of some verses of the Qur'ān, as in his saying that the veil for women resembled a tent." As for ʻAṭṭa Ṭāyil, he says, "He should stop his fight against Islam. He described the attire of the Prophet's wives as tents, and described the commitment of women to stay in their homes, according to God's rule, ʻAnd do stay in your homes,' as a form of backwardness."

As for the issuing of the family law, it deeply angered the organization, and this Ḥanafī admits: "The issuing of family law, which deeply offended the Jamāʻah Islāmiyyah since it was considered a deviation from the Sharīʻah, happened in the twinkling of an eye because the First Lady was behind it. Meanwhile, the codification of the Sharīʻah was never completed after years of debate."

The above delineates the main factors behind Sadat's assassination, as discussed by the most important members of the Jamāʻah Islāmiyyah. Let us consider the following: first, the important role morality and sex played in their thinking, and the focus of most of their efforts on the subject of secluding women from society and their sickly fear of having relationships with women as equal partners and peers. This attitude attributes a basic immorality in human nature, wherein men's eyes are likened to those of wolves and are seen as a means of violating a woman's honor and chastity. Sexual desire seems to play a dominant role in every encounter between a man and a woman, a view that contains within it many psychological problematics.

The second point is the superficiality of their thinking, to the extent that if a woman was president then that would be reason enough to assassinate her.

The third point applies to their total disregard of historical process and social change. These groups cling to the description of attire that suited the Prophet's wife in a specific age and environment. Generally speaking, how people dress is not one of the foundations of doctrine but changes according to living conditions and the times. Most importantly, the modifications introduced to family law, which deeply offended the Jamāʻah, were not in fact onerous and still fall within the pure context of Islam. These modifications concern the interpretation of some Qur'anic texts that relate to divorce, polygamy, and the "compliance" of woman in the case of family problems. The intention was to grant women more rights than they had before. However, the Jamā'ah saw this as a deviation from God's law. Their estimation of women seeking employment outside of the home is much lower than of those religious leaders that Qāsim Amīn opposed over eighty years ago. Seeking employment and going out of the house are seen as behaviors of true unbelief.

On the basis of this backward framework of thinking, the Jamā'ah Islāmiyyah condemned Sadat's practices and spilled his blood. When one thinks about these reasons, one is utterly surprised at the positive images permeating Ḥanafī's descriptions of the Jamā'ah patriotism, sublime goals, and noble objectives. He should compare the sayings of the pillars of the Jamā'ah we have provided with the poetic descriptions heaped upon them, which do not have any basis in reality. Ḥanafī writes, "Everything came to an end at the hands of Egypt's army, as well as at the hands of Egypt's spirit and legacy. This was an expression of Egypt's collective will." He discusses Khālid with the following words: "He fought in order to save Egypt from corruption and tyranny. With the light of belief radiating on his face, he addressed his mother, 'We are free while you are imprisoned.' It is to his credit that Egypt presently enjoys a relative measure of freedom and democratic good tidings. Life has returned to the media, university, and one's honor." The reader must also compare the real reasons for the assassination, as discussed above, with what Ḥanafī writes:

> In reality, Egypt's spirit changed its image positively. The officer Khālid, his comrades, the Jihād Movement and Islamic fundamentalism in general were the executing parties only. They all express a collective consensus in Egyptian society and were the ones to execute this consensus. In this appeared the collective spirit of Egypt, which combines Islam, patriotism, the purity of the youth, and a useful knowledge guided by action.

How can one understand the author's references to "Egypt's soul" and "the complete nationalist consensus" and compare them to the real actions of the Jamā'ah, which is evidenced in their refusal of any slight modification of family laws, insistence on locking women in their homes, rejection of state–religion separation and the principle of democracy, which is the rule of the people?

Both integrity and intellectual objectivity force us to reach a painful conclusion, which is that those who killed Sadat for these superficial reasons did not emotionally connect with or become angry at the abject poverty from which millions of Egyptian people suffer and the corrupt luxury enjoyed by the thieves of the Open Door policy era (*'aṣr al-infitāḥ*). They were perturbed by the *ḥijāb* issue but not moved by the sight of one million people living among the dead in the cemeteries of Cairo. Some of those enraged by the granting of some insignificant rights for women fail to show the same feeling when it comes to oppression, repression, terrorism, falsification of election results, and the incarceration of nationalists with the help of emergency laws. These are the people who become so angry that they resort to murder because of the principle of religion–state separation, but who say nothing whatsoever against American military bases and Egypt's pacts with the West. Furthermore, they defer the struggle with Zionism. These people cannot under any conditions express and represent the spirit or patriotism of Egypt.

Both integrity and intellectual objectivity also force us to a more painful conclusion than before. Sadat's record as ruler was full of flaws; however, in some few instances, as with many other rulers, he followed the flow of the modern era. The real tragedy is that Sadat was not killed because of his many vices but because of these lesser sides of his rule and practice, which I count from my perspective as positive features. The Jamā'ah paid no attention to Sadat's big crimes and showed no desire to rescue the country from his deleterious deeds. However, it was moved to action only after becoming angry at finding that Sadat had some inclination to grant women their human rights, separate religion from politics, and criticize religious arrogance and doctrinal vacillation. These positions taken by Sadat had more to do with the fact that no ruler can deny the experiences of two centuries of progress and evolution in his country and little to do with his implicit or explicit moral excellence.

Finally, one must admit in all honesty and objectivity that the most painful result of this assassination is that it was also an assassination of modernity, which has played a significant role in our lives, particularly in the lives of enlightened intellectuals; it was also an assassination of the modern age, its progress, and the liberation humanity has thus far attained. The Islamists wanted not only to kill Sadat; with him they were killing Newton, Galileo, Voltaire, Qāsim Amīn, Ṭāha Ḥussain, and even Ḥassan Ḥanafī himself, as he is allowed to freely express himself in these articles. The will behind the assassination is also directed toward the pioneers of modernizing society and those who work to remove the curtain of darkness from their sight, or anyone daring to think critically and refuse blind and absolute submission. Their real desire was to kill those principles humanity has struggled to achieve, achievements that stood in contrast to the beliefs of the oppressors, false prophets of any color and hue. However, the fact is that they turned a blind eye to Sadat's real crimes and treasons.

THE IMAGE OF THE FUTURE

Ḥanafī has no doubt about his conviction that the future of our country belongs to what he calls Islamic fundamentalism. Contrary to the thesis that these groups are attracted to the past and the Golden Age so as to avoid the present, Ḥanafī thinks that "the new call of Islamism is future-oriented and grants immense hope to Muslims worldwide. The future has more potential than the past and the true Muslim orients his heart toward the future and not the past." He goes on to say that these groups have liberated themselves from the shackles of the past:

> The third dimension of time follows, which is the past and the need to liberate oneself from the past for the sake of taking off to the future. In this regard, the Salafiyyah movement offers a futurist global vision, and not a return to the past as is prophesized in the Western corpus of social sciences and in the minds of those scholars who have fallen under the influence of the West and its prior judgments. Islam goes forward and does not regress and the future is richer than the past.

However, soon afterward, in many of his writings, Ḥanafī is quick to answer the questions he raises, albeit in a contradictory manner. For example, he discusses the five stages or phases of Islamic history, as detailed by Faraj in *The Neglected Duty*. Here Ḥanafī argues that the fifth stage, futurism, is about "the return to the early caliphate of the first Islamic century and the rule by the traditions of the Prophet, that is to say, a return to the second stage mentioned by Faraj." The author opines that the fifth stage is a symbol of "renaissance and the future of the ummah," which is "the process of the new beginning and return to the first phase, the phase of the beginning." It is clear that this so-called futuristic vision is simply a repeat of a past phase, and in fact is an imitation of it. I find it odd that Ḥanafī's futuristic outlook invokes the past when the future is full of possibilities of which the past never dreamed.

However, the author himself refutes what he wrote earlier. He comments on the thought of the movement saying: "In reality, the past imposed itself on the present because of the crisis of the present and the seclusion of Islamic thought. Very quickly, the present threw its burden on the past and found sufficient justification to carry the banner of rebellion against the state without taking into consideration the historical differences between the present and past." The first thing Ḥanafī mentions when he presents his comments on *The Neglected Duty* is: "The mastery of the raw text in its theoretical treatment or in the description of the present Muslim reality reflects the seclusion of the Jamā'ah from its reality and its persistent search to find an alternative in the old tradition. This has led the Jamā'ah to eliminate history and time from their calculations." He further advocates "The mastery of the past over the present and living in the early phase when the Islamic state was successful." Thus, the author provides the connection between the Jamā'ah and the Islamic Golden Age of the past and the elimination of historical factors from this which has made it impossible for members of the Jamā'ah to ponder the true reality of the present, since they evaluate the present only through the lens of the past. If they are incapable of seeing the present and have secluded themselves from it, wouldn't the futurist vision be impossible for them?

If we put aside theoretical reflection on the possibility of a futuristic outlook on the part of the Jamā'ah and move to the futurist image as seen by Ḥanafī, we see that he emphasizes in many places that Islamic fundamentalism is the future, since the "final salvation of Egypt" happened at its hand. And since other oppositional forces have proved their impotence, people will not waver in joining the organized Islamic movement after it has proved its worthiness and capability: "The masses will join any newly-established Islamic movement the moment the call goes out." Later on he says, "The balance of the Islamic movement will increase in the people's consciences after the disappearance of leftist organizations." Islamic fundamentalism has proved that it is the only movement "capable of leading the masses and standing up to a tyrannical ruler." He expresses his position clearly:

> If the Islamic movement infiltrates present-day life and if its popular balance increases due to the confidence of the people in its capability to achieve, and its legitimacy in both present and past, it will be capable of presenting itself as the unparalleled future of Egypt despite the social and political achievements carried out by secular ideologies. It is the only future alternative.

It is only here, after reading these clear statements, that we see that the author has anchored his ship and that of the whole country in one secure and stable port: Islamic fundamentalism. However, the reader is quickly disappointed when he then takes an opposite position and refutes those he took earlier. Here, he criticizes the Islamist movements because "The psychological conditions in which they grew made them pretty secluded and remote from the masses. In addition, their own psychological and historical conditions made them stumble in fulfilling their role. To this day, God's sovereignty (*ḥākimiyyah*) in Egypt has not been translated politically and socially or in any accurate quantitative measure or clear nationalist program." It therefore becomes clear that the group, described earlier as the only alternative for the future and which realized the masses' hopes and aspirations, is actually secluded from them, closed upon itself, and incapable of offering a clear program. The reader's hopes descend to a final opinion and to the satisfaction that at last Ḥanafī offers a clear perspective when he subjects this movement, praised by him earlier and offered as a last hope for the masses, to the harshest of criticisms.

In all of this, the reader's perplexity increases while he ponders the author's request, which is to translate the *ḥākimiyyah* into an accurate statistical count and a clear nationalist program. Certainly, the reader recognizes that *ḥākimiyyah* leaves authority in the hands of God rather than in human authority or rule. How is it possible to translate this concept statistically and quantitatively? And how does it translate into a clear nationalist program? Does it mean, among other things, that translating divine rule into a human one is the principle that the Jamā'ah principally rejects?

The reader must surely have noticed in the passages quoted above the conflation in Ḥanafī's articles, especially the later ones, of Islam in general and an Islamic organization with a specific worldview, such as the Jihād Movement, or of this Movement and Islamic fundamentalism in general. This conflation has produced dangerous results with respect to the author's assessment of the Movement and his future outlook. These dangerous results are also reflected in the minds of readers as confusion and radical intellectual mayhem.

The author was quite correct to point out the negative influences of the historical and psychological conditions on the Movement. The Movement evolved in the prisons under the influence of torture and terrorism; that is, it appeared under abnormal circumstances that inevitably resulted in a large portion of its thought being of a sickly nature. One member of the group (Mamdūḥ Muḥarram) described the group in his testimony as a product of "sick thought." How does Ḥanafī come to accept this brand of thought as the path of the future? Does he wish his country has as its dominant future ideology the product of the sadism of prison officers or deviant rulers in some of the more unenlightened phases in our history?

Let us follow, in any case, the author's vision of the future and the position of the Jamā'ah Islāmiyyah in it. After saying that it is the only future alternative, he levels criticisms against it on the same page, making this alternative a dark one indeed. In a third step, he offers a new formula, which is that "Nasserism is the near future of Egypt and Islam is its distant future." As for the fourth step, another new formula is offered, where leftist, liberal, and Islamist currents together adopt "populist Nasserism," which becomes the future program for Egypt. It is clear here that in Ḥanafī's words, Islamic fundamentalism retreated from the position of being the only expression of Egypt's future (and the future of the whole Arab world, most probably) to a mere current of thought represented in a large alliance, where all currents of thought are placed under the wing of Nasserism.

The new solution uses a concrete formula of *rapprochement* between the July Revolution and the Muslim Brotherhood Movement. A reader considering this *rapprochement* may become puzzled. The Ikhwān no longer control the Islamist groups that are active nowadays, and the revolution is not Nasser's or Sadat's. It is controlled by a ruler who did not have any direct connection to it in the first twenty-five years of its life. So what kind of revolution does the author mean?

Ḥanafī tries to satisfy everyone: the old parties, the left, Nasserism, and the old and new Islamist groups, that is all the currents that suffered from a history of non-cooperation with each other. Regardless, Ḥassan Ḥanafī invites all of these currents to join in the context of "a mutual respect for the opposite current of thought." The Islamist movement becomes a "wing" and the left becomes another "wing" and the revolution exemplifies the "heart of Egypt." (Notice that Islam was always the heart of Egypt.) Liberal history functions as the head, that is to say, party pluralism in pre-revolution Egypt. This accommodative formula takes the shape of the end of a happy and vulgar Arab movie, where all the heroes marry all the heroines. Finally, "after labor, the mountain produces a mouse": the method of realizing the project of the future shrinks to a request that the Egyptian Revolution offer the Ikhwān an apology and return to them their headquarters in al-Darb al-Aḥmar in Cairo. The author's long and broad analyses end up in an accommodative and vulgar formula of reconciliation, which no one is sure how to execute after the long history of bloody confrontation.

Taking extra precaution so that no harm will ocur, Ḥanafī disavows the Iranian Revolution, calling for revolution in Egypt without "following in the footsteps of other contemporary Islamic revolutions." With these cautious words, which make his unclear position more ambiguous than ever, and which signal another retreat by an author who prefers the language of reconciliation and self-help, after all the efforts he exerted to spread the Iranian revolution in Egypt, Ḥassan Ḥanafī 's epic about Islamic fundamentalism comes to a close.

NOTE

1. *Translator's note*: Veteran Egyptian journalist Mohamed Heikel had this to say about Sadat's assassination during the annual military parade of 1981: "On the stand everybody was either dead, wounded, taking cover or starting up into frenzied activity. Mamduh Salem, the former Prime Minister and ex-policeman, threw chairs in the direction of the President in an attempt to give him some protection. A former deputy Prime Minister was seen by all television viewers sneaking out of the stand to make his getaway. The Vice-President, Husni Mubarak, [currently Egypt's president] was unhurt, as was the Sheikh of al-Azhar, but the President's principal aide-de-camp, General Hassan Allam, his personal photographer, and [Coptic] Bishop Samweel were among those who died" (Mohamed Heikal, *Autumn of Fury: The Assassination of Sadat* (New York: Random House, 1983), 259–60).

9
Islamic Fundamentalism and the Verdict of History

I had no choice but to write critically about this set of Ḥanafī's articles, which tackle a subject of great importance. Taking vacillating positions characterized by both emotion and passion, these articles do not pay sufficient attention to the danger underpinning this extremist Islamist thought and fail to tackle with either honesty or courage the deficiencies of such thought which is discussed by many thousands of Arab youths. From the start, Ḥanafī announces that he will refrain from condemning his subject outright, but instead will adopt an open-minded approach, to learn about the Islamist phenomenon from the vantage of personal experience and interaction with the Islamists. This approach commands respect, especially if applied objectively.

However, to be favorably disposed to such a phenomenon as the Islamists inevitably means turning a blind eye to their errors; the result of ignoring these errors is that the masses remain misinformed abbot this dangerous movement. Certainly, real sympathy with those youths who have believed in this worldview and blindly followed its path occurs only by enlightening them, raising their consciousnesses, and drawing attention to their mistakes. This is a responsible and mature sympathy. Turning a blind eye to the Islamists' dangerous and awesome negativities is a form of intellectual blindness that is at odds with the responsibility of the intellectual to his audience and, specifically, to the younger generations. However, Ḥanafī was incapable of existing outside his own cocoon. He cloaked the group he studied in his own ideas and expectations, while in those situations where he succeeded in conveying the group's ideas with some degree of objectivity, deficiencies were revealed in the form of glaring contradictions between the group's ideology and the ideal example Ḥanafī envisioned for them. An author who cannot maintain a certain detachment from his subject will end up with this result. Far from being a sympathetic yet somewhat objective approach (in any interpretation of these terms), Ḥanafī's treatment of the Islamist Movement is dangerously subjective. That is to say, his treatment is indicative of the absolute egoism of a mind incapable of self-reflection.

What is required is objectivity, which seems a simple demand. However, objectivity is a very difficult position to maintain, involving not only the subject matter under scrutiny, but also the conscience, ethics, and emotional maturity of the author, as well as his sense of responsibility toward both subject and audience. there is a hefty price for this objectivity.

First, when someone strongly criticizes the intellectual orientation of the groups to which the Jihād Movement belongs, one initiates a battle with oneself. One criticizes them while at the same time being fascinated by them. This is one of the rare occasions in which Arab youths found a cause to which they felt they could sacrifice their lives, and many have indeed realized this sacrifice. Those who know me testify to how fascinated I am by these youths, especially on those occasions when they place themselves in grave danger by confronting a tyrannical ruler. This is a rare phenomenon in the midst of the total moral collapse of the Arab people of late. From this angle, a man must wage a battle with his own soul in order to question: in the interest of what cause did these youths carry out these heroic acts and with this rare degree of sacrifice? In the midst of the fear and trembling liable to take hold of one while reading the naming by each member of the "assassination team" of each other as martyr, while still alive, it is necessary to exert tremendous effort to control one's automatic and direct emotional response so that one can overcome the fascination and consider what happened in a neutral fashion. We also must criticize those swept away by their emotionality, such as Ḥassan Ḥanafī, who turned a blind eye to the real reasons leading the Jihād organization to assassinate Sadat. Instead, Ḥanafī put forward the misguided idea that the superficial reasons for Sadat's assassination were just as important (and given more emphasis) than the true, underlying reasons of state oppression and social inequality. Such reasons as Sadat's modification of family law, and his ridiculing of the veil and some prayer leaders in mosques were, in the eyes of the people, on a par with the fateful factors facing Egyptian society. Despite their superficial nature, these reasons completely took hold in the minds of the youth.

Second, when one forces oneself to objectively consider this dangerous topic, one not only initiates an internal battle, but also a bitter battle with the feelings of the masses themselves. When one passes judgment on the killers of a tyrannical ruler, one is going against the grain of a strong popular emotional wave, which is inclined to glorify without reservation and ascribe to them purely nationalistic motives. The average person sees them as heroes and martyrs for one reason; the ruler they killed symbolized every vice hated by the masses and which was, in their eyes, an embodiment of their wretchedness, suffering, defeat, and frustration.

However, the masses should have glorified Sadat's killers for another important and profound reason. During the last years of Sadat's rule, the people were completely paralyzed and incapable of rebellion. The last attempt at starting a popular movement was the January 1977 uprising which almost toppled the thrones of Egypt's oppressive rulers; however, this rebellion occurred during a transitional point in the method of rule itself. From that time, the Egyptian power elite took measures to bar any possibility of such an uprising happening again. Emergency rules were introduced, oppressive measures taken, and many foreign governments were consulted, which in turn were generous in offering their technical and financial advice and help. All of this was done in order to prevent the possibility of a mass rebellion against the regime. Since that time, the people have been hammered time and again without finding someone to effectively lead the confrontation against oppression. Sometimes popular opposition heroically and courageously takes place, as was the case with the professional labor unions. However, the impact was somewhat limited and had only meager effect on political authority. Thus, the dominant general feeling was that nothing or no one could stand up to the evil authority and shake it at its foundations, while at the same time the oppressive measures of the political elite were recharging resentment on a daily basis. The feeling of deficiency reached its height with the September 1981 arrest campaigns, in which Sadat posed a challenge to every unit, group, and sect in Egypt. The masses were in a state then to respond to such a condition.

In the midst of these general feelings of bitterness and resentment, which were accompanied by feelings of paralysis, assassination happened suddenly, and in a place and time remote from people's expectations. The indignant people found in this event an opportunity to express their resentment toward the oppressive policies of the regime and portrayed the assassins as a group of people fulfilling their work in the interest of revolution against the Sadat regime's nationalist retreat, social and economic oppression, and political repression. People wanted to convince themselves that they could do something, that they were not submissive and helpless in the face of repeated blows from the regime. As a result, the people adopted the group of killers that executed this operation, embraced their goals and ignored the real reasons behind the assassination. Furthermore, the people drew comfort from identifying with these heroes; it was as if the people themselves had carried out the operation, and the assassination thus became the achievement of a whole nation rather than merely an operation executed by an isolated group, which had never considered embracing the people's hopes or staging a revolution to ameliorate their suffering.

This is in itself what made an author like Ḥassan Ḥanafī unable to see the real reasons behind the assassination. Instead, he imputed motives to the group that reflected his own hopes. He wished to unify the group's and the people's wishes (or the group's and his own wishes), so that he could overcome his feelings of frustration and hopelessness, as though he himself had participated in this radical and positive act. Therefore, it was necessary that the true motivations for the assassination be ignored in spite of the fact that every word uttered by members of the group cried out the real reason.

Third, however, any objective examination of the Jihād organization would lead someone to disagree with the nationalist Egyptian opposition to the Sadat regime, even if this person is usually sympathetic to this opposition. The nationalist and progressive opposition adopted the cause of the Jihād organization to a large extent, strove to achieve some level of alliance with it, and was sympathetic to the assassins. However, the opposition failed to comprehend the real reasons behind the assassination. To my mind, Sadat was assassinated for daring to defend some social and economic programs—secularism, modernization, and religion–state separation—which the opposition supported, sometimes even more so than Sadat. Thus, the opposition strove to ally itself with the Jihād organization, turning a deaf ear to the clear declarations of the group's members who proclaimed that the proponents of secularism were their historical enemies.

The opposition sympathized with the Jihād organization because it opposed the ruling regime. In the eyes of the opposition, this was "an objective alliance." Furthermore, the opposition imagined that it could soften the group's rigid stands and encourage it to be open to its point of view and mitigate its antagonism. Who knows, perhaps in the final analysis, the two might form a unified front adopting a common program. In this way, the opposition would guarantee the participation of a broad mass foundation on which Islamist groups have depended in order to achieve change.

However, to my mind the most fundamental reason for this alliance was pragmatic. The opposition thought, without expressing itself openly, the following: "The masses considered that the assassination of Sadat was an heroic act executed for social and nationalist reasons that were in conformity with their hopes and suffering. Let us give up our philosophizing and theoretical search for the real reasons behind the assassination, since one of the principles of political activism necessitates exploiting the people's strength of feeling in order to give them hope that they can accomplish something. Therefore, we should not pay attention to the real intentions and reasons for the assassination, but instead go along with the popular opinion that it is the people who carried out this heroic act because of their difficulty and pain. But if we search for the intellectual rationale behind this act, we run the risk of alienating the masses, which is unacceptable to any organized political activism. The people wanted the killing of Sadat to have been carried out for patriotic reasons, because he was engaged in oppression, repression, and in the sale of their resources to foreigners, thus depriving them of their livelihood. After all this, how can we disillusion people by telling them the true reasons? What value does this truth have if it chills their burning passion, extinguishing their hopes and making the assassinated oppressor seem as though he had possessed wider horizons than the martyred and heroic assassins? Isn't turning a blind eye to this reality the preferred position so that people are not demoralized?"

The opposition's position rests on a strong logic, similar to the Platonic notion of the "royal lie." Under some circumstances, reality can be injurious and white lies can be beneficial. Therefore, it becomes inevitable in the course of political action that politicians adopt an attitude capable of boosting the morale of the people.

In spite of the power of the preceding logic, reality cannot so easily be defeated, mainly because the principles of political action should not be dictated by the wishes of the opposition. This is premised on the glaring contradiction between the opposition's discourse and that of the Islamist groups. When these groups have had opportunities to clearly express themselves, we see that their enemy is the secularist and progressive discourse centered on changing society according to modern concepts. An admission to this effect was made by their strategic planner, Khālid al-Zumur; he pointed out that the group had planned to kill Khālid Muḥyī al-Dīn, chairman of the Arab nationalist or Nasserite Tajamu' Party and that the discussion implicitly evolved when they spoke of the high hopes they had initially had for Sadat when he was fighting the left. Many have admitted their enmity to democracy and the principle of the people's rule.

It behoves us to raise the following question from a pragmatic political perspective: is it possible to secure a constructive mass movement by deluding it and promoting the false hope that the killing of a tyrannical ruler was done on its behalf, and not for a narrow-minded group that considers its main concern to be the superficial rites of religion and that does not take into account the daily suffering and worries of the masses? Would that count, from a purely political perspective, as the correct foundation for a movement striving to achieve change for the better or, at least, a conscious oppositional movement? Is it in the interest of the masses to embrace this group's motives and methods of thinking? Can the masses then guarantee that this group will walk the path that will realize the people's hopes? Does the group's intellectual discourse and program exert a positive influence in realizing the masses' wishes on the concrete level? Don't we cause such a mass movement to fall into a bottomless pit if we let it embrace this discourse or even ally itself with accommodative programs or half-baked solutions?

Let us compare the opposition's attitude in Egypt to that in Pakistan, led by the widow of Dhu Faqar Ali Bhutto, as reported by the mass media. Nusrat Bhutto issued a warning to the world and her people in Pakistan about the continuation of Ziyaul Haq's dictatorial regime. She said that the regime's exploitation of Islam for political purposes would ultimately lead to religious extremism with the religious right in the power seat. To my mind, this warning by Mrs Bhutto is an example of a mature opposition endowed with discernment, compared to the naïve attitude of accommodating extremist Islamist discourse as embraced by the Egyptian opposition specifically and the proponent of progressive thought in the Arab world, generally. It would have been easy for Mrs Bhutto to ally herself with those extremists for the purpose of removing the tyrannical authority of Ziyaul Haq from power, taking into account that she harbored personal reasons, in addition to general political reasons, to take revenge on the ruling regime. However, she refrained from doing so. On the contrary, she remained in opposition to the dictator while resolutely distancing herself from religious extremism, and by doing so she snapped the diabolical cord that inevitably leads dictatorships into the dominion of religious extremism. Farsighted people exhibit this brand of thinking, whereas the naïve opposition does not shy away from flirting with dangerous trends that are on the verge of exploding; in fact, when a naïve opposition calls for an alliance with these trends it usually becomes their first victim.

After all of this, let us ponder the example that these extremist currents offer to our youth, to the thousands of youths in this country who unconsciously but passionately embrace this discourse. Do we really accept that the average image of our youth will become that of a person who keeps their eyes closed or stares at the heavens, who neither smiles nor laughs, who shuns the arts, and who refuses to watch television (as Khālid did)? Do we accept the notion of a girl who considers a man looking at her, or talking with her, prohibited (*ḥarām*), who veils herself because she assumes that her femininity is shameful, that men will look at her with desire, and thus she must pay the price for these desires, whereas men do not? Do we want the model for our children to be the submissive youths who suspend all critical thought and who vie in pelting each other with sacred texts instead of engaging in critical and inventive discourse? Isn't the task of the responsible thinker to draw attention to this disease which spreads day by day, even if he knows that by doing this he subjects himself to danger from a group intolerant of logical debate, that resorts to solving problems with the fist whenever it is cornered in debate?

THE ROOTS OF VIOLENCE

Violence is a central, not accidental, phenomenon in extremist groups; it forms an indelible part of their psychological and mental formation and is often their only means of realizing their objectives in society. Certainly, sometimes violence takes the form of heroic sacrifice and for reasons that are not convincing to those who think critically. What is the type of mentality of a young man who carries out these heroic acts for purely nominal reasons and who sacrifices himself for the sake of a *fatwa* from Ibn Taymiyyah about the Tatars dating to an age which is both distant and different from ours? The foundation of such a mentality is blind obedience, as opposed to an analytical one which makes conscious choices. Belief reaches the level of semi stupefaction: the group adopts a pyramid-like hierarchy where the word of the leader at the apex is followed blindly by those at the bottom, not because the latter fear the former, but because they have been trained to listen and obey, and take orders without discussion.

It is necessary to point to the fact that excessive analysis and criticism often lead to abstention from sacrifice, and behavior which resembles, on the surface at least, cowardice. Because of their inclination toward thinking, discussion, and reflection, rational people often exhibit cautious behavior, avoiding both risk and impetuosity. However, this is a general rule. During the Spanish Civil War, for example, a significant number of American and European intellectuals valiantly fought against the Fascist regime in Spain; many sacrificed their lives out of complete conviction to the cause for which they fought.

The same phenomenon was repeated in the resistance movements in the countries occupied by Nazi troops during World War Two, and we see many examples of intellectuals engaging in armed struggles in Latin America. However, it is possible to say in general that the readiness to sacrifice oneself according to blind opinion devoid of conscious analysis or criticism is much greater in shallow thinkers than in those with deliberate and deep thinking. This was the case with Hitler's soldiers and officers, who exhibited high levels of courage, impetuosity, and "heroism," in the absolute meaning of those terms, because of their belief in a cause they followed blindly and never thought to debate or analyze.

I can say that Egypt has been amenable to the spread of this mentality over the thirty years of military rule in the country. In my opinion, an organic connection exists between the political system installed by the July 23 Revolution and the spread of religious extremism and violence. The political system was inclined by its very nature to apply to the people the same behavioral values applied to the military and to establish a relationship between ruler and ruled identical to one between an officer and his troops, and not between equal and rational citizens. The 1952 Revolution opted to create "submissive citizens" who refrained from analyzing, debating, and pondering the future, instead allowing the leader think on behalf of the people. They were only expected to obey orders.

In reality, a thin line separates military rule from religious extremism. In both cases, we find tyrannical thinking, blind opinion, the belief that they possess the absolute truth, and the rejection of others' opinions, to the point of regarding such opinions as both treasonous and a sign of unbelief. In both cases, authority dominates logic, battles or conflicts are resolved by liquidation not dialogue, the right of reason to raise objections and take an autonomous path is expropriated, and the media platforms that cultivate people's critical faculties disappear.

In our perspective, violence is a common denominator of the military regime and extremist Islamist groups. For both, violence is not an accidental phenomenon, but an essential part of their foundations. This fact does not require proof in the case of the military, since direct physical power constitutes an acknowledged principle of the army. As for the extremist religious groups, however, exposing their roots in violence does require some discussion.

A discourse like that of the Jihād organization may lead to a civil war between Christians and Muslims in Egypt; as a matter of fact, this occurred when Jihād members killed the Coptic owners of jewelry stores and expropriated their wealth. They considered this operation to be a *religious duty* and their possession of the money as booty permissible for Muslims. If the Islamists succeeded in their plan to seize power, the country would be drowning in a sea of blood, with the blood of those democrats and progressives who ally themselves with these groups flowing profusely. But this does not shed light on the phenomenon of violence and its role in the formation of these groups. What is more important in this regard is the spread of the concept of *takfīr*, that is, declaring somebody an apostate or an infidel, and the ease with which this condemnation is uttered. So the state is unbelieving (*kāfirah*), and anyone who does not rule by and apply Sharī'ah is a *kāfir*, and anyone, even a Muslim, who does not follow the Islamist framework of thinking is also a *kāfir*. The expression *kāfir* or *kufr* was often used by the defendants in the Jihād case.

Here, we must be conscious of the fact that the characteristic of *kufr*, according to the intellectual framework of these organizations, is not easy to define. It not only expresses a form of opposition, condemnation, or rational criticism, it is a total incrimination, making the spilling of blood and confiscation of wealth permissible, as well as the total "erasure" of an individual from existence. Anyone labeled with this characteristic must therefore be exterminated, cancelled out and removed from the domain of thinking and reality. *Takfīr*, or declaring someone an unbeliever, is equivalent to a judgment of capital punishment, with a moral obligation on the part of the believer to continually bear in mind the punishment until it is possible to act upon it. When the opportunity presents itself, the execution of the judgment is imperative, and is carried out in an atmosphere of certainty: religious duty has been fulfilled which will bring recompense in this life and entry to paradise in the next.

In other words, *takfīr* is the religious equivalent of the acts of imprisonment, oppression, torture, and execution which are controlled by worldly authority. If the government can isolate its opponents, silence, and kill them, that is, "erase" its opponents from existence in one form or another, religious groups can do the same to their opponents, using their own methods. However, with the latter, "erasing" someone from existence does not take a concrete physical form, mainly because these groups do not rule or possess power. If they were to rule, they would apply the formula "erasure from existence" to a much wider domain than has been done by secular governments, however sanguine they may be.

Therefore just as violence constitutes an indelible component of military rule, it is also at the heart of the extremist groups' mental and psychological formation. The extremists' mere use of the expression "someone is an unbeliever" or "this state or institution is an unbeliever" is equivalent to Sadat's "I will grind anyone who dares to oppose me." But the extremists' crushing of their enemies is more violent, because it is done with such unquestioning peace of mind that it does not stand up to the level of consciousness a secular ruler has with respect to the oppression and destruction of his people.

Violence underlies both the discourse and behavior of the military in Egypt and the extremist groups. One must add this factor to the historical environment that produced this type of discourse, that is, the failure of the July 1952 Revolution, which was characterized by military defeats, the predominance of superstition, the slavish flattery of religious fervor, the adoption of the principle of "only one truth," and the elimination of any ideology or individual who would oppose this way of thinking.

It is time now to ask a fundamental question: if the appearance of these extremist organizations is referred to as an "Islamic revival" in cultural and political circles, and if the conditions under which this revival appeared are like the ones we have already described, would this revival be considered a feature of progress in Muslim consciousness, as its proponents and those writers who champion them claim, both nationally and internationally, and who flatter them for different reasons? In reality, the Islamic revival in its contemporary form appears to be dominated by the regression and backwardness that pervaded the Arab and Muslim worlds in the 1970s. In that sense, this revival is a direct reflection of the defeats and frustrations affecting people's consciousness, and is far from being an attempt to overcome these problems. The escape into formalistic rites and blind obedience, ignoring the concrete problems of life, paralysis of critical reason, the return to the past, and overlooking the dramatic changes and transformations produced by many centuries, all of this is but "the discourse of defeat" itself and produces general paralysis in people's consciousnesses. This phenomenon is not the product of the anger of new generations and the failure of the youth to unite with the current regimes, as some scholars such as Saad Eddin Ibrahim argue. All these factors were there up until the mid-1970s, and instead incited the youth to turn to the left. The "discourse of defeat" is a direct expression of the highest form of mental deterioration, and the fruition of the tyrannical tendency or orientation after thirty years of falsifying consciousness. The same mental environment that made Tharwat Abāza Egypt's official man of letters, Anīs Manṣūr and Musṭafa Maḥmūd the most important thinkers and philosophers, and Aḥmad 'Adawiyyah the most popular artist, has made religious extremism the most widespread current among the new generations of youth.

After all of this, one essential point remains for which we must forgive any author sympathizing with these trends. The youths committed to these extremist groups were the only ones able to "achieve" something, regardless of the motives behind this "achievement." These youths were able to put an end to the stagnating conditions that seemed set to continue for many years to come. They threw a huge stone in the muddy lake of Egypt, creating new waves and whirlpools that may one day change into ferocious winds and waves. Compared to this, the democrats, progressives, and secularists did not play any role whatsoever in this sudden turn of events, and it appeared they reached a dead end when this shocking assassination was carried out.

Thus, a real problem with no clear solution appears before the political thinker. It seems as though our country currently has two choices, each worse than the other. We either satisfy ourselves with a progressive and enlightened discourse capable of comprehension, criticism, and analysis but incapable of movement, or we follow in the footsteps of a backward discourse, deficient in comprehension, criticism, and analysis, but the only one with any dynamism! In yearning for a better future, Egypt is facing a real crisis: it is forced to choose between thought without action or action without thought. I think that our salvation will come the day that those who think reach a level in which they are able to apply their thought to the domain of effective and influential action, or when those who act finally understand the value of open-minded thought and enlightened reason.

Part Three

On the Implementation of Sharī‘ah

10
An Invitation to Dialogue

Contrary to what others think, I do believe that engaging in dialogue with the currents of thought that call for the implementation of Sharī'ah is a vital task in the light of contemporary conditions. I think that a responsible media should open the widest door possible for all sides to express their thoughts freely, so that those Egyptians who are undecided can familiarize themselves with the different positions, compare the different arguments of the supporters and opponents of Sharī'ah implementation, and derive their own conclusions from such a dialogue. The following reasons justify such a call to dialogue. The first is the utter importance of the subject matter. The implementation of Sharī'ah is not a simple endeavor and is not merely a step taken by the People's Assembly in Egypt to satisfy certain forces on the ground, which have persistently pushed toward this direction. There are other wider forces within society that insist on such an approach, although they have vague ideas about such a possibility, assuming that both private and social problems will be automatically solved the moment Sharī'ah is implemented. Such an implementation would mean a radical lifestyle change for both the individual and society, leaving an indelible mark on every member of society in their style of personal behavior, their cultural habits, the media to which they are exposed and the education they receive. Furthermore, this implementation would impact the governing style, legal systems, the dispensation of state resources, and the form of the state's foreign policy. In view of the potential for comprehensive change in people's lives, why has our intelligentsia neglected to delve into this dangerously important topic while others have paid only lip service to it?

The second rationale for such dialogue is that there are indeed masses of people who believe in the appropriateness of such an idea and request that it be implemented with both passion and sincerity. Most of these citizens are well-intentioned people who strive to reform themselves and their societies. The familiar image of the man devoted to the idea of implementing Sharī'ah is that of a straightforward and pious individual who belongs to a religious group and regularly attends talks and discussions in mosques frequented by at least one of the important preachers. More often than not, this young man unhesitantly embraces the monolithic view, since he has been not exposed to different perspectives and his general education has usually been meager. Even if we suppose that his profession is in the field of science, such as medicine and engineering, he does not allow his area of specialization to influence his general outlook on life, and remains a prisoner of his narrow worldview. Although we find exceptions, this is a typical portrayal of these people.

Those, like myself, who oppose these masses of well-intentioned albeit misinformed men and women, must deal with them with sensitivity. Many of their critics find it sufficient to describe them as reactionary and rigid; people who want to turn back the clock and who place little value on the facts and the conditions of the modern age. Even if these descriptions were accurate, they fall short in dealing with people who aspire toward reform and who believe that they alone possess the means of salvation for both individual and society.

As mentioned above, the youths' biggest problem is that they have been exposed to one perspective only and are in dire need of exposure to other perspectives, which should be presented to them calmly and without coercion so that they are exposed to new horizons of thinking. What they truly need is dialogue that would take into consideration their good intentions and their desire to achieve reform while drawing their attention to the grave errors their spiritual and intellectual guides have committed. Any other approach would just strengthen their position and lead to more defensive behavior.

This leads to the third rationale for the needed dialogue, since the essential difference among the proponents and opponents of Sharī'ah implementation resides not just in their differences of opinion, but in the difference of their styles of thinking as well. Proponents of Sharī'ah do not justify their arguments on the basis of reason and logic but on absolute belief and obedience. If some use reason in their arguments, they do so in a limited way only. Islamist youths have grown used to servile obedience to the extent that their leaders exercise an immense and indisputable power over them. Thus, their debate, from beginning to end, depends on textual quotations, not just from established texts, but also from the proponents of individual *ijithād,* such as Ibn Taymiyyah and Sayyid Quṭb, whose ideas become more established as they are repeated on every occasion.

The main benefit of dialogue would be to release these youths from the prison of texts to the wider domain of rational thought and its magnanimity. Such dialogue opens new horizons, which are not visible while they remain entrenched in their own groups. Dialogue enables them to use their faculty of reason, portrayed by some as a product of

Satan and not the greatest gift from God. Undoubtedly, the discovery of the world of systematic thinking that uses reason and logic does work to save these youths from committing drastic errors, or at least opens the door for them to independent thinking in matters they have never before subjected to the power of logic.

As for the last rationale for dialogue, it is simply that the dialogue has never taken place in our society. Over the past four decades, in which the degree of polarization has intensified between the religious and secular groups in Egyptian society, no real dialogue has emerged. Each trod its independent path while addressing its supporters with its own internal discourse. If one side levels a critique against its antagonist, it does so from its parochial position without making any effort to understand the other or give them an equal opportunity to freely express their ideas.

For all the above reasons, the mass media should do a favor to the people of Egypt by initiating a genuine and principled dialogue dominated by reason and quiet logic and driven by the desire to attain mutual understanding between the two sides. To my mind, this is the most appropriate time to conduct such dialogue, since many voices are calling for an immediate implementation of Sharī‘ah, as though this were the final solution to our problems. Also, we must critically examine at this time the various attempts to implement the Sharī‘ah in other Arab countries and judge whether the results have been positive or negative; we must be aware of the extent to which such a result would reflect on society.

The question in dispute concerns the future of the whole Arab ummah, and administrative decisions or legal rulings are far from sufficient in finding a solution to this issue. First and foremost, people have to grapple rationally with the issue; if they fail to produce rational solutions, the issue will reignite, which would be dangerous indeed.

At this juncture, we must raise the question: why has this dialogue not yet taken place? What are the reasons that led to the polarization of the Egyptian nation in some of its most important dimensions, and why is it that every group avoids and undermines the others or fails to see any benefit in engaging the other side in dialogue? The essential factor seems to be fear and lack of trust.

There is a real fear, in our Arab societies in general and in Egypt in particular, of debating the nature of religious dogma. If we ponder for a minute the level of the debates about these issues that took place in the first half of the twentieth century, we will discover that they were more courageous and honest than what has been written and said about these issues in more recent decades. There is a lot of evasion when it comes to debating these issues, and many authors try to disguise the meanings they are presumably conveying to their readers. This time, the fear is not of the authority of the state, but of public opinion, which, according to some, ring-fences some issues as not to be challenged.

In many discussions taking place in the last four decades, some individuals have used public sensitivity to their advantage by accusing, on any occasion or without an occasion at all, their ideological enemies of atheism and heresy, as though there were a human authority that judges (*takfīr*) people and denies them paradise. This type of person is easily satisfied with slandering their opponent, knowing full well that the result will be to effectively silence their rival, even in the area of non-religious issues. The same applies to some secularist groups, who hypocritically adopt the same tactics against their religious rivals.

However, these secularist attempts have completely failed, as members of the religious movements exhibit an impermeable logic. If you accept their premises, it will be difficult to reach conclusions different from theirs. Their theory is well integrated, the parts seamlessly interconnected, and the only way to critique it is by debating its premises and intellectual foundations. Half-hearted solutions do not sit well with them; on the contrary, they lead to counterproductive results. They know their supporters and opponents well. If their opponents were to hide under the mask of a meek lamb, their wakeful shepherds would be quick to detect their deception.

So it is fear that has made things so complicated and prevented real opportunities for dialogue. No real dialogue can take place unless the barriers of fear collapse. I do not mean to say that a new cycle of violent confrontation between the two sides must begin, but that each side must have equal opportunity for expression so that each can understand the other's position and evaluate it on the basis of enlightened knowledge and not on the basis of arrogance, extremism, superficial courtesy, and hypocrisy. I do hope that the subjects I am going to present in the next pages will provide a good beginning for fertile dialogue that does not base itself on mutual accusations and fake smiles, but on the quiet contemplation and correct logic which would benefit our society in its current crisis.

11
The July Revolution and the Islamist Groups

The most widespread thesis promoted by the writings of contemporary Islamist movements is that the history of the July 1952 Revolution with regard to these movements has been that of repression, and that religious extremism arose during the long period of incarceration and oppression the members of these groups were subjected to in 1954, 1965, or afterwards. These movements take this thesis for granted and do not subject it to criticism. I do not intend to absolutely deny this claim here but to express certain reservations about it and shed some light on some of the misunderstandings surrounding it.

Proponents of this thesis conclude, on the basis of the violent confrontation in most of the history of the July Revolution between the regime and various Islamist groups, that the Revolution adopted an antagonistic position *vis-à-vis* Islam. Islamist groups, with their strong identifiction with Islam, consider that the violence meted out to them by the regime is evidence of a direct attack on Islam itself.

The preceding conclusion is far from the truth. We cannot confine Islam to this or that group and its destiny cannot be determined on the basis of this or that group languishing in prison or roaming freely in society. Undoubtedly, one of the gravest errors committed by a certain group is to consider itself the sole guardian of Islam, and to induce in people the belief that any attack on it is an attack on Islam itself.

To my mind, the radical proof that abrogates such a conclusion is the fact that the confrontations between the July Revolution and the Islamist groups were political in nature, and were far from being religious or doctrinal. Usually, a confrontation takes place when the regime thinks that a specific religious group begins to pose a danger to the political system and the state, or security and the status quo. It is possible that this thinking was not always right and may have led to grave errors. However, we are not in a position to assess what exactly happened or pass judgment upon it. We limit our task here to evaluating the phenomenon itself and expressing the essential idea that the conflict was in principle political and not doctrinal.

As a matter of fact, no battle over any dimension of Islamic doctrine ever took place during the reign of the July Revolution. In this, the July Revolution differs from many other revolutions, for example, the Atatürk Revolution in Turkey which adopted a clear-cut secularist approach and severely diminished religious institutions, or, on the other hand, the Iranian Revolution, which elevated the status of religious institutions at the expense of other institutions. The July Revolution never did this. It is possible to argue that there was more interest in religious questions during the time of the July Revolution than during the liberal rule which extended from 1919 to 1952. As proof, it suffices to mention the establishment of the Higher Council of Islamic Affairs, which systematically published a large number of books and periodicals and was active in proselytizing (*da'wah*), especially in Africa and South East Asia. Furthermore, the domain of the religious mass media expanded and religious movements were permitted to express themselves with more freedom than that permitted to the secular trends, which had experienced little repression in the preceding era. The religious curriculum expanded in both private and state schools, and a noticeable increase in the number of mosques constructed.

In summary, the claim that the July Revolution, especially in the 1950s and 1960s, oppressed Islam itself because it dealt with some religious movements in a certain way is certainly unfounded since the competition took place on the political plane only. Since politics often takes warped paths, the relationship between the July Revolution and the religious movements was extremely complex. Very often, bloody confrontation would take place after a period of deep *rapprochement*, as was the case in 1954, when the Muslim Brotherhood Movement (the Ikhwān) was close to the Free Officers in their first two years of power.

On the scale of any objective assessment, this relationship between the sides is steeped in many errors, and the only way to exit this impasse is to try and fathom the depth of the relationship between the Islamist movements and the July Revolution.

In those periods of power dominated by an absolute ruler, in which real democracy was blocked, the proponents of this rule followed a style of behavior not too dissimilar from that followed by extremist religious groups in both their thinking and organization. An authority that tolerated no criticism made political decisions, and those controlling the mass media censured their opponents, labeling their ideas as forms of atheism and unbelief. Instead of applying the methods of dialogue and understanding, most political differences were resolved by recourse to violence and power. Servile submission was the greatest "righteousness" a citizen, or any person close to the pyramid of power, was expected to express. Political authority propounded its special genre of "absolute truth," which considered any opposing position as atheistic and false.

But haven't the above been characteristic of the extremist religious movements, as well? Once we remember that whole generations grew up in the context of this special relationship between the ruler and ruled (a relationship that only lacks divine imprimatur), why should we be surprised to discover that a huge number of youth follow, both individually and collectively, in the footsteps of these extremist religious groups, especially after all the oppression to which these groups are subjected? (Indeed, we would be surprised if we encountered a young person growing up in this atmosphere who was unafraid to express their own individual belief or opinion.) The youth join those religious movements that operate on the same principles as the powers-that-be with the difference that the Creator of the Universe and not the ruler is the one to be obeyed.

The confrontation between the July Revolution and religious groups, until the 1970s, appears in a new light: it is based on close proximity and violent tension. What caused this violent outcome was the similarity between the two opposing systems of thought and the almost identical style of behavior of the rulers and ruled in both instances. Also, let us suppose that a certain religious group, that is, the Muslim Brotherhood Movement, had gained the upper hand in the confrontations of 1954 and 1965; its own treatment of the defeated party would have been even bloodier and would in essence have assumed the mantle of a dictatorship, repressing any opposition.

Of course, no one can deny the fact that the differences in the actual programs of both sides are great. Here I am addressing the style of behavior and the pattern of the relationship between the different levels of organization, and the relationship between the top level of the power pyramid and its base. In all of this, the undemocratic direction of the 1950s and 1960s provided fertile ground from which all sorts of oppressive currents, including religious extremism, emerged.

In a nutshell, both sides' use of violence in this period seemed to be the only way to sort out their differences. Certainly, this was a grave error that led to many more errors, from which we still suffer. What is important is that both sides were mistaken, though we must admit that the religious movements endured repression for a lengthy period before resorting to violence, which explains why these movements still say that the pre-1970s era in Egypt was one of oppression and violence. However, the only thing that prevented these movements from achieving their goal of religious domination was violent state repression. When both sides play the language of violence, the defeated have no right to complain about the oppression of the victor.

We now reach the 1970s, which were preceded by an important transitional period following on the heels of the Arab civilizational, social, and military defeat of 1967. In this period of Egyptian history, the emergence of religious movements was generally characterized by scholars as a response to the 1967 defeat and the consequent feeling of public humiliation. This was generally perceived as the response of hopeless and desperate people who found no way out of their situations except by seeking succor from the heavens or the distant past. They envisaged that the darkness and failure of the present could only be ameliorated by a renaissance that would re-embody anew the earliest glories of Islam. Undoubtedly, what promoted this type of thinking was the emergence of a strong current in which religious fervor and mass delusion were intertwined. For example, after the tragic June defeat in 1967, wave after wave of people, for many long nights, sought to catch a glimpse of an apparition of the Virgin Mary in a church in Cairo. Many returned home convinced they had actually seen Mary.

I would like to explain my reasons for rejecting this theory that the emergence of religious groups in Egypt in the 1970s was in response to the defeat. First of all, one will notice that the Egyptian nation's response did not take a religious direction in the years following the 1967 defeat. Even the popularity of the story of the Virgin Mary's apparition was somewhat temporary and was invented by those who wanted to lessen the impact of the defeat on the people. In 1968, the Egyptian nation staged demonstrations requesting the leaders assess their responsibility for the defeat. In 1970 and 1973, demonstrations called for leaders to intensify the war of attrition against Israel. In all of these cases, the masses were demanding the implementation of democracy and the improvement of their standard of living. The religious movements did not play a significant role in these demonstrations. Instead, various secular groups dominated the streets, especially among university students. Therefore, the first and automatic response to the defeat did not come from the religious movements. It is only after the 1973 war that these movements began to spread their influence widely among students, in the halls of the mosques and at the popular level generally. The 1973 war was able to only partially diminish the impact of the 1967 defeat.

On the other hand, if the emergence of religious movements had been a counter-response to the defeat, its emergence would have been linked to programs and plans by these movements to help us overcome that defeat.

However, nothing like this ever took place; the programs of the religious movements, spreading widely in those years, focused on superficial issues, for example, the beard, the veil, segregation, and raising the volume of microphones in the mosques through the use of technology, a practice that was seen as unIslamic. Issues of sexuality and sexual purity, with the resultant calls for separation of the sexes and men's sequestering of women, all played exaggerated roles in public discourse. Men were attracted to the religious movements by appealing to the desire to protect the honor of their women, while women were reminded that their sexual purity and good behavior were essential for a happy life. However, these had nothing to do with the actual life of the people or the major problems from which society suffered. Has even one reader heard of one program sponsored by a religious movement that would ameliorate our economic crisis, or take responsibility for our natural resources, our balance of payment, the relationship between the private and public sectors, our commitment to international banks, and our heavy financial debt? Have the booklets published by these movements contained any clear perspective, amenable to implementation, on the subjects of economic growth, independence and dependence, and the problems of university education, and that of private and public schools? More importantly, has any religious movement envisioned actual plans with the objective of confronting Israel and the powers supporting it by providing weapons to the army and utilizing our national resources for the sake of the war of revenge we all waited for so impatiently after the defeat? Nothing happened with the exception of the utterance of some general statements about the enmity of the Jews to Islam and the rallying of Muslim power.

How can we claim that the spread of religious movements was a counter-response to the 1967 defeat when the programs of these movements lacked any plan that could be implemented in the age of electronic war and the threat of nuclear bombs? No doubt, those from whom we want revenge use the most advanced scientific and technological methods when organizing their societies and planning their daily affairs.

I would like to defend the idea that the mass appeal of the Islamist movements, occurring only in the third part of the 1970s and not immediately following the 1967 defeat, is a clear expression of the totality of the defeat and its psychological impact; the rise of the Islamist movements was never a counter-response to the defeat or an attempt to ameliorate its effects. Rather, the movements' followers clearly were suffering from the internalization of the defeat. Although not conscious of this internalization, every atom of their thought and behavior, especially after they join the movement, testifies to this. They do not use their mind or thought processes, but instead accept simplistic answers from their leaders, answers that are then disseminated to other malcontents. Their lives revolve around repeated, memorized, deeply believed clichés, taught by people perceived as infallible. The follower does not seek innovation or exert any form of analysis or autonomy of opinion; any critical faculty is non-existent. In a nutshell, the follower does not use nine-tenths of the greatest and most sublime faculty with which God has endowed humanity: reason. Is it possible to say that such a person who cancels out their mind in such a way has the means to respond to the defeat? Or are we dealing with someone whose very behavior makes defeat a certainty, gives support to its foundation and proves that the defeat has seeped deeply into the recesses of their personality?

However, in order to be fair-minded, we must point out that the foundations for this negative behavior were established long before the defeat itself. In the authoritarian era, people grew accustomed to obedience and passive listening, giving others the opportunity to think for them and make all the critical decisions on their behalf. Over the years, people's minds became fertile ground for utter obedience, and it became natural for them to think that there was always an external source that contained the solutions to all of their questions and problems. There is only a minor difference between this position and that adopted by the religious movements. If the individual is not expected to contribute in terms of critical thinking, but simply receive and obey orders from superior sources, isn't it more appropriate that these orders are perceived to emanate from those who ascribe their authority to divine sources, rather than from a ruler who, in the final analysis, is a finite human being?

Thus, the long years of authoritarian and oppressive rule prepared the ground for such behavior; the 1967 defeat exacerbated people's sense of vulnerability and weakness to the point where the simplest of preachers could mesmerize tens of thousands of people with passionate but vacuous phrases.

However, our discussion of the spread of religious movements cannot be complete unless we address other factors of support, especially financial, that the movements received from internal and external sources. Undoubtedly, the state turned a blind eye to the activities of religious movements and some even argue that the state trained some members of these movements. This position, either of turning a blind eye or giving material support, was the second major error that the July Revolution committed in its treatment of the religious movement. After the violence of the 1960s came the flirtation of the 1970s. State policy was founded on the philosophy that the youths' joining of these movements was far less dangerous than their joining leftist groups, which seemed to have gained some strength between 1968 and 1973. In other words, the official state policy was to seek the religious movements' assistance to the extent that it would benefit the state and enable it to realize its domestic and foreign objectives. This error was the straw that broke the camel's back. Experience has repeatedly shown that it is impossible to contain these groups in a specific box or use them to meet the objectives of others. Very swiftly, these groups move to realize their own objectives and break away from the limitations within which they were expected to operate. This happened repeatedly in the 1970s, and its bloody consequences were seen in the attack on the Military Academy, the murder of Shaykh al-Dahabī (Minister of Islamic Endowments), and the sectarian conflict, until the situation exploded in the 1980s. The main mistake of official policy in the 1970s was its attempt to balance contradictions that were quite impossible to reconcile: the religious current is simultaneously useful but dangerous; it must be encouraged while being confined to boundaries from which it must not overstep, or it must be given the freedom to operate while remaining under constant surveillance. As we all know, the price paid for failing to follow these guidelines was high indeed.

The second source of support for the religious movements was external. It is not accidental that they began to gather momentum exactly around the same time that the influence of oil began to appear in Egypt, that is, in the early 1970s. If we ponder the form of the Islamic mission adopted by the extremists of these groups, we will find a strong resemblance to that adopted in some Arab countries that raise the banner of Islam, where great effort is expended to ignore the teachings of Islam about social justice, equality, the criticism of usury, and the care and righteousness that must be shown to the poor and weak in society. Most of these movements focus on the superficial aspects of life, such as the outer appearance of a person and their apparel, and the exaggerated segregation of men and women. What is notable is that many of these extremist Islamist movements, although attacking the *Jāhiliyyah* (pre-Islamic) nature of those societies that do not implement God's law, refrain completely from showing any criticism with regard to the way Sharī'ah has been implemented in petroleum-producing countries. Furthermore, these movements do not expose the great gap between the teachings of Islam and the squandering of oil-derived wealth on extreme luxury and over-consumption. Meanwhile, the transfer of some of this wealth to these movements has made them popular, especially among students.

Major errors were committed by the state in dealing with the problem of religious groups. The state's handling of these groups vacillated between extreme repression, which in the long run made the problem worse, and extreme support, which encouraged these groups to transcend their boundaries and increase in strength. These errors led to what we call the "sectarian conflict," which reached its apogee in the event of the Manaṣṣah (when Sadat was assassinated) and in the Muslim Brotherhood uprising in Aṣyūt in Upper Egypt. The natural extension of all of this has been the demand to implement Sharīʿah, a demand that is still very popular nowadays.

12
The Implementation of Sharī'ah: An Attempt at Comprehension

The accumulated mistakes of the past thirty years in Egypt, some of which were committed by the Islamist movement itself and others by the government in dealing with the movement, have culminated in the present explosive situation, in which active Islamist groups declare that the only exit from our problems is an immediate implementation of Sharī'ah. These groups attempt to move their work from the theoretical stage to that of actual implementation.

The responses to such a critical situation have vacillated from one position to its opposite. On the one hand, some have downplayed the importance of the situation, claiming it was exaggerated in order to cover up other social and economic problems in society. On the other hand, others have blown the situation out of proportion and warned us of a dreadful danger on the verge of destroying us. In either case, no rational discussion of the roots of the problems facing us in Egypt and the larger Arab world has taken place. To my mind, the danger is real and to make light of its intensity is misleading.

The claim that the character of the Egyptian nation does not admit that violence and terrorism feature in matters of religion is not a sound thesis, but an intentional act of emotional denial. For many years, the Iranian nation had suffered from the horrors of (the Iranian secret services) the Savak, which killed thousands and left even more physically and mentally scarred. Once the revolution took place in 1979, capital punishment and automatic trials went into effect, and a dark curtain of extremism, dejection, and sullenness fell upon people who had just won their freedom from the dictatorship of an oppressive ruler. I doubt that the Sudanese nation has the temperament to gather in public spaces in order to "enjoy" the sight of hands being cut off or backs being flogged. This did happen, not during the reign of a full-fledged Islamist revolution, but in the wake of a sudden turning to Islam, which was the final cycle in a series of dramatic changes the previous Sudanese regime went through.

One must not underestimate this issue. However, the automatic and hasty counter-responses to the demands for Sharī'ah and the attacks on the proponents of Sharī'ah implementation are useless unless they offer a well-researched and convincing perspective. Therefore, the question calls for a meditative rational discussion on the dimensions of this demand, the possibilities of its implementation and the consequences it may have.

Therefore, what faces us in this analytical discussion that I intend to offer are two questions: first, why? And, second, how?

THE FIRST QUESTION: WHY THE CALL TO IMPLEMENT SHARĪ'AH?

Proponents of Sharī'ah implementation are quick to point out that the rules of Sharī'ah are divinely ordained, whereas positivist laws (*qawānīn waḍi'yyah*) are of human origin. The simple logic behind the penetration of such a thesis into the hearts and minds of millions is that divine rule and human rule are not comparable. The human species is fragile and weak; its age, compared to that of the eternal universe, is no more than a moment, and their being is just a small atom in a boundless universe whose dimensions are measured by millions of light years. Proponents of Sharī'ah tend to raise the following argument: while we possess both divinely ordained and human-made legislation, it is inappropriate to hesitate for a moment in our choice of which is "correct."

As I have already mentioned, this straightforward logic cannot be contested in the mind of any average person; on the contrary, the force of its conviction is clearer than the simplest mathematical formulations. The fact that people live in a state of regression and crisis increases the appeal of this conviction. The more that political, economic, and social crises tighten the noose around their necks, the more the people will come to accept such logic, which asks them: haven't you discovered yet the results of human-made rule? Distancing yourselves from the divine path has caused your tragedies. Why do you not tread this path, if you really desire to save yourselves from the precipice?

Naturally, if the choice had really been between a divine rule and a human one, then the solution would have been immediately apparent. However, the fundamental question is: are we really in a position to choose between divine jurisdiction and human law? In my opinion, the case is far from this; the alternatives offered by the proponents of Sharī'ah exist only in the minds of those who do not deeply ponder matters. My opinion is based on essential foundations: first, Sharī'ah rules, as all admit, mostly reflect very general principles and require the exertion of tremendous effort in order to fill the many gaps these rules possess. The more complicated life becomes, the more significant it is to examine the details of these rules. Undoubtedly, our contemporary age is the most complex since the inception of human history as a result of dramatic technological and scientific progress and the concomitant changes in how we live our lives. These changes created new situations humans had not hitherto known. Therefore, it is imperative for any society to exert immense human effort to translate general religious principles into attainable realities in such a world.

We shall give two examples in this regard. The principle of charity (*iḥsān*) is well recognized in Islam. Many Qur'anic verses extrapolate this principle with the objective of reminding the wealthy that the deprived have a right to some of that wealth. The main intention is to ensure a minimum standard of living for the poor. Thus the principle of charity is an essential element that purports to realize some form of social justice. Amidst the increasing complication and urbanization of modern societies, it becomes imperative that we grasp the general spirit of the principle of charity and strive to narrow the gap between rich and poor. Also, we must exert great effort in identifying the methods that will realize for certain some form of social justice in this complex society. The methods of realizing social justice can extend from the rich giving charity directly to the poor (a useless formula in most contemporary societies), to barring the wealthy from owning the means that enable them to exploit the poor and weak. There are many differences of opinion (which are man-made), about the solutions to this problem, although these differences can be classified under the general religious principle of charity.

The second example is that of Qur'anic principle of *shūrah*, or consultation among the people, which is divinely ordained. As we all know, there is still wide disagreement about this principle and whether or not it is binding on the ruler. What is even more important is that the principle of *shūrah* has been subject to widely divergent interpretations: it can be defined as the murmur of the ruler in the ears of his ministers and close confidants, or the carrying-out of honest and free elections that will lead to the choice of real people's representatives, who form an authoritative body to keep an eye on the conduct of the ruler and establish checks and balances that cannot be overstepped. The divine principle is one; however, the interpretations, which are human-inspired, are quite numerous.

In this regard, I would like to point out the interpretation offered by the Egyptian thinker Khālid Muḥammad Khālid [d. 1996] in a recent article of his in *al-Ahrām* (June 6, 1985). In this article, the eminent Islamic writer defines the principle of *shūrah* as follows:

1) The nation is the source of authority.
2) It is essential that there be separation between the different branches of power.
3) The nation must have the absolute right to choose its president.
4) The nation must have the absolute right to elect its representatives.
5) There must be a courageous and free parliamentary opposition that can topple the government in instances of transgression.
6) There must be party pluralism.
7) There must be a free press, which must be always honored and defended.
8) "Oh brother, this is the Islamic system of power, without any falsification or reduction."

Needless to say, this last line of Khālid Muḥammad Khālid's statement will be vehemently opposed by many Islamist groups as well as by those regimes that vociferously claim that they follow the path of Sharī'ah. Mr Khālid's definition represents the extreme democratic position; however, the principle of *shūrah* can be, from a theoretical perspective at least, interpreted in a much narrower sense. Therefore, what Mr Khālid perceives as the Islamic system of governance is in fact his personal view of this system. We must be grateful for such an enlightened and expansive perspective; however, we must admit that this is not the only perspective that the religious texts contain.

In this regard, the important question is: would Mr Khālid have reached such a definition of authority had he pondered only the general principles contained in the religious texts? Would he have been able to define the principle of *shūrah* as the separation between the different authorities, free parliamentarian election, a strong opposition capable of toppling the government, party pluralism and freedom of the press, had he not been influenced by such weak and mortal human beings as John Locke, Montesquieu, Rousseau and Thomas Jefferson and had not the experiences of the countries that applied democracy before us supported these philosophers' ideas in real life? Would Mr Khālid have been able to interpret the principle of *shūrah* in such an enlightened way had he not acquired democratic proclivities through his reading, general education, and acquaintance with the experiences of modern nations? If someone were to say that he arrived at this definition of the principle of *shūrah* as a result of his deep knowledge of Islamic tradition (*turāth*), why weren't these principles fathomed and implemented in the whole history of this tradition?

Here, we discover that the general principle, subject to various and contradictory interpretations, does need an indispensable human effort in order to be translated into a living human reality. Whenever the conditions of life become more complex, the role of human effort takes primary importance and, to a large extent, general principles depend on such human effort.

The second reason that compels me to argue that it is not a matter of a choice between a divine rule and a human one is that the divine text is not self-explanatory or self-applicable. Human beings interpret and apply divine text. In the process of interpretation and implementation, human desires, interests, and partialities intervene. Only during the Prophet's age were the legislation, and its interpretation and implementation of divine nature: the person in charge of interpretation and implementation was God's messenger. It is only during this Prophetic Age that one can compare divine and human rules. After this time, human beings, with their desires and weaknesses, intervened; it was only through humans that divine legislation was actualized. This is the only explanation for the huge gap among political systems, each of which swears that it implements Sharī'ah in the most appropriate fashion.

What do we conclude from the above? Anyone with a minimum level of reasoning reaches the obvious conclusion that the fundamental objective of the proponents of the implementation of Sharī'ah is impossible to realize. The proponents of this call to Sharī'ah are overcome by an honest desire to reform their societies, and they attempt to dispel human weakness and confusion by resorting to a divine rule that is much more sublime than anything human beings can offer. However, the fragility and partiality of human beings, and their corruption and moral laxity, still accompany them even when they resort to divine legislation. The moment we throw desires and prejudices out the window, they return through the back door.

Rule or governance is first and foremost an essentially human process. As long as those who practice it are human beings, they will impose their feelings and opinions on any text that guides them in their rule, even if that text is divine. Anyone suspicious of this must take a look at all the experiments of implementing the Islamic Sharī'ah, not just in the contemporary Muslim world, but also throughout Islamic history since the age of the Prophet.

The answer of the Islamist movements to our first question, "Why the call to implement the Islamic Sharī'ah?" has been that this implementation simply means the return to the divine rule (the term used by some Islamist thinker is *ḥākimiyyah*), and that divine rules are superior to human ones. However, our preceding analysis has resulted in one significant conclusion, which is that a comparison between divine and human rules is not possible since any rule controlled by humans, even if of divine origin, reflects the desires of human beings, their prejudices, greediness, and their weaknesses. What this means is that the real choice is not between divine and human rules but between a human rule that claims that it speaks in the name of divine revelation and another which admits its human foundation. The danger of the former, which is always accompanied by human errors, is that it paints these errors and desires with the tincture of the sacred, and intentionally mixes the divine root of these rules with their human interpretations. In this sense, this combination insinuates that the whims and faults of the ruler are but a form of obedience to divine revelation, and it endows the weakness of the ruler with an infallibility that is completely undeserved. The second type of rule, that admits its human origins, its partiality and error is less dangerous, since we acknowledge beforehand that this type of rule is made by mortal, fallible beings.

Humanity does repeatedly commit errors in the different experiences of rule it practices and learns from its own mistakes. However, the gravest of errors is the one committed by a ruler who imagines that their desires and narrow interests are but an embodiment of divine will and gives the false impression that whatever they do is inspired by divine legislation. The bitter experiences of our long Islamic history have proven that such rulers have been, very often, the bloodiest and the least concerned about the destiny of their people.

THE SECOND QUESTION: HOW CAN WE IMPLEMENT SHARĪ'AH?

Nowadays, a debate rages about how to implement Sharī'ah. Is it enough to say that Sharī'ah is implemented the moment we impose its penalty codes (*ḥudūd*), that is, must we implement the penalty for theft, which is the chopping off of hands, and the penalty for drinking alcohol, which is to flog the drunkard, or the penalty for prostitution, which is to stone the one who commits this sin? Many reasonable people, even in the heart of the Islamist movement itself, emphasize that the implementation of Sharī'ah is much wider than just the subject of *ḥudūd*. Penalties are the negative side of Sharīʻah. Does that mean that Sharīʻah will not affect and organize the lives of righteous people, that is, those who do not commit theft, prostitute themselves or drink alcohol (and I assume they are the majority)? Undoubtedly, Sharīʻah must be implemented in the positive realms of human life and not in the negative realms alone.

To ponder the question from another perspective: are the problems of society confined to these sins alone? Let us suppose that we applied the *ḥudūd* laws on the thief, the drunkard, and the prostitute and let us suppose that through this we thought that we might be able to extinguish society's ills, would this be sufficient to reform society? Would applying the penalty for theft, instead of increasing productivity and achieving equality of distribution and guiding consumption, solve the economic problem? The same question applies to social and ethical problems. It suffices to look around us at those societies that have applied these penalties with so much intent and energy, the Sudan in the past and Pakistan currently, in order to realize that the implementation of penalties is not sufficient at all in solving ethical, social, and economic problems.

Many have realized the above fact and demanded that efforts to improve society not be confined to the implementation of Sharīʻah alone. Some of those requesting Sharīʻah's immediate implementation went along with this faction in order to promote the idea that Sharīʻah has more positive aspects than just the imposition of penalties. However, I do suspect the latter's position and believe their real efforts are focused on implementing the harsher aspects of Sharīʻah.

Any comprehensive implementation of Sharīʻah is time-consuming and must be gradual in nature. To keep demanding its immediate implementation is unrealistic and the same is true of those meetings or proceedings that call for immediate implementation. What *can* be decided overnight is whether or not to simply issue an order to institute the legal penalties.

It is likely that most of the proponents of immediate implementation believe that the imposition of the penalty rules is the most critical step in the implementation of Sharīʻah, and that everything else will follow. To my mind, this opinion is far from sound: any political system can distract people for years on end with the sight of chopped-off hands and flogged backs, with the stoning to death of sinners. These would never lead to constructive reform in society, and this is what has happened in contemporary experiences of implementing Sharīʻah.

That the current call nowadays is essentially a demand to implement the penalty rules at the expense of other aspects of Sharīʻah was evident when proponents of Sharīʻah passionately applauded the former Sudanese president when he issued his famous edicts, which were confined to the issues of flogging, amputation, stoning, and other penalties. Many declarations of support for what was happening in the Sudan were printed in newspapers published by Islamist movements throughout the Arab world, without any one of their thinkers asking: "Is what is happening in this society truly identical to divine law?" Some Islamic newspapers were even embarrassed when the Numairi regime collapsed after they had praised this regime only a few days before; they attacked the methods Numairi used to implement Sharī'ah, knowing that they had claimed he was following the right path when he was in power.

Two schools of thought exist within the Islamist current in the contemporary Muslim world. The first advocates the automatic implementation of Sharī'ah, and by this it actually means the issuance of the penalty laws, which it asserts is an essential step before later ones. The second school of thought argues that the implementation of penalties should be the final and not the first step, and that what must first take place is the realization of a minimum level of social, economic, and political justice. When this is accomplished, then society can apply penalties, while making sure that no one is unjustly treated.

Undoubtedly, the latter position is based on an admirable logic. A hasty implementation of the penalty rules without first preparing the appropriate social milieu may lead to tragic consequences. How can our consciences accept the chopping off of a person's hands in an era dominated by distress and penury and where the rich plunder the poor? Once implemented, the judgment of amputation cannot be reversed. What would happen if we cut off the hands of a man who steals because he is starving and who later shows repentance? Doesn't God accept repentance from all? This stigma, clear to everyone, will haunt this man and his descendants after him.

Do our consciences accept that we identify the money, stolen out of need, which is in the final analysis an impermanent commodity, with an essential part of man's life and a fundamental factor in his humanity and nobility? For these reasons, proponents of patience in the implementation of penalties have hit the right mark when they declare: secure for people the minimum level of justice and human living before you apply penalty laws.

Let us look at another example. As we all know, the crime of prostitution is to a large extent difficult to prove, and Sharī'ah has stipulated complex criteria for proof, given the harshness of the penalty of stoning. Are we able to equate committing the crime of prostitution in a society that suffers from a housing crisis in which the majority of youth cannot marry since they cannot obtain appropriate housing with those injuries committed in a wealthy society by those who lead lives of opulence? It is true that prostitution is a crime in either case. However, do we blame a person who is forced to remain unmarried indefinitely in the same way that we blame a wealthy person who knowingly commits adultery?

The crimes and evils to which Sharī'ah rules are intended to apply are not absolute evils and cannot be isolated from their social contexts. On the contrary, we can understand their meaning only in the context of change in society and in people's lives. There are many signs that prove that an automatic implementation of the penalty rules before a minimum of social justice has been achieved will in all probability lead to grave oppression against the people. In the Sudan, where people still suffer from starvation, the museum display of amputated hands is the best proof of this oppression.

Having said all of that, the proponents of patient implementation of the penalties have not yet raised the following question: what does securing a minimum level of standard of living mean in a country like Egypt? This simply means finding solutions to the problems of growth, unemployment, starvation, poverty, housing, and education, in addition to most of the problems we have been facing for the past several decades. In light of our constant population growth and continuous national and international crises, there is no proof at the moment that a solution is going to be found soon.

Thus the parameters of the impasse resulting from the call for a hasty implementation of Sharī'ah come to the fore: if we were to initiate the process of implementing Sharī'ah at this time without preparing the appropriate social ground for it, we would commit grave errors and do wrong to people. If we waited until social conditions are ripe, then our problems would be taken care of without resort to the implementation of Sharī'ah.

This brand of analysis, and another which I presented in these pages, is not an invitation to hopelessness but to using one's reason. I would like to convey the following message to our tens of thousands of youths who have pure intentions and a sincere desire to reform themselves and their societies: do not accept everything that is being said to you uncritically. Once you use your minds critically, you will realize, like many did after so many bitter experiences in the Sudan, Pakistan, and the Gulf, that the notion that reform will follow on the heels of an automatic implementation of Sharī'ah is an exaggerated fiction; and a person in charge of implementing Sharī'ah would always remain partial, prejudiced, oppressive and ignorant, like any other human being (you should consult history about this). The solution we all dream of will not follow on the heels of hasty decisions but will come after a long struggle against poverty, ignorance, disease, underdevelopment, and dependency on outside forces, and most importantly, after a long battle with the human self that becomes comfortable with easy solutions, simple formulas, and noisy slogans.

The message I would like to convey to official decision makers is that in dealing with the Islamist movement, neither extreme violence nor extreme flirtation is useful. The encounter should be based on an extended democratic dialogue, and the solution to this problem should not be placed in the hands of the ministries of the interior or the security forces.

All I hope for is that the ideas I have presented will pave the way for a quiet and rational contemplation based on the language of logic and not on that of the sword, since resorting to the sword in these matters is the refuge of the weak.

13
The Implementation of Sharī'ah: A New Dialogue

The journalistic debates in which I have recently participated (both inside and outside of Egypt) and which have taken the form of either dialogue or heated intellectual debate have taught me that supporters of an opinion defended by a certain author do not usually send written comments. Only the opponents write letters. The supporter may express their appreciation over the phone or in a personal meeting but the opponent possesses a strong incentive that drives them to shoulder the burden of writing and responding to the author.

I must express my own happiness at the wide response I personally received to the three articles I published in the daily *al-Ahrām* on "The Religious Question in Contemporary Egypt." The written responses I have received express an opposing position. Since this brand of critical opposition does help in the continuation of dialogue and the expression of its various dimensions, I have found it useful to discuss the ideas of my opponents, not for the sake of engaging in a formalistic debate with them, but so as to discover novel dimensions for the dialogue taking place nowadays around the contemporary call to implement Sharī'ah.

Some responses I have received express ideas that open new avenues of dialogue, while others do not add anything to the subject matter at hand, since they misrepresent what I wrote. I will begin with an example of the latter responses since they deal with an erroneous methodology that has lately become widespread in our intellectual life. This methodological pitfall appears because many critics or commentators discuss not what is written but what they imagine is written. They also interpret what is written in a way that has no relevance to the source, in order that they give themselves the opportunity to carry their criticism in the way they wish. To my mind, this type of dialogue is a waste of time since the objective of the original writer would be then confined to shedding a new light on his meanings and objectives, although they had been clear before. In this, dialogue does not advance a bit. However, drawing one's attention to these intellectual pitfalls is always useful.

For example, Dr 'Abd al-Raḥmān 'Ayyād, vice president of the Supreme Court, devoted a large section of his article in the daily *al-*

Ahrām entitled "The Rational Discourse and Sharī'ah Implementation," to defending the general principles of Sharī'ah, as though my previous article placed these principles in doubt. What I have asserted and still assert is that the increasing complexity of life brings us face to face with new situations that cannot be gauged on the basis of general principles, but need great attention to the minute details. This kind of effort has to be "human." Whenever a society preserves a general principle, such as the principle of *shūrah* or consultation, this society must also add to it human effort, which becomes more significant the more complex our lives become. There is no doubt that the civilizational space that separates the conditions of our contemporary life from the historical conditions in which Sharī'ah was revealed has become so huge that we must admit to the increasing importance of human effort that must be expended in order to convert the general principle into a series of ideas and detailed measures that can be implemented in a very complex society.

The above applies to Dr 'Ayyād's objection, which states that human desires do not intervene in the implementation of Sharī'ah alone, but in any other legislation or civilization. This is exactly what I meant and I do not see any difference of opinion between the author and me. The partiality and weakness of human beings will always accompany us, even in the process of implementing Sharī'ah, since it is humans who will convert the letters and words of Sharī'ah into a dynamic and concrete reality. This person, like you and me, does err and take positions in conformity with their desires and whims, as history has proven. And naturally, those who implement human legislation err and take sides, as well. Dr 'Ayyād could have saved himself the immense effort he exerted in order to prove a reality that no reasonable person denies.

Dr Fawqiyyah Ḥussein Maḥmūd, Professor of Philosophy at the College of Women in Cairo University, strongly objects to what she calls, "His [Zakariyya's] own narrow presentation of the person who approaches religious texts, since to him this person has abandoned the faculty of his reason in order to be an automatic executor of the texts." This is an objection to an opinion the writer imagined, since I never talked about the person who "approached religious texts" but about those youths who are moved by passion and energy to join religious groups which demand absolute obedience, not just to religious texts but also to the leaders of the group. The reader is well aware that the category of the "readers of religious texts" is much wider than the one of which the professor speaks, since the former includes people who study religious texts with a highly rational methodology. Therefore, distorting my words to include all of those who study religious texts falsifies my true objectives; she has created a fictitious enemy who is not amenable to criticism.

A third example of this arbitrary reading is that of Mr Aḥmad 'Abd al-Raḥmān Ibrahīm, an Egyptian teacher who was working in Saudi Arabia and who is currently employed in Algeria. He objects to my stated opinion that the conflict between the Nasser regime and the Muslim Brotherhood Movement was political in nature, and that it had nothing to do with Islam. He argues that the Muslim Brotherhood were advocating a "totalistic vision" of Islam, an Islam to be implemented in all walks of life, whereas Nasser, described by the writer as a secular ruler, advocated a "partial vision" of Islam. On the basis of this, the author concludes that the conflict centered on Islamic doctrine (*'aqīdah*). Here, I would like to raise the following question in the mind of our esteemed writer: did the conflict arise when Nasser began to debate the doctrinal ideas of the Ikhwān on "totalistic Islam," similar to the debates in the court of the 'Abbasid caliph al-Ma'mūn, who when not buying their ideas placed them under arrest and executed some of their leaders, or was it primarily a conflict over political authority? Has our esteemed writer forgotten that the "totalistic Islam" the Ikhwān advocated also included the legal and political systems and that such advocacy was based on the stripping of political authority and governing from the Nasserite system?

I take the last example from a witty letter written by Mr Nabīh Naṣr Rizq of Alexandria who objects to my lack of conviction about the apparition of the Virgin Mary after the June 1967 war, saying: "The apparition of the blessed Virgin and Saint Mary in the Church of Zaytūn in Cairo on April 2, 1968 was a true reality not subject to dispute. And I have only one word to say to the esteemed Professor: Come yourself and take a glance at the reality of the apparition of the pure Virgin so that you will discover the light and smell the odor of incense."

It is clear that my opinion hurt his religious feelings and I think that such sensitivity is unnecessary, since the number of Muslims who participated in such a belief and who came to the church by the thousands every day exceeded that of Christians. The primary goal was to criticize one of the non-rational patterns of thought that became widespread among many in one of the most difficult times in contemporary Arab history. As for the content of the apparition itself and whether or not it took place, he has the right to believe in whatever he wishes. The same right must apply for those convinced that the era of miracles is over and that the miracles of our era are those of the transistor, the satellite, and the computer. We must understand that the difference between the two groups is over methodological reasoning and not over religious issues.

These few examples of objection do not add, I am afraid, to the dialogue we are advocating. However, these responses have raised other serious problems, whose discussion sheds new light on our subject matter.

TOTALISTIC ISLAM

Professor Fawqiyyah Ḥussein Maḥmūd objects to my thesis that the implementation of Sharī'ah requires a radical change in every aspect of our lives and draws our attention to the fact that "we are already Muslim and we do already follow the essence of Sharī'ah. What the esteemed Professor advocates will only effect the heedless. Far from being comprehensive, change is about the adaptation of the forms, since we already follow the contents of Sharī'ah."

Clearly, the person advocating such an opinion has never taken into account the presence of those groups whose extremism reaches the level of accusing an entire society of unbelief, and that groups which believe in Sayyid Quṭb's thesis that our societies live in the *jāhiliyyah* of the twentieth century advocate changes far more comprehensive than mere formalities. However, let us put this point aside and give the task of responding to Professor Maḥmūd's opinion to Dr Aḥmad 'Abd al-Raḥmān, a colleague of hers who takes an oppositional view of my ideas. In his assessment of the position of the Muslim Brotherhood Movement, the mother organization of most contemporary Islamist movements in Egypt, he argues: "The Islamist groups have sprung up in order to realize a central doctrine, which is the doctrine of 'total Islam'—an Islam that covers thought, worship, ethics, economics, politics, art, literature and every aspect of human life in order to stamp it with its distinguished mark." He goes on to argue that, "In the view of the Islamists, the oppression of Islam itself and its totalistic conception of life is one oppression and any partial application of Islam is equal to apostasy." What this means in essence in the view of the main representatives of the Ikhwān is that the current Muslim regimes' partial application of Islam is a form of apostasy, and what is required to ameliorate the situation is a complete application of Islam.

I have left the response to Professor Maḥmūd's objection to someone who shares her position in opposing my views and who represents the largest contemporary Islamist movement. Can the members of such a movement and other movements that are more extreme than the Ikhwān be classified under the category the esteemed Professor calls "the heedless"? This is an internal question, which I leave for her to take care of.

What faces us in essence is to debate that call or invitation that is attractive on the surface, that is, the invitation to a complete form of Islam. My main objection to this discourse is that it opens wide the door to conceptual seclusion and civilizational stagnation. In their quest for realizing "total Islam," the proponents of such a position will have an opportunity to advocate shutting the gate to external civilizational influences, with the excuse that such influences represent an alien and intellectual crusade, and that "total Islam" contains everything that we need. It is possible then for rigid totalitarianism to arise in the context of this call, that will freeze history in one era, refusing to admit progress and evolution while burying its head in the sands of "the past Golden Age" and denying the brilliant achievements occurring in our contemporary age.

The proponents of "total Islam" (*Islām shāmil*) advocate the implementation of one perspective in the domains of philosophy, economics, politics, the arts, and literature. Therefore, what do we do with those systems of thought appearing in the world independently of Islam? Do we take a similar position to that of famous men of religion who asserted that the gravest error committed by the ʻAbbasid caliph al-Ma'mūn was to pave the way for Greek philosophy to enter the world of Islam? What do we do with the currents of art and literature appearing in society that did not know Islam? Wouldn't a strict and rigid application of the principle of "total Islam" lead to the rejection of all the above and the drawing of a heavy curtain between us and the currents of thought, literature, and art so widespread in the contemporary world?

Let me give a simple example of an opinion I have recently discussed with some of my students about an artistic topic. As the reader well knows, some Muslim countries (Egypt is not one of them) ban the art of sculpture completely on the premise that sculpture is a statue and statues are banned in Islam. The question I raised was as follows: if sculpture was banned in an age when reverting to polytheism was still possible, why is there still fear that people would look at a statue in a public place as an object of worship? Is the possibility of reverting to polytheism viable in our contemporary Muslim society, even one in a million? If the possibility is not likely, then why do we deny ourselves the appreciation of a sublime art that cultivates our tastes and adds beauty and harmony to our lives? Undoubtedly, we thought this in Egypt, which is why our public squares are adorned with sculptural works, some of which possess a sublime artistic value. But wouldn't it be possible that some among us would advocate applying "total Islam," destroying idols and banning statues, as some Muslim countries have done? Wouldn't it be possible for such censorship to be repeated in the domains of thought and creative literature and lead us to gloomy and melancholic lives where such things as music, dance, sublime art, sculpture, universal systems of thought, television programs, and theater are prohibited? These are not distant possibilities: this has already taken place, either partially or completely, in some Muslim countries. Those who live in some Arab countries know how the schools of music, from example, suffer at the hands of women students who belong to some Islamist groups which declare that music promotes shamelessness, moral laxity, and polytheism. The same applies to the other domains of the arts, intellectual and scientific trends, and technological innovations.

I do not argue that these results would be inevitable if "total Islam" were to be implemented, but affirm that such a call would open the floodgates to the proponents of these ideas; it will be difficult for others to withstand their strong current.

In their assertion of the capability of Sharī'ah to reflect the changes of the age, a good number of the respondents have pointed out the famous hadīth, "You are cognizant of the affairs of your life." What has escaped the attention of those people is that this particular hadīth absolutely stands in contradiction to the principle of "total Islam." If running the affairs of this life is left to the effort of human beings and the nature of their age and conditions, the principle of "total Islam" leads, according to the quoted hadīth, to limiting someone's ability to run the affairs of their life in a manner that they know best. If the hadīth implicitly contains a separation between the affairs of this life, whose organization is left to humans, and the affairs of religion as stipulated by Sharī'ah, the call to "total Islam" would be in danger of removing this separation and subjecting all aspects of life to one religious perspective. In his fascinating summary published in the daily *al-Ahrām* by Mr Muḥammad Aḥmad Farghalī, he has not strayed from the spirit of the hadīth quoted above when he asserts that religion represents only one of the many sides of an individual's life.

READING THE PRESENT FROM THE PERSPECTIVE OF THE PAST

The words of the esteemed thinker Khālid Muḥammad Khālid inspired me to delve into this topic when he offered a definition of the concept of *shūrah,* which I pointed out in preceding chapters. He maintains that this principle contains the idea of separation of the spheres of power, freedom of establishing political parties, freedom of the press and the opposition, etc. What attracted my attention was that when Mr Khālid discussed my ideas in the pages of another newspaper, he did not tackle the central points of my discussion of his ideas, which were as follows: would he have been able to offer such a definition of the principle of *shūrah* had he not been a proponent of democracy and had he not been influenced by human intellectual and philosophical currents that came before him?

To my mind, the above issue is fundamental and pondering it deeply will reveal to us that traditional debates surrounding the question of Sharī'ah implementation are futile. Mr Khālid, as an enlightened contemporary thinker, asserts that he has discovered the full meaning of democracy and its different dimensions in the Islamic heritage. However, to my mind this is quite impossible since the principle of separation between spheres of power is a modern concept. In the same vein, the media and political parties had no presence in the era Mr Khālid is talking about. What our esteemed teacher Khālid Muḥammad Khālid has in mind is that we can discover in Islamic tradition certain principles; if we exert some effort in interpreting them from the perspective of contemporary concepts, we would see in them what we can measure against the democratic principles of the present era. As for finding these principles literally, without any form of ambiguity, in tradition, as Mr Khālid seems to suggest, it would be impossible to be convinced of such a position.

Let us suppose that a good number of the experts in religious affairs have read the same texts, which unambiguously contain, according to Mr Khālid's assertion, all the principles of modern democracy—would they reach similar results to those of Khālid's? Do these texts by themselves express these principles regardless of their intellectual formation, political orientation, and the economic and social interests of those who read them? Are those principles found in such a way that it is impossible for two people to differ over their interpretation in the way that healthy eyes will never differ over the green color of grass?

Both logic and reality point to a different position. If these texts were shown to Shaykh Ibn Bāz of Saudi Arabia, he would not have discovered any democratic principle or he would have avoided those texts and focused on entirely different ones, which also belong to Islamic tradition, texts that would allow him to substantiate his ideas and preferred interpretations.

Many a reader and interpreter of Sharī'ah texts engages in a reductionist approach, which no one can deny. For example, such a reader imposes their own ideas on what they read and selects what is more fitting to their point of view. Someone could construct a whole system of thought on the basis of the hadīth, "There is no preference between an Arab and a non-Arab except by piety." Another would assert the Qur'anic principle, "And We have raised some of them above others in rank"[1] or "And God gives sustenance to whom He pleases without reckoning."[2] In every case, the reader would choose, from the flexible Islamic principles, that which fits his objectives; the reader would turn a blind eye to the principles that contradict his objectives and keep affirming to others and himself that he receives his inspiration from tradition and Sharī'ah.

What is the actual result of all of this? The fundamental result is that human beings, with all of their desires and self-interests, are the ones who guide the texts, whereas the texts do not guide them. The second result is that the call to implement Sharī'ah, a call that is so attractive to millions of well-intentioned people, will not lead to our salvation from our aimlessness, since its impact will be determined by the people who carry out the implementation.

If the implementation of Sharī'ah were placed in the hands of reactionary people, who control huge wealth and flourish by exploiting others, they would use Sharī'ah to realize their abusive objectives and find texts to justify this. On the other hand, if someone like Khālid Muḥammad Khālid were charged with the task of implementing Sharī'ah, we would certainly see a democratic implementation in the modern meaning of the term. Therefore, it is the type of people and not Sharī'ah itself that will guarantee the type of implementation, and this point has been sufficiently proven by all the contemporary implementations of Sharī'ah.

This reductionist attitude is similar to the methods of proponents of a scientific interpretation of the Qur'ān. As we all know, there is a community of scholars that specializes in interpreting the Qur'ān scientifically and in discovering the most novel scientific theories in its text. If we leave aside the fundamental result of such an approach, as noted by Dr Aḥmad 'Ukāshah in his important article in the daily *al-Ahrām*, stipulated that the established texts of the Qur'ān would be subject to the changes and transformations of accompanying science day after day. If we set aside this observation, we will discover that what these scholars are doing is a human imposition: a scientific theory is discovered in the Qur'ān only after it has already been attained by virtue of human reason. If any of these exegetes were able to discover a scientific theory, on the basis of his interpretation of the Qur'ān, before it is discovered by science, we could believe in the usefulness of such exegesis. In reality, the exegetes always begin to search for the Qur'anic verses that support scientific discoveries only after these discoveries have been made by human reason. This kind of exegetic effort is useless: it would never change people's lives or science one bit.

In this context, a famous example comes to mind. In our childhood, the verse "God knows what every female bears, and that of which the wombs fall short of completion, and that in which they increase. And there is a measure with Him of everything"[3] was interpreted by our teacher as meaning that the gender of the unborn fetus was unknowable to humans. Many books in Qur'anic exegesis took this perspective until a few years ago. However, with the progress of science, it is possible for humans to know the gender of the fetus before birth; afterward, some exegetes began to offer new interpretations saying that this verse does not actually discuss the fetus but the future destiny of the fetus. Why this confusion, which shakes people's confidence in the works of these exegetes? Undoubtedly, this is due to the imposition of the religious text on the scientific domain.

It is certainly a grave mistake to impose one's views on the text instead of letting the text serve as one's guide. Plenty of such convoluted and mistaken examples appear in and affect our lives, especially when we agree with the call for implementation of Sharī'ah, which looks simple on the surface.

BETWEEN PRINCIPLE AND APPLICATION

I would like to begin this section by quoting from a letter I received from Mr Ayman Aḥmad Yūnus, an Egyptian working in Saudi Arabia, in which he says: "Praise be to God that all sorts of political systems have been tried in the history of modern Egypt, and praise be to God that all have failed to fulfill their commitments in advance of the cause of people. Why do not we, therefore, try to apply Sharī'ah? Sharī'ah has not had a chance yet to be implemented like other systems." This opinion is quite widespread and assumes that other systems have been tried but that Sharī'ah has not yet been tried.

Is it true that other systems have been tried and that they have failed? This opinion is not defended by Islamists alone, but also by a great number of leftists and Nasserites. However, in principle, I do not accept this opinion, since these other systems were in power for such limited times. Take the example of the liberal period in modern Egypt. It lasted only thirty years, from 1923 to 1952. In this period, it faced thousands of hurdles, at the fore of which was the British occupation and the resistance of the Palace and other political parties to the British. In addition, the level of social and economic growth was too low to successfully apply the new political system since such an implementation requires a high level of capitalist development. As for socialism, the period of its implementation did not last more than five years, from 1961 to 1965, and was followed by a decade in which its meager achievements were erased one after the other, until it completely disappeared in the mid-1970s. In this period of five years, its application was half-hearted. Most of the people chosen to guide and protect the new experiment were chosen on the basis of their personal loyalty to the ruler and not on the basis of their political conviction or their readiness to sacrifice for the sake of principle. Then how do we claim that other systems have been tried?

As for the second issue, that stipulates that Sharī'ah has not been applied before and that now is the time to apply it, this sounds like it would be a new experience and that Egyptian society should try this new process. However, Sharī'ah *has* been tried, more so than any other system, if we carefully consider Islamic history. Even in the contemporary era, four Muslim countries have applied Sharī'ah: first, the earliest, Saudi Arabia; second, Pakistan, one of the largest Muslim countries in the world; the Sudan, the largest Arab country, and Iran, the pioneer of the largest Islamic revolution in the contemporary period.

Therefore, the question of the application of Sharī'ah is not really new: before us stand several experiments from both the past and present. However, proponents of the Islamist movement would have us believe that the application has not yet taken place and our salvation lies in such implementation.

What surprises me is the fact that the calls to implement Sharī'ah have increased since the failure of the Sudanese experiment. How can we deny the lessons of history? Had I been in a leading position in the most extremist of Islamist groups, I would have gathered my people upon hearing of the failure of the Sudanese experiment and told them: let us be patient in our call to implement Sharī'ah, study our steps and the causes behind the failure of the Sudanese experience so that we do not repeat its mistakes in the future. And let us analyze the mistakes of the Iranian experiment after carrying out the most fascinating revolution, which attracted the sympathies of even the opponents of the Islamic movement. And let us review the factors that led to the application of Sharī'ah in Pakistan, which resulted in the assassination of opponents, the flogging of journalists and the rise of a dictatorial regime in the country. Also, let us study the reasons behind placing Islam, in the process of applying Sharī'ah in the rich Gulf countries, in the service of protecting the wealthy of the political elite instead of putting that immense wealth in the service of Islam.

Contemporary experiments in applying Sharī'ah have all been failures and have produced systems of rule that oppose the message of justice and righteousness preached by the heavenly revelations and not just by Islam. Weren't these failures enough to convince the proponents of Sharī'ah to pause and reflect, to prepare a written plan of action that would prevent the repetition of the tragedies and follies that have been linked to the recent applications of Sharī'ah?

Some are trying to wash their hands of the Sudanese and other experiments, as did Dr Ahmad 'Abd al-Raḥmān Ibrahīm in a letter in which he writes, "To take Numairi as an example has no scientific value." However, another writer who belongs to the same camp, Mr Wahbī Aḥmad Dahab, a member of the Sudanese Legislative Council, responds to Dr 'Abd al-Raḥmān by saying: "As for the application of the Islamic Sharī'ah in the Sudan, that is to say, the penalty rules, I would like to say that the Sudanese people have responded well since the application of the penalty rules protected their souls and property." To this clear position, we must add what is known about the Muslim Brotherhood Movement, which hailed the Numairi experiment of applying Sharī'ah, as Dr Faraj Fūda proves in his important book, *Before the Fall*.[4] So the same groups that blessed the Sudanese experiment during the Numairi regime are trying to wash their hands of this experiment after its fall and discover, like Dr 'Abd al-Raḥmān, that the experiment failed because the government that carried out the process of application was essentially secular.

In the preceding, I have discussed contemporary experiments of Sharī'ah implementation. As for the experiments of past history, they form a long series of failures. Despotism was the rule and oppression formed the foundation of the relationship between rulers and ruled. Furthermore, such Sharī'ah principles as justice, righteousness, and *shūrah* were mere words of propaganda used to justify the actions of rulers who often disregarded anything connected to these sublime principles.

Undoubtedly, the practices of the proponents of Sharī'ah implementation (however they differ on the details of such implementation), to constantly invoke the experience of the Rightly-Guided Caliphs, and especially that of Caliph 'Umar b. Khaṭṭāb, is proof that they have found nothing to invoke from the long period in which Sharī'ah was implemented. This implementation, lasting around thirteen centuries, was in reality a negation of Sharī'ah principles and a deviation from its path.

As mentioned above, the proponents of Sharī'ah application invoke the age of the Rightly-Guided Caliphs, and especially that of Caliph 'Umar b. Khaṭṭāb. Do these esteemed preachers realize that Caliph

'Umar was a unique and exceptional personality? If the experiments of past centuries and the present time have failed to produce a unique ruler like 'Umar, why do Islamists toy with the impossible hope of returning to 'Umar's age? If the template of righteousness, justice, and goodness has declined over the centuries and reached rock-bottom in contemporary experiments of Sharī'ah implementation, on what basis do the proponents of application hope that the next experiment they advocate applying in Egypt would be the one to succeed where others have failed throughout Islamic history?

Some of those who object to my writings accuse me of commingling the poor implementation of Sharī'ah with the principle of application or "the legitimacy of application," according to Professor Fawqiyyah Ḥussein Maḥmūd. However, what do we do when all cases of application known throughout Islamic history, except the very first whose uniqueness cannot be easily repeated, failed to realize justice, remove oppression, and establish a society in which human exploitation of each other totally disappears? Do we cling to the fiction that the 'next' application will succeed without offering any program that will make sure that this next time will not be marred by the grave mistakes committed in past experiments?

In order to justify this call, its proponents offer us cloudy and floating expressions that can be interpreted in any number of ways. Let us read what Professor Mahmūd says: "What is required is the ethical elevation of the human self, and the basis of such elevation is the fulfillment of actions with the fear of God." What if a person in a position of authority puts forward the claim that he fears God, while hiding other intentions? How can we enable millions of people to achieve a high ethical status, how many years will that take, and what methods do we use to achieve all of this? Dr Aḥmad 'Abd al-Raḥmān forwards the following claim: "Islam absolutely prohibits tyranny, and the Qur'ān presents definitions of both justice and tyranny that bar any leaning towards injustice and corruption. Justice is defined as the right of every human being to obtain the fruit of his work and bear the consequence of his mistakes." It is true that the Qur'ān has absolutely forbidden tyranny. However, has this prevented tyranny from taking place throughout Islamic history and reaching its climax in the contemporary experiments of Sharī'ah application? Have the accurate definitions of tyranny and justice prevented rulers from offering their own definitions to suit their own whims and interests? Do the proponents of Sharī'ah in the oil-producing countries agree with the principle that justice means that a human being receives the fruit of his work (*thamarat 'amaluh*)?

Dr ʻAbd al-Raḥmān ʻAyyād admits that "The phenomenon of partisanship and whimsical behavior in applying Sharīʻah was exacerbated when the first Umayyad Caliph Muʻāwiyah deviated from the preceding rule and established a dictatorial political system, which was at odds with the general principles of Islam." Do take note of the expression "exacerbated when Muʻāwiyah deviated from the preceding rule." How much time has elapsed since Muʻāwiyah deviated, and how much oppression and tyranny has taken place ever since at the hands of rulers, each of whom asserts that he completely applied Sharīʻah, without any oppression or deviation?

I do hope that the authors of such general judgments and composers of these statements will take the time to offer honest answers to these questions without, I hope, supporting their claims by pointing to someone like the Caliph ʻUmar, who was an exception. If they are self-reflective, they will discover that humans often impose their whims and biases on any rule or legislation. That is why in the modern era, the effort of human legislation has been focused on offering guarantees to the process of power, and democratic systems have moved to affirm the principle of checks and balances between the different institutions and power spheres of society. The main objective of all of this is to reduce the influence of human whim and bias to the minimum and establish boundaries that would limit the deviant behavior of a ruler.

DREAM AND REALITY

The proponents of the application of Sharīʻah have a rosy dream; however, they suffer from the problem of not exerting sufficient effort to translate this dream into the language of reality. In the process of such translation, it is essential to absorb the lessons of the past and present and understand their implications. Thousands of details and accurate checks must be established so that deviant rulers do not have a chance to exploit the flexibility of generalities in realizing their own objectives. Also, it is important to carefully ponder the possibility of such a call to apply Sharīʻah and its viability in the contemporary era, and to understand the reasons why the efforts to apply Sharīʻah have no connection whatsoever to the grinding problems from which the Egyptian citizens suffer every minute of their lives.

One of the main components of this rosy dream is the thought that our problems would automatically disappear the moment Sharīʻah was applied. How? No one has the answer. It is most likely that the proponents of Sharīʻah believe in the depth of their hearts that divine care will protect us the moment Sharīʻah is applied. Thus, heavenly forces will interfere to solve our problems without us having to exert any effort to do this. In the midst of the elation produced by these enchanting and attractive expressions, doesn't it occur to someone to raise the question: did this ever happen in the Sudan or Pakistan when Sharīʻah was applied? Didn't the problems of these countries increase in the context of those systems that claimed to only apply the rules of Islam?

Another component of this dream is that no one seems to have cared about raising a question about the party that will initiate and protect such application. Would that party be the men of religion? Would we create a new priestly class and a new papacy? Would it be specialized men of religion? Would we find a new group of people who combine specialization in religion and knowledge of contemporary sciences? Then, would we have the right to question the source of these unbelievable capabilities that enable the members of such a group to carry their heavy burden of responsibility for the affairs of rule and the running of a complex and problem-laden society?

One of the main characteristics of this rosy dream, as in any other dream, is that it tends to exaggerate things. Such dreamers imagine that the prohibition of alcohol, for example, will guarantee societal reform, while forgetting that the ruling classes in those Muslim countries applying Sharīʻah still consumed alcohol. Those dreamers forget that Muslim societies suffer from problems much worse than alcohol consumption or women's veiling or lack thereof. In any crisis-laden society such as ours, we must give priority to the problems from which we suffer in terms of resources, economy, finance, education, and health, and not to the segregation of the sexes or the sequestering of women behind closed doors.

Finally, this rosy dream leads its followers to exaggerate the ability of the rulers in the utopian society they want to establish, to develop the teachings of religion so that that society will be capable of facing the challenges of the twenty-first century. Is there justification for such hope?

In order to answer this question, let us give one example only. For many years, the Muslim world was unable to determine the start of the lunar calendar and Muslims still differ on the start of the day of fasting or the beginning of festivities. The basis of such disagreement was the insistence of interpreting the word "sighting" *(ru'yah)* in the famous hadīth, "Begin your fasting after sighting it and end it after sighting it," based on seeing the moon with one's own eyes. This position does not admit that new technological systems can do a better and more accurate accounting of the beginning of the lunar calendar. Every year the question of "sighting" comes to the fore, and religious institutions and organizations, official and non-official, reject any interpretation not based on sighting the moon with the human eye.

We have not heard over the past decades that the Islamic groups requesting the application of Sharī'ah have shown any flexibility on this simple question of determining the lunar calendar. Next year, the beginning of the month of Ramadan will probably be determined by Shaykhs who will strain their weak eyes during sunset; and it is likely that many Arab countries in the coming years will fail to reach a consensus on the precise beginning of Ramadan. If we face such great rigidity over this simple question, will we be content with the ability of these religious institutions and groups to adapt their doctrine so as to face the challenges of the computer age and travels in the cosmos? Doesn't this clear example make us suspicious of the aspirations they offer in the name of their rosy dream?

A large number of the people who have objected to my articles have used the pretext that there is a wide mass appeal to apply Sharī'ah. I cannot but agree with this. However, all I can say is that we have lived in a Muslim country and have always known balanced religious citizens who fulfill their obligation of worship through their constant and tireless efforts to advance themselves and their society; the scream (*ṣayḥah*) to apply Sharī'ah was uttered in soft voices without affecting the daily affairs of the people. This is the image of religion our nation has known over many generations. The present tendency of applying Sharī'ah, in spite of its speedy dissemination, is a new and alien phenomenon in the area of rational and quiet religiosity of the Egyptian people. Like any alien phenomenon, we must trace its origins to accidental factors, such as oppression, political and intellectual tyranny, and the absence of viable opposition and criticism. Also, we must trace it to external factors, such as the effort exerted by the controllers of oil wealth to safeguard their riches, and the effort made by those forces standing in opposition to our progress to find ways to numb our minds, to destroy our unity, and to divert our attention from our real enemies, both nationally and internationally.

NOTES

1. Qur'ān: 43: 32.
2. Ibid., 2: 212.
3. Ibid., 13: 8.
4. Faraj Fūda, *Qabla al-Suqūṭ* (Cairo, 1985).

A Selected Bibliography in Contemporary Arab Thought

'Abd al-Fattāḥ, N., ed. *The State of Religion in Egypt Report* (Cairo: Al-Ahrām Center for Political and Strategic Studies, 1996).

'Abd al-Laṭīf, K. *Salāma Mūsa wā ishkāliyat al-nahḍah* (Beirut: Dār al-Ṭalī'ah, 1982).

——. *Mafāhīm multabasah fī'l fikr al-'arabī al-mu'āṣir* (Beirut: Dār al-Ṭalī'ah, 1992).

——. *Qirā'āt fī'l falsafah al-'arabīyyah al-mu'āṣirah* (Beirut: Dār al-Ṭalī'ah, 1994).

——. *al-Fikr al-falsafī fī'l maghrib: qirā'āt fī a'māl al-Jābīrī wa'l 'Urwī* (Casablanca: Ifrīqyyah al-Sharq, 2001).

'Abd al-Malik, A. *Dirāsāt fī'l thaqāfah al-waṭaniyyah* (Beirut: Dār al-Ṭalī'ah, 1967).

'Abdallah, I.S. "al-Kawkabah: al-ra'smāliyyah al-'ālamiyyah fī marḥalatī mā ba'da al-imberiāliyyah." *Al-Ṭarīq*, volume 56(4), July–August 1997.

——. "al-'Arab wa'l 'awlamah: al-'awlamah wa'l iqtiṣād wa'l tanmiyyah al-'arabiyyah." In Markaz Dirāsāt al-Wiḥdah al-'Arabiyyah, *al-'Arab wa'l 'Awlamah* (Beirut: Markaz Dirāsāt al-Wiḥdah al-'Arabīyyah, 1998).

Abdel-Malek, A. "The Occultation of Egypt." *Arab Studies Quarterly*, volume 1(3), Summer 1979.

——. *La pensée politique arabe contemporaine* (Paris: Seuil, 1970).

Abdelrazik, A. *L'Islam et les fondements du pouvoir*, tr. Abdou Filali-Ansary (Paris: La Découverte, 1994).

Abou Nasr, M. *L'idéologie nationale arabe dans le discours de Gamal Abd-El Nasser, 1952–1970* (Thesis: Paris: Université de Paris, 1979).

Abū'l Majd, A.K. *Ḥiwār lā muwājaha: dirāsāt ḥawla al-islām wa'l 'aṣr* (Cairo: Dār al-Shurūq, 1988).

——. "Ḥawla nadwat al-ḥiwār al-qawmī al-dīnī." In Markaz Dirāsāt al-Wiḥdah al-'Arabiyyah, *al-Ḥiwār al-qawmī al-dīnī* (Beirut: Markaz Dirāsāt al-Wiḥdah al-'Arabiyyah, 1989).

——. *Ru'yah islāmiyyah mu'āṣirah* (Cairo: Dār al-Shurūq, 1992).

——. "Ṣūrat al-ḥālah al-islāmiyyah 'ala mashārif alfiyyah Jadīdah." *Wijhāt Nadhar*, volume 1(11), December 1999.

——. "Min ajl wiḥdah thaqāfiyyah 'Arabīyyah." In Sayyid Yāssīn, ed., *al-'Arab wa taḥadiyyāt al-qarn al-ḥādī wa'l 'ishrīn* (Amman: Mu'assassat 'Abdul Ḥamīd Shūmān, 2000).

Abū Zayd, N. "al-Khiṭāb al-dīnī al-mu'āṣir: āliyātuhu wa munṭalaqātuhū al-fikriyyah." *Qaḍāyah Fikriyyah*, volume 8, 1989.

——. *Mafhūm al-naṣṣ: Dirasah fī 'ulūm al-Qur'ān* (Cairo: al-Hay'ah al-Miṣriyyah, 1990).

——. *al-Tafkīr fī zaman al-takfīr* (Cairo: Dār Sīnā, 1995).

Abu-Deeb, K. "Cultural Creation in a Fragmented Society." In Hisham Sharabi, H., ed. *The Next Arab Decade: Alternative Futures* (Boulder, CO: Westview Press, 1988).

Abu-Rabi', I. *Contemporary Arab Thought: Studies in Post-1967 Arab Intellectual History* (London: Pluto Press, 2003).

——. *Intellectual Origins of Islamic Resurgence in the Modern Arab World* (Albany: State University of New York Press, 1996).

——. "The Concept of the 'Other' in Modern Arab Thought: From Muḥammad 'Abduh to Abdallah Laroui." *Islam and Christian-Muslim Relations*, volume 8(1), 1997: 85–97.

'Ālim, M. A. *al-Wa'y wa'l wa'y al-zā'if fī'l fikr al-'arabī al-mu'āṣir* (Cairo: Dār al-Thaqāfah al-Jadīdah, 1986).

——. "Nadhariyat al-thawrah 'indā Mahdī 'Āmil wa adawātīhah al-ma'arifiyyah." In Markaz al-Buḥūth al-'Arabīyyah, *al-Nadhariyyah wa'l mumārasah fī fikr Mahdī 'Āmil: Nadwah Fikriyyah* (Beirut: Dār al-Fārābī, 1989).

——."Naqd al-Jābīrī li'l 'aql al-'arabī." In Maḥmūd Amīn al-'Ālīm, *Mafāhim wā qaḍāyah ishkāliyyah* (Cairo: Dār al-Thaqāfah al-Jadīdah, 1989).

——. *Mafāhīm wā Qaḍāya ishkālīya* (Cairo: Dār al-Thaqāfah al-Jadīdah, 1989).

——. *al-Fikr al-'arabī bayna al-'awlamah wa'l ḥadāthah wā mā ba'da al-hadātha.* In *Qaḍāya Fikriyya*, volume 19–20, 1999.

Amīn, S. and Burhān Ghalyūn, *Ḥiwār al-dīn wa'l dawlah* (Casablanca: al-Markaz al-Thaqāfī al-'Arabī, 1996).

Amin, S. *Unequal Development: An Essay on the Social Formations of Peripheral Capitalism* (New York: Monthly Review Press, 1976).

——. The Arab Nation: Nationalism and Class Struggles (London: Zed Press, 1983).

——. "al-Thaqāfah wa'l aydiyūlūjiyyah fi'l 'ālam al-'arabī al-mu'āṣir." *Al-Ṭarīq*, volume 52(1), May 1993.

——. *Les défis de la mondialisation* (Paris: L'Harmattan/Forum du tiers-monde, 1996).

——. *Fī muwājahatī azmatī 'asṣrinah* (Cairo: Sīnā Li'l Nashr, 1997).

——. *Capitalism in the Age of Globalization* (London: Zed Books, 1998).

——. *Delinking: Towards a Polycentric World* (London: Zed Press, 1990).

Arkoun, M. *Essais sur la pensée islamique* (Paris: Éditions Maisonneuve et Larose, 1977).

——. "The Adequacy of Contemporary Islam to the Political, Social, and Economic Development of Northern Africa." *Arab Studies Quarterly*, volume 5(1 and 2), Spring 1982: 34–53.

——. *Pour une critique de la raison islamique* (Paris: Éditions Maisonneuve et Larose, 1984).

——. *Arab Thought*, tr. Jasmere Singh (New Delhi: S. Chand and Company, 1988).

——. "Islamic Studies: Methodologies." In John Esposito, ed., *The Oxford Encyclopedia of the Modern Muslim World*, volume 2 (New York: Oxford University Press, 1995).

Aruri, N. "The Recolonization of the Arab World." *Arab Studies Quarterly*, volume 11(2 and 3), Spring/Summer 1989.

Asad, T. *Genealogies of Religion: Discipline and Reasons of Power in Christianity and Islam* (Baltimore, MD: Johns Hopkins University Press, 1993).

——. "Europe Against Islam: Islam in Europe." *The Muslim World*, volume 87(2), April 1997.

'Aṣfūr, J. *Hawāmish 'alā daftar al-tanwīr* (Cairo: Dār Su'ād al-Ṣabāh, 1994).

'Azm, S.J. *al-Naqd al-dhātī ba dah al-hazīmah* (Beirut: Dār al-Talī'ah, 1969).

——. *Naqd al-fikr al-dīnī* (Beirut: Dār al-Talī'ah, 1969).

——. "Mā hiya al-'awlamah?" *Al-Ṭarīq*, volume 56(4), July–August 1997.

——. *Dhihniyat al-taḥrīm: Salmān Rushdī wā ḥaqīqat al-adab* (Damascus: Dār al-Mada, 1997).

——. *Mā ba'da dhihniyat al-taḥrīm: qirā'at al-āyāt al-shayṭāniyyah* (Damascus: Dār al-Mada, 1997).

——. "Sur l'islam, la laïcité et l'Occident." *Le Monde Diplomatique*, September 1999.

——. "Mā hiya al-'awlamah?" In Ḥassan Ḥanafī and Ṣādiq Jalāl al-'Azm, *Mā al-'awlamah?* (Damascus: Dār al-Fikr, 1999).

'Azmeh, A. *al-'Ilmāniyyah min mandhūr mukhtalif* (Beirut: Markaz Dirāsāt al-Wiḥdah al-'Arabīyyah, 1992).

——. "Aslamat al-ma'rifha wā jumūḥ allā 'aqlāniyyah al-siyāsiyyah." In *Qaḍāyah Fikriyyah*, volumes 13 and 14, 1993: 407–19.

——. "al-Dīn wa'l dunyah fī'l wāqi' al-'arabī." In *Qaḍāyah Fikriyyah*, volumes 13 and 14, 1993.

——. "Nationalism and the Arabs." *Arab Studies Quarterly*, volume 17(1 and 2), Winter and Spring 1995.

Bennabi, M. *Islam in History and Society*, tr. Asma Rashid (Islamabad: Islamic Research Institute, 1988).

——. *The Problem of Ideas in the Muslim World*, tr. Mohamed El-Mesawi (California: Dār al-Ḥaḍāra, 1994).

——. *On the Origins of Human Society*, tr. Muhammad Taher al-Mesawi (Kuala Lumpur: Open Press, 1998).

Bishrī, Ṭ. *Bayna al-'urūba wa'l islām* (Cairo: Dār al-Shurūq, 1968).

——. "Ḥawla al-'urūbbah wa'l islām." In Markaz Dirāsāt al-Wiḥdah al-'Arabīyyah, *al-Ḥiwār al-qawmī al-dīnī* (Beirut: Markaz Dirāsāt al-Wiḥdah al-'Arabiyyah, 1989).

——. *Al-Ḥiwār al-islāmī al-'ilmānī* (Cairo: Dār al-Shurūq, 1996).

——. *Bayna al-jāmi'ah al-dīnīyyah wa'l jāmi'ah al-waṭaniyyah fi'l fikr al-siyāsī* (Cairo: Dār al-Shurūq, 1998).

——. "Al-Waḍ' al-dīnī fī miṣr bayna al-manṭūq bihī wa'l maskūt 'anhū." *Wijhāt Nadhar*, volume 1(4), May 1999.

Boullata, I. *Trends and Issues in Contemporary Arab Thought* (Albany: State University of New York Press, 1990).

Charaffeddine, F. *Culture et idéologie dans le monde arabe* (Paris: L'Harmattan, 1994).

Charfi, A. "La secularisation dans les sociétés arabo-musulmanes modernes." *Islamochristiana*, volume 8, 1982.

Daher, A. *Current Trends in Arab Intellectual Thought* (Washington, DC: Rand, 1969).

Djait, H. *La personnalité et le devenir arabo-islamique* (Paris: Seuil, 1974).

——. *Europe and Islam: Cultures and Modernity* (Berkeley: University of California Press, 1975).

Eickelman, D. "Islam and the Languages of Modernity." *Daedalus: Journal of the American Academy of Arts and Sciences*, Winter 2000.

El-Affendi, *Turābī's Revolution: Islam and Power in Sudan* (London: Grey Seal Books, 1991).

El-Kenz, A. "al-Islām wa'l hawiyyah: mulāḥādhāt lī'l baḥth." In Markaz Dirāsāt al-Wiḥdah al-'Arabiyyah, *al-Dīn fi'l mujtama' al-'arabī* (Beirut: Markaz Dirāsāt al-Wiḥdah al-'Arabiyyah, 1990).

——. *Algerian Reflections on Arab Crises*, tr. Robert W. Stooky (Texas: University of Texas Press, 1991).

Elmandjra, H. *Retrospective des futurs* (Casablanca: Ouyoun, 1992).

——. *al-Ḥarb al-ḥaḍāriyyah al-ūlah* (Casablanca: 'Uyūn, 1994).

——. *La décolonisation culturelle: defi majeur du 21ème siècle* (Marrakech: Éditions Walīlī, 1996).

Fandy, M. *Saudi Arabia and the Politics of Dissent* (New York: Palgrave, 1999).

Faris, H.A. "Constantine K. Zurayk: Advocate of Rationalism in Modern Arab Thought." In George N. Atiyeh and Ibrahim M. Oweiss, eds, *Arab Civilization: Challenges and*

Responses, Studies in Honor of Constantine K. Zurak (Albany: State University of New York Press, 1988).

Filali-Ansari, A. "Islam and Secularism." In Gema Martin Munoz, ed., *Islam, Modernism, and the West* (London: I.B. Tauris, 1999).

——. "Can Modern Rationality Shape a New Religiosity? Mohamed Abed Jabri and the Paradox of Islam and Modernity." In John Cooper, Ronald Nettler, and Mohamed Mahmoud, eds, *Islam and Modernity: Muslim Intellectuals Respond* (London: I.B. Tauris, 1998).

Fūda, F. *Qabla al-suqūṭ* (Cairo: No Publisher, 1985).

——. *al-Nadhīr* (Cairo: al-Hay'ah al-Miṣriyyah, 1992).

Gallagher, N. "Islam v. Secularism in Cairo: An Account of the Dar Hikma Debate." *Middle East Studies*, volume 25(2), April 1989.

——. "The Life and Times of a Moroccan Historian: An Interview." In Bassam el-Kurdi, ed., *Autour de la pensée de Abdallah Laroui* (Casablanca: Le Centre Culturel Arabe, 2000).

Ghalyūn, B. "al-Islām wa azmat 'alāqāt al-ṣulṭah al-ijtimā'iyyah." In Markaz Dirāsāt al-Wiḥdah al-'Arabīyyah, *al-Dīn fī'l mujtam' al-'arabī* (Beirut: Markaz Dirāsāt al-Wiḥdah al-'Arabīyyah, 1990).

——. Ightiyāl al-'aql: miḥnat al-thaqāfah al-'Arabīyya bayna al-salafiyya wa'l taba'iyyah (Cairo: Madbūlī, 1990).

——. *Le malaise arabe: l'État contre la nation* (Paris: La Découverte, 1991).

——. *Naqd al-siyāssa: al-dawla wa'l dīn* (Beirut, 1991).

——. "Binā' al-mujtama' al-madanī al-'arabī: dawr al-'awāmil al-dākhiliyyah wa'l khārijiyyah." In Markaz Dirāsāt al-Wiḥdah al-'Arabīyah, *al-Mujtama' al-madanī fī'l waṭan al-'arabī* (Beirut: Markaz Dirāsāt al-Wiḥdah al-'Arabīyyah, 1992).

——. "La fin de la stratégie nationale: Strategie et nouvel ordre mondial." In *Jusoor: The Arab American Journal of Cultural Exchange and Thought for the Future*. Spring–Summer 1993.

Ghannūshī, R. *Maqālāt: ḥarakat al-itijāh al-islāmi bī tūnis* (Paris: Dār al-Karawān, 1984).

——. "Ayatū hadāthah? Laysa mushkiluna ma' al-hadāthah." *Qirā'āt Siyāsiyyah*, volume 2(4), 1992.

——. "The Battle Against Islam." *Middle East Affairs Journal*, volume 1(2), Winter 1993.

——. *al-Ḥuriyyāt al-'āmmah fī'l dawlah al-islāmiyya*h (Beirut: Markaz Dirāsāt al-Wiḥdah al-'Arabīyyah, 1993).

——. "Islamic Movements: Self-Criticism and Reconsideration." *Middle East Affairs Journal*, volume 3(1–2), Winter/Spring 1997.

——. *Muqārābāt fī'l 'ilmāniyyah wa'l mujtama' al-madanī* (London: al-Markaz al-Maghārībī li'l buḥūth wa'l Tarjamah, 1999).

——. "Secularism in the Arab Maghreb." In John L. Esposito and Azzam Tamimi, eds, *Islam and Secularism in the Middle East* (New York: New York University Press, 2000).

Ghazālī, M. *al-Islām al-muftara 'alyhī bayna al-shuyū'iyyīn wa'l ra'smāliyyīn* (Cairo 1952).

——. *Our Beginning in Wisdom*, tr. Ismā'īl R. al-Faruqi (Washington, DC, 1953).

Grunebaum, G.E. *Modern Islam: The Search for Cultural Identity* (Berkeley: University of California Press, 1962).

Guazzone, L. *The Islamist Dilemma: The Political Role of Islamist Movements in the Contemporary Arab World* (London: Ithaca Press, 1995).

Haddad, Y. "Muslim Revivalist Thought in the Arab World: An Overview." *The Muslim World*, volume 76, July–October 1986.

Hafez, Y. "The Novel, Politics and Islam: Haydar Haydar's Banquet for Seaweed." *New Left Review*, Number 5, September–October 2000.

Ḥāfiz, Y. *al-Hazīmah wa'l idiūlūjiyyah al-mahzūmah* (Beirut: Dār al-Ṭalī'ah, 1979).

Haj, S. *The Making of Iraq, 1900–1963* (Albany: State University of New York Press, 1997).

Hamdi, M. *The Politicization of Islam: A Case Study of Tunisia* (Boulder, CO: Westview Press, 1998).

Hammoudi, A. *Master and Disciple: The Cultural Foundations of Moroccan Authoritarianism* (Chicago, IL: University of Chicago Press, 1997).

Ḥanafī, Ḥ. *al-Turāth wa'l tajdīd* (Beirut: Dār al-Tanwīr, 1981).

——. *al-Turāth wa'l tajdīd: mawqifunā min al-turāth al-qadīm* (Cairo: al-Markaz al-'Arabī, 1982).

——. *al-Dīn wa'l thawrah fī miṣr*, volume 8 (Cairo: Madbūlī, 1989).

——. *Muqadimah fī 'ilm al-istighrāb* (Cairo: al-Dār al-Faniyyah li'l Nashr wa'l Tawzī', 1991).

——. "al-Fikr al-'arabī al-mu'āṣir." In Maḥmūd Amīn al-'Ālim, ed., *al-Fikr al-'arabī 'alā mashārif al-qarn al-ḥādī wa'l 'ishrīn* (Cairo: Qaḍāyah Fikriyyah, 1995).

——. "al-Yasār al-islāmī: turāth al-sulṭah wa turāth al-mu'āraḍah." *Al-Qāhirah*, number 164, July 1996.

Ḥawwā, S. *al-Madkhal ilā da'wat al-ikhwān al-muslimīn* (Amman: al-Maṭba'ah al-Ta'āwuniyyah, 1979).

——. *Hādhihī tajribatī wa hādhihī shahādatī* (Cairo: Mu'assassat al-Khalīj al-'Arabī, 1988).

Haykal, M.H. *Ḥarb al-thalāthīn sanah: 1967 al-infijār* (Cairo: Markaz al-Ahrām li'l Tijārah wa'l Nashr, 1990).

——. "Ḥiwārāt ma' al-Qaddāfī." *Wijhāt Nadhar*, volume 1(4), May 1999: 4–14.

——. "Ḥadīth mustadrad 'an al-siyāsah al-dākhiliyyah." *Wijhāt Nadhar*, volume 2 (17), June 2000.

——. *'Ām min al-azamāt: 2000–2001* (Cairo: al-Misriyyah li'l Nashr al-'Arabī wa'l Duwalī, 2001).

——. *al-'arabī al-tā'ih* (Cairo: al-Miṣriyyah li'l Nashr al-'Arabī wa'l Duwalī, 2001).

Hilāl, A. "Azmat al-fikr al-liberalī fī'l waṭan al-'arabī." *'Ālam al-Fikr*, volume 26(3–4), January–June 1998.

Hourani, A. *Arabic Thought in the Liberal Age, 1798–1939* (Cambridge: Cambridge University Press, 1970).

——. "The Arab Awakening Forty Years After." In *Studies in Arab History: The Antonius Lectures, 1978–87*, ed. Derek Hopwood (London, 1990).

Hudson, M. *The Precarious Republic: Political Modernization in Lebanon* (New York: Random House, 1968).

Humphreys, R. *Between Memory and Desire: The Middle East in a Troubled Age* (Berkeley: University of California Press, 1999).

Huwaydī, F. *al-Qur'ān wa'l sulṭān* (Cairo: Dār al-Shurūq, 1982).

——."'An al-'ilmāniyyah wa tajaliyātihah." *Al-Maqālāt al-maḥdhūrah* (Cairo: Dār al-Shurūq, 1998).

——. "al-Khiṭāb al-islāmī fī 'ālam mutajaddid." In Sayyid Yāssīn, ed., *al-'Arab wa taḥadiyyāt al-qarn al-ḥādī wa'l 'ishrīn* (Amman: Mu'assassat 'Abdul Ḥamīd Shūmān, 2000).

Ibrahimi, A. *al-Maghrib al-'arabī fī muftaraq al-ṭuruq fī dhil al-taḥāwwulāt al-duwaliyyah* (Beirut: Markaz Dirāsāt al-Wiḥdah al-'Arabīyyah, 1996).

Idrīs, S. *al-Muthaqaf al-'arabī wa'l ṣultah: bahth fī riwāyat al-tajribah al-nāṣṣiriyyah* (Beirut: Dār al-Adab, 1993).

Imārah, M. *al-A'māl al-kāmilah li 'Abd al-Raḥmān al-Kawākībī* (Cairo: al-Hay'ah al-Miṣriyyah al-'Āmmah li'l Ta'līf wa'l Nashr, 1970).

——. "Mawqi' al-fikr al-islāmī al-ḥadīth min al-itijāh al-liberalī." *Al-Ṭalī'ah*, volume 8(8), August 1972.

——. *al-Jadīd fī mukhaṭaṭ al-'ālam al-gharbī tijāh al-muslimīn* (Cairo: International Institute of Islamic Thought, 1983).

——. *al-Dawlah al-islāmiyyah bayna al-'ilmāniyyah wa'l sulṭah al-madaniyyah* (Cairo: Dār al-Shurūq, 1988).

——. *al-Ghazw al-fikrī: wahm am ḥaqīqhah* (Cairo: International Institute of Islamic Thought, 1988).

——. *Fikr al-tanwīr bayna al-'ilmāniyin wa'l islāmiyyin* (Cairo: International Institute of Islamic Thought, 1993).

——. *al-Islam wā uṣūl al-ḥukm lī 'Alī 'Abd al-Rāziq: Dirāsah wā wathā'iq* (Beirut: Mu'assassat al-Dirāsāt, 1994).

——. *al-A'māl al-kāmilah li'l Imām Muḥammad 'Abduh*, 5 volumes (Cairo: Dār al-Shurūq, 1995).

Jābīrī, M.Ā. *al-Khiṭāb al-'arabī al-mu'āṣir* (Beirut: Markaz Dirāsāt al-Wiḥdah al-'Arabiyyah, 1982).

——. *al-Dimūqraṭiya wa ḥuqūq al-insān* (Beirut: Markaz Dirāsāt al-Wiḥdah al-'Arabīyyah, 1994).

——. *al-Masa'alah al-thaqāfiyyah* (Beirut: Markaz Dirāsāt al-Wiḥdah al-'Arabīyyah, 1994).

——. *al-Masa'alah al-thaqāfiyyah* (Beirut: Markaz Dirāsāt al-Wihdah al-'Arabiyyah, 1994).

——. *al-Muthaqafūn al-'arab fī'l ḥadārah al-'Arabīyyah* (Beirut: Markaz Dirāsāt al-Wiḥdah al-'Arabīyyah, 1995).

——. *Mas'alat al-hawiyah: al-'urūbah, al-islām wa'l gharb* (Beirut: Markaz Dirāsāt al-Wiḥdah al-'Arabīyyah, 1995).

——. *al-Dīn wa'l dawlah wā taṭbīq al-sharī'ah* (Beirut: Markaz Dirāsāt al-Wiḥdah al-'Arabīyyah, 1996).

——. "al-'Awlamah, niẓām wa aydiyūlūjiyyah." In al-Majlis al-Qawmī li'l Thaqāfah al-'Arabīyyah, *al-'Arab wa taḥadiyāt al-'awlamah* (Rabat: al-Majlis al-Qawmī li'l Thaqāfah al-'Arabīyyah, 1997).

——. *Naḥnu wa'l turāth* (Casablanca: al-Markaz al-Thaqāfī al-'Arabī, 1993).

——. "al-Falsafah: fann siyāghat al-mafāhīm." *Al-Sharq al-Awṣat*, Number 6619, January 11, 1997.

——. *Qaḍāyah fī al-fikr al-mu'āsīir* (Beirut: Markaz Dirāsāt al-Wiḥdah al-'Arabīyyah, 1997).

——. "al-Mujtam' al-madanī: tasā'ulāt wā āfāq." In 'Abdalla Ḥamūda, ed., *Wa'y al-mujtama' bī dhātihī: 'an al-mujtama' al-madanī fī'l maghrib al-'arabī* (Casablanca: Dār Ṭubqāl, 1998).

——. "al-'Arab wa'l 'awlamah: al-'awlamah wa'l hawiyyah al-thaqāfiyyah." In Markaz Dirāsāt al-Wiḥdah al-'Arabīyyah, *al-'Arab wa'l 'awlamah* (Beirut: Markaz Dirāsāt al-Wihdah al-'Arabīyyah, 1998).

——. *al-'Aql al-akhlāqī al-'arabī* (Casablanca: al-Markaz al-Thaqāfī al-'Arabī, 2001).

Jad'ān, F. "al-Salafiyyah: ḥudūduhah wa taḥawulātuhah." *'Ālam al-Fikr*, volume 26, January–April 1998.

Jalāl, S. "al-Yasār al-'arabī wa sosiolojiyat al-fashal." *'Ālam al-Fikr*, volume 26, January–April 1998.

Janḥānī, H. *al-Taḥawwul al-iqtiṣādī wa'l ijtimā'ī fī mujtama' ṣadr al-islām* (Beirut: Dār al-Gharb al-Islāmī, 1985).

——. "al-Mufakkir wa'l sulṭah fī'l turāth al-'arabī al-islāmi." In al-Tāhir Labīb, ed., *al-Intillejensia al-'Arabiyyah* (Tunis: al-Dār al-'Arabiyyah li'l Kitāb, n.d.).

Kanafani, G. "Thoughts on Change and the 'Blind Language'." In Ferial J. Ghazoul and Barbara Harlow, eds, *The View from Within: Writers and Critics on Contemporary Arabic Literature* (Cairo: American University of Cairo Press, 1994).

Kant, I. "What is Enlightenment?" In *Kant: Political Writings*, ed. Hans Reiss (Cambridge: Cambridge University Press, 1991).

Khālid, K.M. *From Here We Start*, tr. Ismā'īl R. el-Faruqi (Washington, DC, 1953).

——. *Naḥnu al-bashar* (Cairo: Angelo, 1959).

——. *Azmat al-huriyyah fī 'ālam*ina (Cairo: Angelo, 1972).

——. *al-Dimūqratiyah abadan*, 4th edn (Beirut, 1974).

——. *Muwāṭinūn lā ra'āyah*, 7th edn (Beirut, 1974).

Khatibi, A. "Double Criticism: The Decolonization of Arab Sociology." In Halim Barakat, ed., *Contemporary North Africa: Issues of Development and Integration* (Washington, DC: Center for Contemporary Arab Studies, 1985).

Kugelgen, A.V. "A Call for Rationalism: 'Arab Averroists' in the Twentieth Century." In *Alif: Journal of Comparative Poetics*, number 16, 1996: 97–132.

Labdaoui, A. *Les nouveaux intellectuels arabes* (Paris, 1993).

Labib, F. and Nehad Salem, eds. *Clash of Civilizations or Dialogue of Cultures* (Cairo: Afro-Asian Peoples' Solidarity Organization, 1997).

Lahbabi, M. *De l'être à la personne: Essai de personnalisme réaliste* (Paris: PUF, 1954).

——. *Le personnalisme musulman* (Paris: PUF, 1964).

——. *Le monde de demain: Le Tiers-monde accuse* (Casablanca: Sherbrooke, 1980).

Laroui, A. *L'idéologie arabe contemporaine* (Paris: Maspero, 1970).

——. *The Crisis of the Arab Intelligentsia: Traditionalism or Historicism?* (Berkeley: University of California Press, 1976).

——. *Les origines du nationalisme marocain, 1830–1912* (Paris: Maspero, 1977).

Lowrie, A.L., ed. *Islam, Democracy, the State and the West: A Round Table with Dr. Hasan Turabi* (Tampa, FL: World and Studies Enterprise, 1993).

Mabrūk, M.I. *Amerika wa'l islām al-nafi'ī* (Cairo: Dār al-Tawzī' wa'l Nashr al-Islāmiyyah, 1989).

——, ed. *al-Islām wa'l 'awlamah* (Cairo: al-Dār al-Qawmiyyah al-'Arabīyyah, 1999).

Malkāwī, F., ed. *al-'Aṭā' al-fikrī li'l Shaykh Muḥammad al-Ghazālī* (Amman: al-Ma'had al-'Ālamī li'l Fikr al-Islāmī, 1996).

Masīrī, A. "al-Ru'yah al-ma'rifiyyah al-imberialiyyah." *Qirā'āt Siyāsiyyah*, volume 2(4), 1992: 137–59.

——. "The Imperialist Epistemological Vision." *The American Journal of the Islamic Social Sciences*, volume 11(3), Fall 1994: 403–15.

——. *al-Insāklubīdyyah al-ṣuhyūniyyah*, seven volumes (Cairo: Dār al-Shurūq, 1999).

Merad, A. *Le réformisme musulman en Algerie de 1925 à 1940: Essai d'histoire religieuse et sociale* (Paris: Mouton, 1967).

Milad, Z. "Islamic Thought and the Issue of Globalization." *Middle East Affairs Journal*, volume 5(1–2), Winter–Spring 1999.

Mouaqit, M. "Mohamed Abed Al-Jabri: Rationalisme et laïcisme." In M.Y. Retnani, ed., *Penseurs maghrebins contemporains* (Casablanca: Éditions Eddif, 1997).

Moughrabi, M. "The Arabic Basic Personality: A Critical Survey of the Literature." *International Journal of Middle East Studies*, volume 9(1), February 1978.

Munīf, A. *The Trench* (New York: Pantheon, 1990).

——. *Cities of Salt* (New York: Vintage, 1991).

——. "al-Thaqāfah wa'l muthaqqaf fī'l mujtama' al-'arabī." In Sayyid Yāssīn, ed., *al-'Arab wa taḥadiyyāt al-qarn al-ḥādī wa'l 'ishrīn* (Amman: Mu'assassat 'Abdul Ḥamīd Shūmān, 2000).

Murquṣ, E. *Tārīkh al-aḥzāb al-shuyū'īyyah fī'l waṭan al-'arabī* (Beirut: Dār al-Ṭalī'ah, 1964).

——. *al-Mārkisiyah wa'l sharq* (Beirut: Dār al-Ṭalī'ah, 1968).

——. *al-Mārkisiyah fī 'asrina* (Beirut: Dār al-Ṭalī'ah, 1969).

Mūsa, S. *The Education of Salāma Mūsa*, tr. L.O. Schuman (Leiden: E.J. Brill, 1961).

——. *Mā hiya al-nahḍah*? (Cairo: Mu'sassat Salāma Mūsa, n.d.).

Mustafa, S. "Arab Cultural Crisis and the Impact of the Past." *The Jerusalem Quarterly*, Number 11, Spring 1979.

Mustafa, Y. "Azmat al-muthaqaf al-'aqlānī." In Maḥmūd Amīn al-'Ālim, *Qaḍāyah Fikriyyah, al-Fikr al-'arabī 'ala mashārif al-qarn al-wāhīid wa'l 'ishrīn* (Cairo: Dār Qaḍāyah Fikriyyah, 1995).

Nābulsī, S. *Thawrat al-turāth: Dirāsa fī fikr Khālid Muḥammad Khālid* (Beirut: Dār al-Turāth, 1991).

Najjar, F. "Islamic Fundamentalism and the Intellectuals: The Case of Nasr Hamid Abu Zayd." *British Journal of Middle Eastern Studies*, 27(2), 2000: 177–200.

——. "The Debate on Islam and Secularism in Egypt." *Arab Studies Quarterly*, volume 18(2), Spring 1996: 1–22.

——. "Book Banning in Contemporary Egypt." *The Muslim World*, volume 91(3 and 4), Fall 2001: 399–424.

Naqqāsh, F. *Yawmiyyāt al-mudun al-maftūhah* (Cairo: Dāral-Thaqāfah al-Jadīdah, 1987).

——. *al-In'izāliyyūn fī miṣr: radd 'ala Tawfīq al-Ḥakīm wa Luwes 'Awad* (Cairo: al-Hay'ah al-Miṣriyyah al-'Āmmah li'l Kitāb, 1996).

Qaraḍāwī, Y. *Ghayr al-muslimīn fī'l mujtama' al-islāmī* (Cairo: Maktabat Wahba, 1977).

——. *al-Islām wa'l 'ilmāniyyah wajhan lī wajh: rad 'ilmī 'ala Fu'ād Zakariyya wa jamā'at al-'ilmaniyyīn* (Cairo: Dār al-Ṣahwah, 1978).

——. *al-Ḥall al-islāmī, farīḍah wa ḍarūra*h (Beirut: Mu'assassat al-Risālah, 1989).

——. *Islamic Awakening Between Rejection and Extremism* (Herndon: International Institute of Islamic Thought, 1991).

——. *Limādha al-islām?* (Beirut: Mu'assassat al-Risālah, 1993).

——. *al-Ḥulūl al-mustawrada wa kayfa janat 'alā ummatina* (Beirut: Mu'assassat al-Risālah, 1995).

——. *al-Ṣahwah al-islāmiyyah wa humūm al-watan al-'arabī wa'l islāmī* (Beirut: Mu'assassat al-Risālah, 1997).

——. *al-Shaykh al-Ghazālī kamā 'araftuhū: rihlat nisf qarn* (al-Manṣūrah: Dār al-Wafā', 1997).
——. *al-Muslimūn wa'l 'awlamah* (Cairo: Dār al-Tawzī' wa'l Nashr al-Islāmiyyah, 2000).
——. *Priorities of the Islamic Movement in the Coming Phase*, tr. S.M. Ḥassan al-Banna (London: Awakening Publications, 2000).
Sa'īd, S. *Bourquiba: sīra shibh muḥarammah* (London: Riad El-Rayyes Books, 2000).
Saaf, A. *Politique et savoir au Maroc* (Casablanca: Nouvelle Collection Atlas, 1991).
Sagiv, D. "Judge Ashmāwī and Militant Islam in Egypt." *Middle Eastern Studies*, vol. 28(3), July 1992.
Said, E. *Orientalism* (New York: Vintage Books, 1978).
——. *Culture and Imperialism* (New York: Alfred A. Knopf, 1993).
——. "The Other Arab Muslims." In *The Politics of Dispossession* (New York: Vintage Books, 1995).
——. *Representations of the Intellectual* (New York: Vintage Books, 1994).
——. "The Arab Right Wing." In *The Politics of Dispossession* (New York: Vintage Books, 1995).
——. "The Formation of American Public Opinion on the Question of Palestine. In *The Politics of Dispossession* (New York: Vintage Books, 1995).
——. "Ignorant Armies Clash by Night." In *The Politics of Dispossession* (New York: Vintage Books, 1995).
——. *Reflections on Exile and Other Essays* (Cambridge, MA: Harvard University Press, 2000).
——. *The End of the Peace Process: Oslo and After* (New York: Pantheon, 2000).
—— "America's Last Taboo." *New Left Review*, volume 6, November/December 2000.
——. *The End of the Peace Process: Oslo and After* (New York: Pantheon Books, 2000).
Salvatore, A. "The Rational Articulation of Turāth in Contempoary Arab Thought: The Contributions of Muhammad 'Ābid al-Jābīrī and Hasan Hanafī." *The Muslim World*, volume 95(3 and 4), 1995: 191–214.
——. *Islam and the Political Discourse of Modernity* (London: Ithaca, 1997).
Sāyigh, A., ed. *Costantine Zuryak: 65 sanat min al-'aṭā'* (Beirut: Maktabat Beisān, 1996).
Sayyid, L. *Mabādi' fī al-siyāsah wa'l adab wa'l ijtimā'* (Cairo, 1963).
Sayyid, R. "Contemporary Muslim Thought and Human Rights." *Islamochristiana*, volume 21 (1995): 27–41.
Shafīq, M. *al-Islām fī ma'rakat al-ḥadārah* (Beirut: al-Nāsher, 1991).
——. *Qaḍāyah al-tanmiyyah wa'l istiqlāl fī'l ṣirā' al-ḥadāri* (Beirut: al-Nāsher, 1992).
——. *Fī al-ḥadāthah wa'l Khiṭāb al-ḥadāthī* (Casablanca: al-Markaz al-Thaqāfī al-'Arabī, 1999).
Sharabi, H. "Islam and Modernization in the Arab World." In Jack Thompson and Robert Reischauer, eds, *Modernization of the Arab World* (New York: Van Nostrand, 1966).
——. *Arab Intellectuals and the West: The Formative Years* (Baltimore, MD: Johns Hopkins University Press, 1970).
——. *Neopatriarchy: A Theory of Distorted Change in Arab Society* (New York: Oxford University Press, 1988).
——, ed. *Theory, Politics, and the Arab World* (New York: Routledge, 1990).
Sharqāwī, M. *Salāma Mūsa: al-mufakir wa'l insān* (Cairo: Dār al-Hilāl, 1968).
Shehab, S. "Philosopher Faces Apostasy Charge." *Al-Ahram Weekly*, May 8–14, 1997.

Shukrī, G. *Min al-arshīf al-sirrī li'l thaqāfah al-miṣriyyah* (Beirut: Dār al-Ṭalī'ah, 1975).
——. *Egypt: Portrait of a President* (London: Zed Books, 1981).
——. *al-Nahdah wa'l suqūṭ fī'l fikr al-miṣrī al-ḥadīth* (Beirut: Dār al-Ṭalī'ah, 1982).
——. *Salāma Mūsa wā azmat al-ḍamīr al-'arabī* (Beirut: Dār al-Āfāq al-Jadīdah, 1983).
——. *Aqwās al-hazīmah: wa'y al-nukhbah bayna al-ma'rifah wa'l sulṭah* (Cairo: Dār al-Fikr, 1990).
——. *Aqni'at al-irhāb: al-bahth 'an 'ilmāniyyah Jadīdah* (Cairo: al-Hay'ah al-Miṣriyyah al-'Āmmah li'l Kitāb, 1992).
——. Bidāyat al-tārīkh: min zilzāl al-khalīj ilā zawāl al-soviet (Cairo: Dār Su'ād al-Sabāḥ, 1993).
——. "Man la yakhāf al-Shaykh al-Ghazālī?" In his *Thaqāfat al-niẓām al-'ashwā'ī: takfīr al-'aql wa 'aql al-takfīr* (Cairo: Kitāb al-Ahālī, 1994).
——. *al-Khurūj 'alā al-naṣṣ: tahadiyyāt al-thaqāfah wa'l dimūqratiyyah* (Cairo: Dār Sīnā, 1994).
——. *Diktātoriyat al-takhalluf al-'arabī* (Cairo: al-Hay'ah al-Miṣriyyah al-'Āmmah li'l Kitāb, 1994).
——. *Mira'āt al-manfa: asi'lah fī thaqāfat al-nafṭ wa'l harb* (Cairo: al-Hay'ah al-Miṣriyyah al-'Āmmah li'l Kitāb, 1994).
——. *Mudhakarāt thaqāfah taḥtadir* (Cairo: al-Hay'ah al-Miṣriyyah al-'Āmmah, 1995).
——. "'Abdul Nāṣṣer wa'l muthaqaffūn." In his *Mudhakārāt thaqāfah taḥtadir* (Cairo: al-Hay'ah al-Miṣriyyah al-'Āmmah li'l Kitāb, 1995).
Sonbol, A.E. *The New Mamluks: Egyptian Society and Modern Feud'Alīsm* (Syracuse: Syracuse University Press, 2000).
Sonn, T. "Secularism and National Stability in Islām." *Arab Studies Quarterly*, volume 9(3), Summer 1987: 284–305.
Springborg, R. "The Arab Bourgeoisie: A Revisionist Interpretation." *Arab Studies Quarterly*, volume 15(1), Winter 1993.
Sprinker, M. *History and Ideology in Proust: À la recherche du temps perdu and the Third French Republic* (London: Verso, 1998).
Tamimi, A. "Democracy: The Religious and the Political in Contemporary Islamic Debate." *Encounters: Journal of Inter-Cultural Perspectives*, volume 4(1), March 1998: 38.
——. *Rachid Ghannouci: A Democrat within Islamism* (New York: Oxford University Press, 2001).
Tizīnī, T. *Ṭarīq al-wudūḥ al-manhajī* (Beirut: Dār al-Fārābī, 1989).
——. "Naḥwa 'ilmāniyyah takūn madkhalan lī mashrū' 'arabī nahdawi jadīd." *Al-Ṭarīq*, volume 55(6), 1996.
——. *Min al-istishrāq ilā al-istighrāb al-maghribī: Baḥth fī'l qirā'ah al-Jābiriyyah li'l fikr al-'arabī* (Ḥoms: Dār al-Dhākirah, 1996).
——. "Mahdī 'Āmil: mā alladhī tabaqqā minhū?" *Al-Ṭarīq*, number 4, July–August 1997.
Turābī, H. *Nadharāt fī'l fiqh al-siyāsī* (Umm al-Faḥm: Markaz al-Dirāsāt al-Mu'āṣirah, 1997).
Ukāshah, T. *Mudhakarātī fī'l thaqāfah wa'l siyāsah* (Cairo: Dār al-Shurūq, 2001).
'Ulwi, H. *Fi'l dīn wa'l turāth* (Jerusalem: Salāḥ al-Dīn, 1975).
——. "Naḥwa ta'sīl 'aqlāniyyah ijtimā'iyyah." *Al-Nahj*, volume 7, 1996.
'Umar, A., ed. *al-Duktūr Fu'ād Zakariyya Bāḥithan wā muthaqaffan wā nāqidan: kitāb tidhkārī* (Kuwait: University of Kuwait Press, 1998).

'Urwī, A. "al-Taḥdīth wa'l dimūqrāṭiyyah." *Āfāq: Majallat Itihād Kuttāb al-Maghrib*, 3–4, 1992.

——. *Awrāq* (Casablanca: al-Markaz al-Thaqāfī al-'Arabī, 1996).

——. *Mafhūm al-'aql*, chapter one (Casablanca: al-Markaz al-Thaqāfī al 'Arabī, 1996).

——. *al-'Arab wa'l fikr al-tārīkhī* (Casablanca: al-Markaz al-Thaqāfī al-'Arabī, n.d.)

'Uways, S. *al-Tārīkh al-ladhī ahmilūhu 'alā dhahrī*, three volumes (Cairo: Dār al-Hilāl, 1987).

Wahba, M. "The Meaning of Ishtirākiyyah: Arab Perceptions of Socialism in the Nineteenth Century." *Alif: Journal of Comparative Poetics*, Number 10, 1990: 42–55.

Wahbah, M. "al-'Aql al-'arabī wa'l 'ilmāniyyah." In Maḥmūd Amīn al-'Ālim, ed., *al-Fikr al-'arabī 'alā mashārif al-qarn al-ḥādī wa'l 'ishrīn* (Cairo: Qaḍāyah Fikriyyah, 1995).

Wald, A. *The New York Intellectuals: The Rise and Decline of Anti-Stalinist Left from the 1930s to the 1980s* (Chapel Hill: University of North Carolina Press, 1987).

Wannās, M. "al-Dīn wa'l dawla fī Tūnis: 1956–1987." In Markaz Dirāsāt al-Wiḥdah al-'Arabīyyah, *al-Dīn fī'l mujtama' al-'arabī* (Beirut: Markaz Dirāsāt al-Wiḥdah al-'Arabīyyah, 1990).

Yāfūt, S. *al-Manāhij al-Jadīdah li'l fikr al-falsafī al-mu'āṣir* (Beirut: Dār al-Ṭalī'ah, 1999).

Yahya, M. *Waraqah Thaqāfiyah fī'l radd 'alā al-'ilmaniyyīn* (Cairo: al-Zahrā' li'l I'lām al-'Arabī, 1988).

Yāssīn, S. *Taḥlīl maḍmūn al-fikr al-qawmī al-'arabī* (Beirut: Markaz Dirāsāt al-Wiḥdah al-'Arabīyyah, 1980).

——. *al-Shakhsīiyyah al-'Arabiyyah bayna sūrat al-dhāt wā mafhūm al-ākhar* (Cairo: Maktabat Madbūlī, 1993).

——. *al–Turāth wa taḥadiyāt al-'asr* (Beirut: Markaz Dirāsāt al-Wiḥdah al-'Arabīyyah, 1985).

——, ed. *al-'Arab wā taḥadiyyāt al-qarn al-ḥādī wa'l 'ishrīn* (Amman: Mu'assassat 'Abdul Ḥamīd Shūmān, 2000).

Zakariyya, F. "al-Falsafah wa'l dīn fi'l mujtama' al-'arabī al-mu'āṣir." In Markaz Dirāsāt al-Wiḥdah al-'Arabīyyah, *al-Falsafah fī'l waṭan al-'arabī al-mu'āṣir* (Beirut: Markaz Dirāsāt al-Wiḥdah al-'Arabīyyah, 1985).

——. *Khiṭāb ilā al-'aql al-'arabī* (Kuwait: Kitāb al-'Arabī, 1987).

——. "al-'Ilmāniyyah ḍarūrah ḥaḍāriyyah." *Qaḍāyah Fikriyyah* (1989).

——. *al-Ḥaqīqa wa'l khayāl fī'l ḥarakah al-islāmiyyah al-mu'āṣirah* (Cairo: Sīnā, 1988).

——. *al-'Arab wa'l namūdhaj al-amerīkī* (Cairo: Maktabat Miṣr, 1990).

——. *Laïcité ou islamisme. Les Arabes à l'heure du choix* (Paris: La Découverte, 1991).

——. "People Direct Islam in any Direction they Wish." *Middle East Times*, May 28–June 3, 1991.

Zawāhīrī, A. *al-Ḥiṣād al-murr: al-Ikhwān al-Muslimūn fī sittīna 'āman* (no publication information).

Zghal, A. "Le retour de sacre et la nouvelle demande idéologique de jeunes scolarises: Le cas de la Tunisie." *Le Maghreb Musulman*, 1979.

——. "al-Istrātijiyya al-Jadīdah lī harakat al-itijāh al-islāmī: munāwara 'an al-ta'bīr 'an al-thaqāfah al-siyāsiyyah al-tūnisiyyah." In Markaz Dirāsāt al-Wiḥdah al-'Arabiyyah, *al-Dīn fi'l mujtama' al-'arabī* (Beirut: Markaz Dirāsāt al-Wiḥdah al-'Arabīyyah, 1990).

Ziadeh, M. "Taqyīm tajribat harakatī al-qawmiyyīn al-'arab fī marhalatiha al-ūla." In Markaz Dirāsāt al-Wiḥdah al-'Arabīyyah, *al-Qawmiyyah al-'Arabīyyah: fī'l fikr wa'l mumārasah* (Beirut, 1980).

Zurayk, C. *Tensions in Islamic Civilization* (Georgetown, Wahington, DC: Center for Contemporary Arab Studies, 1978).

——. "Abiding Truths." In *al-A'māl al-fikriyyah al-'āmmah li'l dokṭor Costantine Zurayk*, volume 4 (Beirut: Markaz Dirāsāt al-Wiḥdah al-'Arabiyyah, 1994).

Index